AN INTRODUCTION TO THE THEATRE

FRANK M WHITING

Adjunct Professor, University of Utah
Professor Emeritus, University of Minnesota

Harper & Row, Publishers

NEW YORK   HAGERSTOWN   SAN FRANCISCO   LONDON

AN INTRODUCTION TO THE THEATRE

FOURTH EDITION

Sponsoring Editor: James B. Smith
Project Editor: Robert Ginsberg
Designer: Andrea C. Goodman
Production Supervisor: Marion Palen
Compositor: The Clarinda Company
Printer and Binder: The Murray Printing Company
Art Studio: Vantage Art Inc.
Cover photograph: Stock, Magnum

An Introduction to the Theatre, Fourth Edition

Library of Congress Cataloging in Publication Data

Whiting, Frank M
    An introduction to the theatre.

    Bibliography: p.
    Includes index.
    1. Theater. 2. Drama-History and criticism.
I. Title
PN1655.W5   1978   792   77-17905
ISBN 0-06-047089-5

CREDITS

Figure 5:5 Novosti Press Agency (APN). *Figure 5:6* Idaho State University. *Figure 5:7* Utah State University. *Figure 5:8* Williamstown Theatre (Stephen Boyd). *Figure 5:9* Act Two. *Figure 5:10* Theatre Collection, The New York Public Library at Lincoln Center, Astor, Lenox and Tilden Foundations. *Figure 5:11* Act Two. *Figure 5:12* Jack Hamilton. *Figure 5:13* Meadow Brook Theatre. *Figure 5:14* Mark Ahlstrom. *Figure 5:15* University of North Carolina.

Figure 6:1 Northwestern University. *Figure 6:2* Children's Theatre Company. *Figure 6:3* Photographic Laboratories, University of Minnesota. *Figure 6:4* Photographic Laboratories, University of Minnesota. *Figure 6:5* Act Two. *Figure 6:6* Martha Swope. *Figure 6:7* Martha Swope. *Figure 6:8* The Cleveland Play House. *Figure 6:9* Act Two.

Figure 7:1 Granger.

Figure 9:3 Theatre Collection, The New York Public Library at Lincoln Center, Astor, Lenox and Tilden Foundations. *Figure 9:4* Culver. *Figure 9:5* Theatre Collection, The New York Public Library at Lincoln Center, Astor, Lenox and Tilden Foundations. *Figure 9:7* From Constantin Stanislavski, *My Life in Art* (New York: Theatre Arts Books, 1948), copyright 1924 by Little, Brown and Company, copyright 1948 by Elizabeth Reynolds Hapgood. *Figure 9:8 (a)* Act Two, *(b)* Nordstrom, *(c)* Act Two, *(d)* Guthrie Theatre. *Figure 9:9* Robert C. Ragsdale — Toronto. *Figure 9:10* Robert Clayton. *Figure 9:11* Theatre Collection, The New York Public Library at Lincoln Center, Astor, Lenox and Tilden Foundations. *Figure 9:12* Irene Corey, Everyman Players.

Figure 10:1 Camera Press, Photo Trends. *Figure 10:5* Kallitza Mavroulis. *Figure 10:8* Theatre Collection, The New York Public Library at Lincoln Center, Astor, Lenox and Tilden Foundations. *Figure 10:10 (b)* Bernard Weinrich. *Figure 10:12 (a)* Editorial Photocolor Archives. *Figure 10:15* Redrawn from illustrations by Irwin Smith for Marchette Chute, *An Introduction to Shakespeare* (New York: Dutton, 1951). *Figure 10:17 (a)* Rockefeller Theatrical Prints Collection, Yale School of Drama Library *(b)* ANTA. *Figure 10:19* Courtesy of the New-York Historical Society. *Figure 10:21* Theatre Collection, The New York Public Library at Lincoln Center, Astor, Lenox and Tilden Foundations. *Figure 10:23* James Sneddon. *Figure 10:25* Pasadena Playhouse. *Figures 10:26 (a)* Squire Raskins, *(b)* Photographic Laboratories, University of Minnesota, *(c)* Ohio State University. *Figure 10:27* Redrawn from Harold Burris-Meyer and Edward C. Cole, *Scenery for the Theatre* (Boston: Little, Brown, 1938). *Figure 10:28 (a)* University of Minnesota, *(b)* Southwest Missouri State College, *(c)* Fort Raleigh National Historic Site. *Figure 10:29 (a) Illustrated London News, (b)* Hastings and Willinger, *(c)* Roger Cannon. *Figure 10:30 (a)* Peter Smith, *(b)* Duff Johnson, courtesy of Ralph Rapson, architect. *Figure 10:31 (a)* Mears, *(b)* University of Texas. *Figure 10:32* Act Two.

Figure 11:1 Sid Perkes, Utah State University. *Figure 11:3 (a)* Devonshire Collection, Chatsworth. Reproduced by permission of the Trustees of the Chatsworth Settlement. *Figure 11:4* The Metropolitan Museum of Art, Harris Brisbane Dick Fund, 1931. *Figure 11:5* First published in *The Magazine of Art*, September, 1901. *Figure 11:6* Theatre Collection, The New York Public Library at Lincoln Center, Astor, Lenox and Tilden Foundations. *Figure 11:7 (a), (b)* Theatre Collection, The New York Public Library at Lincoln Center, Astor, Lenox and Til-
...versity of Minnesota.
...a Foundation, Geneva.
...iversity Photo Studio.
...Two. *Figure 11:12* John
...*ure 11:15 (a)* Gary W.
...Minnesota, *(c)* Guthrie
..., University of Colora-
...lkup, *Dressing the Part*,
...*ure 11:18* Theatre Col-
...ter, Astor, Lenox and

. *Figure 12:16 (a)* Act
niversity of Wyoming,
on Yunker and Terry
t Scales. *Figure 12:27*

irg, *(c)* Photographic
ographic Laboratories,
eddes Collection, Hu-
stin. *Figure 13:4* From
nard Electric Co. *Fig-*
sy of Ward Leonard
l Present, courtesy of
, June 18, 1887. *Figure*
16 Kliegl Bros. *Figure*
liegl Bros. *Figure 13:21*

iversity of Utah, *(b)*
D. Redington, SUSC
Shakespeare Festival,
Hopkins Eisenhower
14:5 (a) Photographic
Laboratories, University of Minnesota, *(b)* Children's Theatre Co. *Figure 14:6*
Asolo State Theatre.

PART THREE
ARCHITECTS, DESIGNERS, AND TECHNICIANS
279

PART FOUR
PROFESSIONAL WORK IN THE THEATRE
435

Chapter 14
PROFESSIONAL WORK IN THE THEATRE   439

PREFACE

An Introduction to the Theatre attempts to compress between the covers of a single volume a brief but comprehensive view of the theatre in the belief that it is wise for the beginning student to examine the whole before plunging into a detailed study of any one of the numerous arts and crafts that make up the complex fabric of stage art.

Part One is concerned with plays and playwrights, for the play is the theatre's central and enduring core. Live acting is recorded only in the memories of those who experience it. Scenery, lights, and props are struck after the final performance and playhouses fall into decay, but the script remains to provide an enduring link with the past. Part Two considers acting and directing — acting, because it is even older and more indispensable to theatre than playwriting, and directing, because the director, especially in the modern theatre, is the central and unifying force in transforming the play from the script into a living production. Part Three considers the architects, artists, and craftsmen who provide the environment in which the actors perform, while Part Four consists of a single chapter on the theatre as a profession.

Needless to say, one hopes that this division into parts will not prevent the reader from gaining an overall view of the theatre as a complex but organic whole. Divisions, whether based on subject matter, geography, or chronology, are a matter of arbitrary convenience, and all have their inherent advantages and disadvantages. So vast is the subject of theatre that even a lifetime of study cannot hope to exhaust possibilities for further discovery. Consequently, in writing *An Introduction to the Theatre* the problem has not been one of finding things to say but rather of deciding what to leave unsaid. For the sake of condensation, it has been necessary at times to employ generalizations, while the exceptions that such sweeping statements frequently arouse have had to be ignored. The temptation to be original rather than fundamental — to advance new ideas and theories at the expense of those that are well established and basic—has also been avoided. Yet in spite of such limitations it is hoped that the conscientious reader will, upon finishing the book, have gained a fundamental knowledge of theatre that will need no serious revision as he or she progresses to a more detailed consideration of any one of the arts and crafts that, through combined effort, make up the whole.

As to this fourth edition, we live in a swiftly changing age when even our most basic assumptions seem constantly to require adjustment, modification, and updating. In response, roughly a third of the book has been rewritten. Photographs are mostly new, but only where they serve to illustrate a point as well as or better than the old ones. Many of the old favorites remain. I have tried to avoid the temptation to be new or different just for the sake of novelty.

Special gratitude is due to a number of people: to Lousene Rousseau, my invaluable guide and editor during the preparation of the first two editions; to Jeff Meeks, who piloted me through the third; and to James B. Smith and Robert Ginsberg for the present edition. Scores of people assisted in the collecting of photographs; special thanks are due to Charlotte Solomon Guindon of the Guthrie Theatre and to Douglas Allan, publicity director at Stratford, Ontario. On a more personal level I must mention my son Professor Gordon C. Whiting, Professor Arthur H. Ballet, and a number of unknown critics who provided me with unusually thorough and scholarly advice. Finally, my thanks to Josinette, who once more typed the manuscript and nursed me through the birth pains of this fourth edition.

Frank M Whiting

TO THE TEACHER

There are many ways in which an introductory theatre course can be organized, and most of the best teachers will insist on organizing it in their own way—which is as it should be. Good courses, like people, have personalities.

During my own years as a teacher of such courses I experimented with numerous approaches: lumping all the arts and crafts together around the life and philosophic background of each period (a "history of the theatre" approach), working from the known to the unknown (beginning with today and working backward to the theatre's heritage), emphasizing present theory and practice, and emphasizing factual backgrounds. I finally ended, however, as I had begun and very much as the present text is organized: by dividing theatre into its customary components and then considering the historical facts, followed by highlights from modern theory and practice in each case. This approach, while never followed slavishly, seemed to be the most natural and clear and the least pretentious. It is the way in which most college curricula are divided (acting, directing, design, etc.). It also afforded a chance to include guest instructors for one lecture in each of the areas, thus introducing students to our staff as well as to the theatre. Needless to say, whatever the approach, the student should eventually gain a rounded image of the theatre as a whole.

Perhaps more important than the organization is the imaginative use of supplementary resources and materials. Many teachers make extensive use of films and filmstrips; many include visits to other theatres; some require a limited amount of backstage crew work; many insist on attendance at live plays (especially when high-quality productions are available); and almost all teachers require the reading of a few plays. Fortunately, a number of excellent anthologies are now available to assist in this last requirement.

All good introductory courses will, of course, relate theatre to the rest of life, especially to the humanities and the other fine arts. The depth to which this is done, however, will depend to some extent on the time available and the basic interests of the students involved. In many colleges an introductory theatre course is now offered as a general appreciation course; in others it is essentially a beginning course for prospective theatre majors. It is hoped that the arrangement of *An Introduction to the Theatre* is clear and simple enough so that the teacher wishing to do so may, within limits, rearrange the reading assignments to harmonize with his or her approach.

PART
ONE

PLAYS AND PLAYWRIGHTS

CHAPTER 1

WHY THEATRE?

When this book first appeared in the early 1950s, the legitimate professional theatre in America seemed about to fulfill the chronic prediction of its pessimists by dying. *Variety*, the trade magazine of professional entertainment, estimated that on an average night fewer than 65,000 people would be found attending the professional theatre whereas tens of millions would be watching television and movies, to say nothing of other forms of entertainment. Then by the late 1960s the traditional theatre faced another threat to its existence. This time the threat came not from without but from within, as youthful rebels, reacting to an ugly war and governmental corruption, turned against theatre as a tool of the Establishment. The old theatre, they cried, was dishonest and decadent. What was needed was a new theatre: a theatre that would move from the playhouse into the streets, "where the action was"; a theatre that was relevant to immediate problems; a theatre that was spontaneous and dedicated to the destruction of obsolete, traditional values; a theatre using unabashed nudity, four-letter words, and insults, among its more potent weapons.

But by the mid-1970s the old living theatre appeared to have weathered these threats to its existence. Legitimate professional theatres were springing up in cities all across the nation. Colleges and universities had constructed hundreds of magnificent playhouses and were pouring millions into the support of theatre programs. Professional dinner theatres were to be found in most of the larger cities. And the old Broadway commercial theatre "just kept rollin' along." Competition from movies and television seemed to have stabilized into something more like a family partnership than cutthroat rivalry, and the youthful rebellion had subsided, leaving a residue of fresh thinking and new techniques that promised to revitalize the theatre and shake it from its old ruts. The legitimate theatre seemed on the threshold of an exciting period of renewal. The "fabulous invalid" had once more regained its health. Like the phoenix, that miraculous bird of Egyptian mythology that consumed itself in fire then rose again from the ashes, the theatre was once more alive and well and living in the United States.

But even so, average American citizens still regard theatre as something distinctly peripheral to their existence. They are skeptical, puzzled, and a little annoyed by all the attention, and especially the money, being "lavished" on theatre by universities, foundations, and arts councils. Were theatre a matter of entertainment alone, such skepticism might well be justified, but in its finer moments theatre is not only entertainment; it is something more. In such moments its playwrights, actors, directors, and designers have sought for the meaning of existence with the same passion and sincerity that have characterized the work of great scientists, philosophers, and theologians. For in its essence the art of theatre rests on a common foundation with all learning: on the human capacity to explore, wonder, and reflect. Most of our lives drift along in a hubbub of the trivial, the confused, and the habitual, our vision numbed by the blind staggers of conformity. But occasionally, alone on some hilltop under the stars, on the timbered shore of a lake under the northern lights, at the bedside of a sick child, or simply at a glimpse of April's crisp watercress in a hillside spring, the trivial, confused, and habitual disappear, and an awareness of meaning and beauty sweeps over us. It is with moments such as these that great art deals, and it is primarily with the theatre as an art that this book is concerned.

On the other hand, it would be dishonest to pretend that theatre always functions on the level of "great art," for few words have a wider range of connotation. As an imitation of life the theatre eventually embraces almost everything that life embraces, including much of life's chaos. Consider, for example, some of the contrasting attitudes toward theatre throughout the ages.

To the ancient Greeks, the theatre was a religious ritual commanding the devotion of the best minds in the community; to the Romans, on the other hand, it eventually became little more than a degraded pleasure—a project by slaves for the titillation of their masters. To the early Church, the theatre was an evil to be crushed, along with thievery and prostitution; to the same Church a few centuries later, some of the great mystery and miracle plays became almost holy rites. To many entertainers, from strolling players to television comedians, the theatre has usually been regarded as a means of earning a living through a few jokes and antics designed to catch the momentary fancy of the general public. To great playwrights, on the other hand, it has provided a means of probing honestly and fearlessly for the meaning of life and the mystery of existence. To some parents the theatre is an evil bound to wreck the personality and character of any child who succumbs to its lures; to many teachers and some psychiatrists it is practically a panacea for all personality and character ills.

THE THEATRE'S HERITAGE

But even if the revival of the American theatre during the 1970s had not occurred—even if the professional theatre in America were now dead—the theatre would still be worthy of study and concern, for unlike its amazing twentieth-century offsprings—motion pictures and television—the live theatre has exerted an influence on human civilization for over 2500 years. To those who distrust anything not of their own generation, the theatre's age may brand it as old-fashioned, but to most of us the theatre's heritage commands deep respect, for it represents the cumulative accomplishments of all ages. Left naked and alone at birth, we would be helpless and ignorant. It is our tremendous inheritance from the past that provides the knowledge and skills on which civilization rests. Each of us owes a staggering debt to those who have gone before, and so it is with theatre; for although movies, radio, and television have

other arts, is frequently forgotten. Booth Tarkington once wrote: "A country could be perfectly governed, immensely powerful and without poverty; yet if it produced nothing of its own in architecture, sculpture, music, painting or in books, it would some day pass into the twilight of history, leaving only the traces of a creditable political record."[2] America today faces such a challenge. In spite of its recent setbacks, America's wealth, energy, military might, and material power remain impressive, but in the realm of culture and great ideas it has only recently begun to prove itself. Let us not forget that Rome also excelled in most of the ways that America has done: its engineers were without equal; its armed might was supreme; its financiers amassed untold wealth; its politicians wrangled with undignified fervor; its swimming pools were as lavish as those of Florida or California. And yet after approximately five centuries of control of the entire Western world, Rome left little to excite the mind and admiration of people comparable in lasting glory to the contributions of the little city of Athens, which controlled but a fraction of the earth's surface and held world leadership for less than a century. One Greek play, *Oedipus the King*, probably outweighs all the words and deeds of the entire Roman senate. Were it not for the achievements of its architects, sculptors, lawyers, and a few of its early Latin poets and philosophers, Rome's reputation today would be sorry indeed.

THE THEATRE AS A FINE ART

Unlike most human creations, the arts tend to endure. The banquet once consumed and the automobile once burned out disappear and are soon forgotten, but great art continues: "A thing of beauty is a joy forever." Art reaches across the barriers of time and space. It penetrates the barriers of creed, race, and nationality. Through its magic we share experiences with Sophocles, Shakespeare, Goethe, Strindberg. *The Trojan Women* and *Lysistrata* have as much significance for belligerent nations today as they had for Athens and Sparta 2500 years ago. *Electra* and *King*

---

[2]"The Indiana University Auditorium," published in commemoration of the completion of Indiana University's auditorium and theatre in 1941.

Lear have left modern audiences more genuinely and deeply moved than anything our own age has to offer. Present-day productions of *The Birds* and *The Merry Wives of Windsor* have provoked gales of laughter that have literally stopped the shows for almost minutes at a time. Styles in the material things of life may change and grow old-fashioned; but the fundamental experiences of human nature—the exuberance of youth, the thrill of young love, the sting of ingratitude—these are the heritage and common property of all people and all ages.

As Tyrone Guthrie has pointed out, the English language shelters a vast treasure house of dramatic literature. To let this wealth of drama lie unproduced would be an incredible waste. It would be like a very rich man who kept a priceless collection of paintings locked away where not even he could see them, or a land where great symphonies were available on paper but were never played.

Without quibbling over which is the greatest of the arts, let us remember that the theatre makes its appeal on two levels: the aesthetic and the intellectual. On the aesthetic level the theatre, like music, painting, and dancing, makes its contribution to the emotional needs of people and to their hunger for the beautiful. On the intellectual level, many of the greatest ideas ever conceived were first expressed in dramatic form. Moreover, ideas and concepts originated by philosophers, theologians, and scientists have often been popularized and communicated via the theatre. No other branch of human learning can point with pride to a more impressive list of great names. No other field of literature can equal the drama in the total extent of its contributions.

It is odd that in spite of such a heritage parents often try to discourage any desire on the part of their children to study the theatre and odd that some excellent students who are attracted by theatre should resist their impulse to associate themselves with it because they feel that for some mysterious reason it is not quite respectable. For the legitimate theatre not only has a long and glorious heritage, but it is still important today. Even in 1952, when the professional theatre was at one of its lowest ebbs, Professor Barnard Hewitt was able to observe:

> Paradoxically, the prestige of the professional living stage remains largely undiminished. It may in fact be higher than it was in 1900 or even in 1929, for with the decline in the number of plays, the quality on the average has

risen. At any rate, the stage wields an influence on the rest of theatre in America out of all proportion to its size and scope.[3]

One reason for the comparatively high quality of legitimate drama may lie in the quality of its audience. To its sorrow financially but to its credit artistically, it has lost most of its audience of tired businessmen, 12-year-old intelligences, thrill seekers, and others who regard any form of theatre as a mere matter of entertainment. It may be significant that playwrights like Eugene O'Neill arrived on the American scene after the movies had begun to drain away the theatre's popular audience. If we are justified in assuming that the quality of the audience has an influence on the quality of playwriting, then one of the brightest hopes for the future of legitimate drama lies in the outstanding quality of the audiences now attending university theatres and professional repertory theatres throughout the country. In educational background, taste, and intelligence, such audiences are probably equal or superior to any audiences in the long history of the theatre. As Arthur Miller pointed out in 1974, "The central fact is that [universities] contain an audience that is seeking rather than jaded, open to fresh experiences rather than nostalgic for what it has comfortably known."[4]

THE THEATRE AS EXPERIENCE

The human hunger to share experience, according to Tolstoi, is the basic impulse behind all art; John Dewey further amplified this idea in his book *Art as Experience*. Even the richest of lives can touch directly but a fraction of the potential range of human experience; fortunately, we can also accumulate experience indirectly, especially through the theatre and other arts. Moreover, experience gained via art, while not normally as intense as that gained through personal involvement, has other qualities that in some ways make it a greater value. Direct personal involvement in a deeply painful or traumatic life experience may so cloud and con-

[3]Barnard Hewitt; "Theatre U.S.A.: Actual and Potential," *Quarterly Journal of Speech*, December 1952, pp. 385–386.
[4]*University of Michigan Theatre Program* for Arthur Miller's *Up from Paradise*, April 1974.

FIGURE 1:1   The fun and excitement of sharing in a theatrical experience can begin at an early age. Children's audiences at the University of Utah.

fuse our awareness that all meaning is distorted or destroyed, but from the safety of a darkened auditorium the meaning and significance of a similar experience, involving someone else, can become clear and strangely enjoyable. We have been detached from the painful, personal features. We watch with deep involvement and compassion, but we are in a position of godlike superiority; we are able to observe, empathize, sympathize, and understand, but we are not required to take direct action or suffer unpleasant consequences. We enjoy with an attitude of detachment that has come to be known as *aesthetic distance*.

There are those today who maintain that aesthetic distance has been overemphasized and misinterpreted. In some respects they are undoubtedly right. Certainly it was a mistake, when the principle was first articulated, for its overly enthusiastic disciples to assume that aesthetic distance could easily be shattered by acting or directing that was too convincing, or that it could be destroyed by placing actors too close to the audience. From the director or actor's standpoint, the opposite is almost invariably the problem—that is, how to decrease the distance and make the play convincing enough so that the audience will become involved—that is, will feel, or empathize with, the lives and problems of the characters.

Thus the customary view that the director and actor must maintain a delicate balance between aesthetic distance (detachment) on the one hand and empathy (involvement) on the other is misleading. In the conventional theatre with a conventional play, sufficient detachment is practically inevitable, while it is almost impossible to achieve too much involvement.[5] Even when a play is superbly performed, and the audience is said to be "carried away," we are somehow still aware that we are watching a play, not life itself. We do not try to prevent the murder of Desdemona or call the police; we know that Ophelia will recover in time to take a charming curtain call; we realize that Hamlet does not really mean, "The rest is silence," and that he will perform again tomorrow night. No, the danger that a conventional play will be mistaken for real life hardly ever occurs except in very young children or in very abnormal

[5]Texts on the subject sometimes cite amateur accidents—a chair that unexpectedly breaks under an awkward actor, a balcony that sways under an overweight Juliet, an actor embarrassed by a forgotten line or a fit of coughing—as examples of shattered aesthetic distance (or underdistance). But although in such cases we may underdistance toward the performers, at the same time we may overdistance toward the play—the work of art itself.

adults; on the contrary, the struggle to secure deeper involvement is constant. In fact, producers of thrill movies like *Jaws* take pride and profit from the fact that many members of the audience momentarily lose their detachment and scream when the great white shark suddenly rams itself onto the deck. Yet even in such extreme cases, audiences realize that they are watching a movie and that they are not actually on the deck of that small fishing rig. Aesthetic distance has been maintained to an extent that permits them to enjoy the experience — to love the fact that for a moment they almost thought the shark had them.

INTIMACY OF THE THEATRE EXPERIENCE

There is another aspect related to sharing experience via the theatre that should not be overlooked. This is the legitimate drama's quality of intimacy — perhaps its one solid advantage over its more prosperous offspring of the mass media.

In the theatre the process of stimulation and appreciation functions in two directions at once — from actor to audience and from audience to actor. As a result, something resembling a chain reaction of stimulus and response may reach proportions that can result in an "inspired" performance. With the living actor and an intimate theatre, this sharing of experience can be heightened to a degree that is difficult to achieve in any mechanical media.

It now seems strange that although intimacy was the one certain element that gave theatre an advantage over its rivals of the mass media, nothing was done to capitalize on it during the first half of the twentieth century as the American theatre was steadily losing ground to these rivals. In fact, the theatre, caught in the toils of realism, first struggled to move in the opposite direction: It abandoned asides and soliloquies; it frowned upon curtain calls and undue applause; college textbooks and professors misinterpreted and overemphasized aesthetic distance; and, worst of all, the commercial theatres outside New York tended to grow larger and larger until the distant actor or actress became more impersonal to those in the back half of the house than the shadows on a movie screen. Ironically, almost every major "reform" tended to drive audience and performers further apart, until the professional theatre was driven

supremacy and war may be highly moral as well as brilliantly entertaining, whereas the same play has often been censured by the general public as shockingly indecent.

Related to this is the fact that the comparative cost of producing a play, especially on the noncommercial level, is trivial compared with the cost of producing either a movie or a television show. Those creative enough to do so can experiment with the production of new scripts, new staging techniques, and new acting and directing styles without encountering the overwhelming hazards, restrictions, and other problems that neutralize so many creative ideas in the realm of the mass media.

To summarize, the legitimate theatre, because of its long and outstanding history, because of its contribution to both the aesthetic and the intellectual needs of people, because of the quality of its audience, because of its strong bond between audience and performer, because of its power to increase and enrich experience, and because of its value to those who participate in its production, seems destined to live on for another few thousand years. It is the logical training ground and starting point for the student of any or all theatre arts, for living theatre is the root, the parent, from which all others have sprung.

CHAPTER 2

CLASSIC DRAMA

Just when the first play was written no one knows. The theatre's origin has been traced as far back as Egypt in the year 4000 B.C.,[1] and it probably extends much further. For our purposes, however, the real beginning is comparatively definite: It centers in Greece during the fifth century B.C. The first important date seems to be 534 B.C., when Thespis, a man justly or unjustly hailed as the world's first actor, won the first tragic contest. Such an item becomes insignificant, however, when placed beside the overwhelming fact that during the single century from 500 B.C. to 400 B.C., the little city of Athens gave the world four of its greatest playwrights: Aeschylus, Sophocles, Euripides, and Aristophanes.

The factors responsible for this amazing burst of creative energy—and it expressed itself in all arts and sciences, not just in theatre—have never been entirely explained, even though volumes have been written on the subject. Certainly religion had something to do with it, for the Greeks had developed a friendly, personal, human attitude toward their

[1] George Freedley and John A. Reeves, *A History of the Theatre* (New York: Crown, 1941), p. 2.

gods—an attitude that emphasized the here rather than the hereafter, an attitude that called for expression, not repression. Politics played a part: Democratic in spirit if not always in practice, Athens produced a generation of citizens bursting with pride, curiosity, and independence. Finally, the very pattern of historical events in the early years of the period set off a surge of national exuberance seldom if ever equaled. At Marathon, Thermopylae, Salamis, and Platea, the Greeks, fighting against overwhelming odds, had covered themselves with undying military glory. It requires no strain of the imagination to realize the emotional and intellectual potentials that such events must have engendered. In all probability, life never held more promise for the future, the privilege of living never seemed more exciting, and the thirst to share and enjoy experi-

FIGURE 2:1 The classic tradition still lives. A performance of Euripides' *Hecuba* in the ancient (reconstructed) theatre at Epidauros.

ence never infected humankind to a healthier degree than during these few short years commonly referred to as "the Golden Age."

In a sense the theatre provided an almost perfect medium of expression for this surging spirit of Greece, though its purpose and nature must not be confused with the more common forms of dramatic entertainment found today. To the Greeks the theatre was not primarily a form of romantic escape. It was not primarily an art for the select few. It was not primarily an avenue of self-expression for the stage-struck. It was rather a vital, living experience that probed into some of life's most basic problems with courageous honesty, and it was shared by the entire community.

Its origin lay in religious ceremonials, not to an omniscient or perfect God, but to a complex and imperfect one, Dionysus—a being with godlike powers and immortality but with an emotional nature that ranged from the sublime and the beautiful through love, fertility, and madcap drunkenness down to the most terrifying forms of Freudian darkness and revenge. In other words, Dionysus was the god of the emotional, the subconscious, and the irrational forces in people—forces that range from ecstasy to terror. Plays were presented during three of the four religious festivals held annually in his honor: the Lesser (rural) Dionysia in December; the Lenaean festival in January, which stressed comedy; and the Great (city) Dionysia in the springtime, which emphasized tragedy. The excitement and anticipation that preceded the city Dionysia—rehearsals, ceremonials, torchlight parades—seem to have affected practically everyone in Athens. Business, politics, and even war came to a standstill; the play was the thing. Consequently, it should not be surprising to learn that the men responsible for the plays were not narrow specialists; they were leaders in thought and often in action.

GREEK TRAGEDY

AESCHYLUS

Aeschylus (525–456 B.C.), first of the great playwrights, had been an outstanding soldier at both Marathon and Salamis; it is likely that every Athenian knew and respected him. Consequently, when he wrote he had ideas and experiences to share, and as a result his plays have scope and surging power. They feature heroes, kings, and gods caught up in volcanic crises. Since he was a founding father in the city as well as in the theatre, his faith in his country was firm, his belief in the gods unshakable, and his hope for the future of humanity unlimited.

Of the 90 plays he is supposed to have written, only seven complete scripts remain: *The Suppliants, The Persians, Prometheus Bound, The Seven Against Thebes,* and *The Oresteia,* which is actually a group of three plays *(Agamemnon, The Choephori,* and *The Eumenides)* that form one of the world's most famous trilogies.

The first play of the trilogy, *Agamemnon,* begins at dawn as signal fires bring news to the queen, Clytemnestra, that Troy has fallen and that Agamemnon, the king, will soon be home. The dramatic intensity of this news is apparent when we learn that Clytemnestra hates Agamemnon because ten years before he had sacrificed their daughter, Iphigenia, in order that the Greek fleet might sail against Troy. Moreover, in his absence the queen has taken a lover, Agamemnon's mortal enemy, Aegisthus. The play moves swiftly. Clytemnestra and her paramour plot the king's death. We see Agamemnon return, accompanied by his mad and visionary mistress, Cassandra. We see him greeted by a cordial but false show of affection, and finally we see him walk up the purple carpet into his palace and to death. The first play ends as his murderers appear before the chorus, boldly justifying their deed because of crimes Agamemnon had committed against them.

The second play, *The Choephori,* begins many years later. The murder of Agamemnon has gone unavenged. Aegisthus and Clytemnestra have firmly established themselves as king and queen; but they have underestimated the drive for revenge on the part of Agamemnon's children, Electra and Orestes. In this second play these children, goaded by Apollo, are reunited after years of forced separation. The trap is soon laid, and Clytemnestra and Aegisthus meet death at the hand of Orestes. Instead of peace, however, this act of revenge launches a pack of Furies upon Orestes, for he is now guilty of the blood of his own mother.

The third play of the trilogy, *The Eumenides,* again centers on Orestes, who after years of torture finally appeals for a trial in the Athenian court of justice. After much debate the goddess Athena herself intervenes to acquit him, and thus the long, terrible blood feud comes to an end.

This account can, of course, serve only as the barest suggestion of

FIGURE 2:2   The Guthrie Theatre's production of *The House of Atreus*, a modern adaptation of the *Oresteia* by John Lewin. Directed by Tyrone Guthrie; designed by Tanya Moiseiwitsch.

what this Greek tragedy is about. It indicates none of the poetic richness, the penetrating ideas, or the dramatic energy that make Aeschylus great. Nor does it reveal such defects as his carelessness regarding details and motivation. Yet this very disregard for detail points toward his strength, which lies in the boundless energy and unrestricted scope of his imagination, thought, and expression.

SOPHOCLES

Not so colorful as a man but greater as a playwright was Sophocles (496–406 B.C.), whose personal life and writing both seem to have verged on perfection. His craftsmanship has been held up as a standard for 25 centuries. No other playwright who thought so deeply has ever expressed himself with such technical perfection. Motivation, suspense, dramatic irony, poetry, and balanced judgment are among the things of which he was master. Seven of his plays, *Oedipus the King*, *Electra*, *Oedipus at Colonus*, *Ajax*, *Antigone*, *The Trachiniae*, and *Philoctetes*, have been preserved; and at least one of them, probably *Oedipus the King*, *Electra*, or *Antigone*, should be required reading for every student in theatre. Anyone with sufficient imagination to respond to the dramatic intensity that surges through these plays should find no difficulty in understanding why Sophocles is universally considered one of the greatest writers of all time.

Oedipus the King is regarded by many as the most perfect tragedy ever written. In the century following its first production, Aristotle used this play to illustrate many points in his great critical work, *The Poetics*. In particular, he praised its involved plot, where every incident is somehow so interwoven in a cause-and-effect relationship with other incidents that not only motivation but a supreme effect of dramatic irony is achieved. As the tragedy begins, the city of Thebes is being racked by plague; death, sorrow, and suffering are everywhere. Into the crisis steps the young King Oedipus. He stands before his people in the morning sunlight, strong, proud, and confident; his words ring with conviction as he pledges every ounce of strength in lifting the plague, certain beyond a shadow of a doubt that he is right, so secure in his position that a word of caution from his brother-in-law, Creon, is interpreted as treason and a warning from the blind prophet, Tiresias, as lunacy. Yet only one terrible hour later this confident and proud man, faced with the fact of his hideous though unintentional crimes, gouges out his own eyes, for they had been blind to the truth. As he leaves for a life of self-imposed exile, the chorus speaks:

> Make way for Oedipus. All people said,
> "That is a fortunate man";
> And now what storms are beating on his head!
> Call no man fortunate that is not dead.
> The dead are free from pain.[2]

Read this play the next time overbearing pride and self-sufficiency threaten to take possession of you. Perhaps Sophocles was sounding a

[2]Sophocles, *King Oedipus*, trans. W. B. Yeats from *The Collected Plays of W. B. Yeats* (New York: Macmillan, 1928). Copyright 1934, 1952 by Macmillan Publishing Co., Inc.; reprinted by permission.

FIGURE 2:3 Sophocles' *Oedipus the King.* The opening production at the Festival Theatre in Stratford, Ontario; directed by Tyrone Guthrie; designed by Tanya Moiseiwitsch.

warning to his own city of Athens, which at that time stood proud and confident. Or was it a warning to any man, woman, group, or nation that grows too proud and confident?

It would be misleading to imply that only one universal idea, the danger of overbearing pride, is found in *Oedipus the King.* Sophocles is concerned with many ideas, among them the ironic truth that people with eyes often see less well than those who are blind. We are also challenged by the nobility and strength with which Oedipus searches out the truth, no matter who suffers or how great the cost. Beyond such themes or ideas there is rich imagery and beauty in the language, and finally there is the terrible fascination of the struggle itself, for every move that Oedipus makes only serves, by some ironic twist of fate, to draw the meshes of doom more securely about him.

EURIPIDES

Last of the great Greek tragic writers was Euripides (480–406 B.C.). Expressions such as "Aeschylus wrote of the gods, Sophocles of heroes, and Euripides of men" suggest some of the basic differences between Euripides and the older masters.

The relationship of the playwright to his environment is nowhere more apparent than in the examples of Aeschylus and Euripides. The first, born of a wealthy and fairly privileged family, lived at the time of Marathon—when Athens was young and full of hope. Euripides, although only 45 years younger, found himself in a world that had already started to decline into a series of tyrannies and into a senseless war with Sparta that was eventually to destroy Athens. Doubt, suffering, and skepticism appear to have become his early companions. Not that he was a malcontent or hopeless pessimist, for almost any thinking person born without a film over his or her eyes would have felt the same. He was simply a freethinker and humanitarian thrust into a world where war, profit, blind obedience, and intolerance were rapidly gaining the upper hand. His plays clearly reflect the environment in which he lived. In 416 B.C., for example, the Athenians sent a brutal military expedition against the island of Melos. Successful in battle, they slaughtered the men and took the women prisoners. The following year in *The Trojan Women* Euripides depicted an almost identical crime with a burning pathos generally regarded as the most powerful attack ever hurled against war. While this is the outstanding example, many other plays of Euripides show a close and unmistakable relationship between what he saw and what he wrote.

Throughout most of his plays runs a thinly veiled skepticism of the gods, a disregard for the supernatural or the accidental, and a fascination with the human and psychological motives behind peoples' acts. In *Medea*, for example, we are concerned less with a struggle of the individual against fate than with the inner struggle of a woman torn between the devouring passions of love and revenge.

It must be admitted that the plays of Euripides are spotty and un-

FIGURE 2:4 Euripides' *The Trojan Women* at MacAlester College; directed by Mary Gwen Owen. Note the realistic style of production in contrast to the ritualistic style of the Guthrie productions in Figures 2:2 and 2:3. Both approaches can be effective.

even in comparison with those of Sophocles. Perhaps his discouragement with life in general resulted in the disregard for dramatic technique that frequently mars his work, although many of the things that seemed like carelessness to Victorian critics are now recognized as carefully calculated strokes of bitterness and irony. Victorian critics, for example, assumed that his frequent use of the *deus ex machina* (the mechanical use of a god to provide a contrived solution) was simply a lazy way of untangling a hopelessly involved situation, whereas we now recognize that some of these pat, conventional solutions proposed by the gods are shockingly ironic and were undoubtedly recognized as such by Greek audiences.

Euripides died in exile, having known little of the success and fame that were to be heaped upon him almost as soon as he was gone; for in the century that followed, he became the most popular of the three tragic playwrights. This probably accounts for the fact that 17 of his tragedies have been preserved, plus one satyr play, *The Cyclops*. This is the only complete satyr play that has come down to us, even though the rules required that each group of tragedies had to be followed by one of these strange burlesques.

CHARACTERISTICS OF GREEK TRAGEDY

Before going further, several general characteristics of Greek tragedy deserve amplification.

1. Greek tragedy does not always end in the death of the main characters or the protagonist. As we shall see later in discussing Aristotle's *The Poetics*, the subject matter is always serious and of magnitude, but the leading character is sometimes left alive and free, redeemed and to a certain extent ennobled through suffering.

2. A single Greek tragedy lasts only slightly more than one hour. Three tragedies plus one satyr play were presented each day. In fact, the entire *Oresteia* trilogy requires approximately the same playing time as either *Hamlet* or *King Lear*. This fact throws some light upon the much discussed problem of the three classic unities: *time*, which required that the action take place within a single day; *place*, which required that the action be confined to a single locality; and *action*, which required that there be but one plot. Although the individual plays within a Greek trilogy quite naturally obeyed these unities, the entire trilogy did not. Moreover, no rigid insistence upon the unities is found in either the Greek plays or the writings of Aristotle. This erroneous concept originated centuries later through misinterpretation of Aristotle by overzealous French and Italian critics.

3. Immediately apparent to anyone reading a Greek tragedy is the importance of the chorus. Much of the finest poetry, some of the dramatic action, and many of the ideas are given to the chorus. To understand

this we should remember the religious origin of drama. At first, an audience plus the chorus with its leader was the whole show. Then Thespis added one actor, Aeschylus a second, and Sophocles a third, but even with three actors the chorus still remained a very important part of Attic drama.

4. To the Greeks, tragedy was designed to serve a definite purpose. That purpose, according to Aristotle, was to effect a catharsis, a purgation of the soul through pity and fear. While no one today seems certain of exactly what this means, it was probably nothing as mysterious as one is often led to believe. Almost everyone has experienced something not unlike it when, obsessed with petty troubles and worries (final exams, tea parties, public performances), he or she has been forced to pause for an experience (personal tragedy, contact with nature, a religious experience) that has swept life's pettiness away.

GREEK COMEDY

Comedy, like tragedy, was clearly associated with the worship of Dionysus. Its origin lay principally in rites of fertility and reproduction. The phallus (symbolic male sex organ) was prominently displayed, which partially accounts for the Victorian rejection of Greek comedy as shocking and obscene. But although important in the plays by Aristophanes, sex was invariably secondary to satire, and perhaps the most amazing thing about Aristophanic comedy is the total freedom that this satire enjoyed. At a time when Athens was fighting for survival in a war even more stupid and tragic than most wars, Aristophanes produced plays that unmercifully flayed war, Athenian leaders, and Athenian institutions. In fact, the audience seems to have enjoyed the ridicule of anyone or anything important, whether the ridicule was funny or not. In a surprising number of instances real people were impersonated without so much as changing their names. Even mild-mannered Socrates suffered the indignity of finding himself caricatured as little more than a muddle-headed buffoon suspended between earth and heaven in a basket. Tradition has it that with characteristic good humor, the great philosopher rose from the audience to take a bow and show that he too enjoyed the fun.

ARISTOPHANES

Aristophanes (c. 448 – c. 385 B.C.) was by no means the only comic writer of the period, but everyone agrees that he was the greatest. Moreover, he is the only one to have had several of his comedies preserved in their entirety. After reading them, one comes to view Aristophanes as a man of astonishing brilliance and devastating wit. Absolutely fearless, he seems to have held nothing sacred. He ridiculed whomever and whatever his fancy selected. He was a conservative, constantly crusading for a return to the good old days, always opposing the new or the progressive — which included both Socrates and Euripides. His plays are frequently defective in technique and dramatic structure. Obviously he could have done better had he tried, but it is altogether characteristic that such a hell-raising old genius would not want to try. As a matter of fact, conscientious care regarding details would probably have destroyed the audacious, breathtaking mixture of ribaldry, satire, and poetic fancy that is the essence of his fascination. One moment we have a passage that is a gem of tender, unexcelled lyricism; next we are plunged into a scene so lusty and bawdy that even modern audiences are sometimes thoroughly shocked.

Most of his plays — *The Frogs*, *The Birds*, and *The Clouds*, for example — take their titles from his choruses, whose antics undoubtedly provided much of the merriment. A brief sketch of *The Frogs* may give some inkling of the mad brilliance and originality with which his mind worked.

Both Sophocles and Euripides appear to have died in the same year, 406 B.C., and Athens suddenly found itself without a major tragic poet. To any ordinary mind this would have occasioned nothing more than a stuffy tribute. Not so with Aristophanes. This was material for his next comedy! It begins as Dionysus, alarmed by the absence of a first-rate tragic poet, decides to visit Hades and demand the return of Euripides. Accompanied by his servant Xanthias, he sets out disguised as Hercules, the only person to have made the dangerous journey successfully. The slapstick possibilities afforded by equipping slightly tipsy, roly-poly Dionysus with the club and lion skin of Hercules are obvious, but this is only the beginning. Arriving at the door of Aeacus, judge of the dead, Dionysus announces himself as Hercules and receives such a vicious

FIGURE 2:5 Aristophanes' *The Birds* at the University of Utah; designed by Howard Gee; costumes by George Maxwell.

tongue-lashing that he falls to the ground overcome with fear. (Hercules, on his previous journey, had strangled the old man's watchdog.) Finally recovering his wits, Dionysus changes places with Xanthias on the theory that it is safer to be the servant than the master. Again the door opens, but this time a beautiful maid of Persephone appears to welcome him. Before Xanthias can join the waiting dancing girls, however, Dionysus again forces him to change places, just in time to be caught by a raging landlady. Finally the two are apprehended by guards of Aeacus. To escape torture, Dionysus protests that he is a god. To make sure, they torture him and Xanthias anyhow, on the theory that if either is a god he should feel no pain. God or not, Dionysus does feel it, and a hilarious endurance contest follows.

After a half-hour of such buffoonery, Dionysus and Xanthias arrive at the realm of Pluto, where they find not only Euripides but also Aeschylus and Sophocles. Soon a great trial is under way to decide which of the three playwrights deserves to return. Sophocles, quite in character, graciously withdraws, but the battle rages between Aeschylus and Euripides. Finally it is settled by literally weighing the verse of each, which of course makes Aeschylus the winner. Played as the Greeks must have played it, the comic possibilities are practically unlimited.

MENANDER AND THE NEW COMEDY

The plays of Aristophanes and his contemporaries are classified as *Old Comedy*. Approximately a century later this was replaced by another form, known as *New Comedy*, with Menander (c. 342 – c. 291 B.C.) as its leading playwright. Until very recently Menander's fame rested chiefly on the high praise heaped upon him by Quintilian and other ancients who had access to his works, and on the use of many of his plays as acknowledged models by Roman writers, including Plautus and Terence. Then in 1905 portions of three of his plays were discovered in Egypt; and in 1959 his first complete play, *The Curmudgeon (Dyskolos)*, which had recently been found in Switzerland among a collection of old papyri, was translated by Gilbert Highet and published in America.[3] The play tends to reinforce most of the impressions scholars had already formed about Menander. Its contrast to Aristophanic comedy is striking, for Menander's work is a pleasantly exaggerated, gentle, and somewhat sentimental little comedy that could be performed today by the most puritanical group without cutting a single line. Many plays by Aristophanes if produced in a similar environment could retain little more than the title! All of the characters in *The Curmudgeon* are essentially honest and good. The wealthy young lover wins his rustic sweetheart in a most honest and upright fashion. In his own words, "There is no prize that can't be won by work and application." Even the curmudgeon, the irascible old father of the girl, is won over by good deeds rather than trickery and is finally forced partially to accept his fellow men and make peace with them. Sir Richard Steele, the great champion of sentimental comedy, would have loved it.

In general, the following contrasts exist between New and Old Comedy: (1) New Comedy no longer indulged in personal or political satire. Athens, occupied by the Macedonians at this time, was humbled and content to accept quietly whatever freedom or enjoyment was al-

[3]*Horizon*, July 1959.

lowed. (2) The chorus, a vital factor in Old Comedy, entirely disappeared in New Comedy. (3) The plots of New Comedy usually centered on a love story: the pursuit of a young girl by an amorous young man, with old men and parents as the chief obstacles. (4) There was an obvious tendency to use stock characters in New Comedy, though these characters often show a surprising depth of humanity. (5)Perhaps because the New Comedy playwrights lived in an age of sadness and poverty, the plays show traits of wisdom, tender irony, and resignation.

In any event, the discovery of *The Curmudgeon* is one of the important literary finds of our time. It adds a small but pleasing gem to the close of a great age, the Golden Age of Greece.

ROMAN DRAMA

Perhaps the main point that needs to be explained about Roman drama is the lack of it. True, the Romans could boast of three important playwrights, Plautus, Terence, and Seneca. But Plautus and Terence wrote when the empire was young and even then did little more than adapt and translate from the Greek; while Seneca—well, Seneca is an isolated phenomenon, a sort of accident. Reasons for Rome's sterility in drama, especially after the great empire matured, are not hard to deduce. A native drama of some promise had begun to develop; then Rome became a conqueror, and among its early victims was Greece. Now, what does a conqueror do after defeating a nation whose art is obviously superior to its own? One practical solution is to dismiss such art as unimportant, the work of an inferior race. Consequently, though Romans might condescend to enjoy theatre, the work—writing, acting, technical effects, and all the rest—was left to slaves—Greek slaves if possible, often rather brilliant and clever fellows, but of course an inferior race. It is therefore not surprising to learn that Terence began his career as a slave; that Seneca was a foreigner, a Spaniard; and that Plautus, though not a slave, was a rough Italian jack-of-all-trades in the early days before Romans had learned to regard themselves with proper racial dignity. Contrast all this with the social and religious prestige of a playwright at the time of Aeschylus, and you have at least one reason for Rome's inferiority in the realm of playwriting.

PLAUTUS

So much for the great Roman plays that were not written; now a few words about the good ones that were. The first to have any of his plays preserved was Plautus (Titus Maccius Plautus, c. 254–184 B.C.). According to tradition, his colorful life included adventures as an actor, soldier, merchant, and grinder of meal. He turned to playwriting when he was past middle age and seems to have scored an immediate success. The rough and rowdy vigor of his life carried over into the spirit of his comedies in a way that engendered enthusiastic response from the noisy crowds that appear to have made up the early Roman audience. He knew this audience, he knew theatre, and he wrote to please, with no thought of literary immortality. It is ironic that more of his plays (21) have been preserved than of any other classic playwright.

There is a sameness about his plots; in fact, all evidence points toward the conclusion that there was a sameness about the plots of all Roman comedy. The basic theme ordinarily centers around a young lover and his amours. To gain the object of his affection he is almost always assisted by a clever rogue of a slave. Mistaken identity or deliberate deception are almost invariably involved. The plot of *The Haunted House (Mostellaria)* is typical. In the absence of his father, Philolaches purchases the freedom of a beautiful slave girl, then runs through his father's wealth in riotous living. At the height of one of his wild parties, news arrives of the father's return. In desperation the young man turns to his clever slave, Tranio. The slave's first frantic act is one of sheer inspiration: He frightens the old man away from the house with a story that it is haunted. The ruse has barely succeeded when a moneylender descends upon Tranio, demanding the return of a large sum Philolaches had borrowed. This arouses the father's suspicion, but Tranio saves the situation by a hastily inspired announcement that the boy borrowed money to buy a new house. Things relax for a moment as the old man pays the moneylender; then the bottom drops out of everything as he suggests to Tranio that they inspect the new house. But the ever-resourceful slave is equal to the situation. He goes to a neighbor's house and explains to the kindly owner that the father is suffering from a delusion that the house is his. Would the neighbor humor the old man by allowing him to inspect the dwelling? Permission is granted, and an inspection tour full of

FIGURE 2:6 *Amphitrion 38.* The 1938 Giradoux adaptation of the famous comedy by Plautus, with Alfred Lunt and Richard Whorf as Jupiter and Mercury.

hilarious misunderstanding results. Finally the entire deception collapses, and Tranio barely escapes the mortal wrath of the enraged father by taking refuge on an altar. In the meantime Philolaches and his lawyer friend have had time to sober up and plead for forgiveness, but neither the situation nor Tranio is really saved until it is discovered that the slave girl purchased by Philolaches is none other than the long-lost daughter of the father's best friend!

TERENCE

In many ways Terence (Publius Terentius Afer, 185–159 B.C.) was the direct opposite of Plautus. Whereas Plautus wrote for the common man in his audience, Terence catered to the elite. Refinement, scholarship, and polish were among the virtues he tried to cultivate. He had been brought to Rome as a slave, but his master quickly recognized the boy's intellectual potential and set him free. It appears that Terence resolved to prove his gratitude by humbly being as perfect as possible in the eyes of the Roman upper class. Consequently, while his plots and characters are drawn from the same sources as those of Plautus, there is nothing of the boisterous originality of his predecessor. Literary merit appears to have been his objective. According to George E. Duckworth, "Terence writes with a lightness and grace that are almost Greek and which reflect the linguistic interest of his friends of the Scipionic circle; Plautus writes with an exuberance and freedom that reveal his knowledge of the theatre and his audience."[4]

The care with which Terence wrote is indicated by the fact that although he finished his first play, *Andria*, at the age of 19, he managed to write only five more before he was drowned at sea about 16 years later. All six of his plays have survived, however, and together with those of Plautus have had tremendous influence on the history of comedy. It was Plautus and Terence rather than Aristophanes who were held up as models during the Renaissance, and among those who borrowed from them were Molière and Shakespeare.

SENECA

The one important writer of Roman tragedy was Seneca (Lucius Annaeus Seneca, c. 4 B.C.– A.D. 65). Seneca is an outstanding figure in Roman history. Not only was he a playwright but he was also one of Rome's leading Stoics and Nero's tutor—incidentally, he met his death at the hand of his famous pupil. Among Seneca's literary works are nine, possibly ten, tragedies. It seems probable that they were written not to

[4]George E. Duckworth, *The Complete Roman Drama*, vol. 1 (New York: Random House, 1942), p. xxxii.

be acted on the stage but simply to be read or declaimed. They tend to be exercises in rhetoric and Stoic philosophy rather than imaginative dramatic poetry. Speeches are frequently of excessive length, while entrances and exits are often unmotivated.

It is not surprising that Seneca had difficulty in writing tragedy, for its basic ingredients, pity and terror, were taboo to the Stoic. Seneca seems to have compensated for their lack by introducing ghosts, bloody deeds, and gory descriptions — all acts of violence, but a violence that tends to be cold and detached like the detachment of a medical student calmly hacking away at a cadaver. But in spite of Seneca's Stoicism, his plays still have many merits. Moreover, they are interesting to us because of the enormous influence they exerted. Critics and playwrights in France and Italy came close to making Seneca the theoretical model of tragedy for all time, and while this veneration did much harm it also resulted in much good. Even in England, Shakespeare and the other Elizabethans borrowed Seneca's five-act form, his ghosts, his blood and thunder, and other items too numerous to mention. Certainly a man of such influence cannot be ignored.

THE ORIENTAL THEATRE

Westerners often assume that the muse of drama lay dormant from the death of Seneca in A.D. 65 until her reawakening in religious drama during the late Middle Ages, but in doing so they forget the softer, more sensuous world of the Orient, where during that period she enjoyed some of her most colorful achievements. India, China, Japan, and other Eastern countries developed theatres of beauty and imagination, even though none rivaled the Greeks in the theatre's most essential element, dramatic literature.

INDIAN THEATRE

In India the origin of theatre appears to have been closely associated with religious ritual, just as it had been in Greece. Legend even informs us that the classical Hindu theatre was a gift from Brahma himself. In both form and content the drama of India stands midway between East and West, and it is therefore much easier for us to understand than other Oriental forms. Whereas the plots of Japanese and Chinese plays are usually slight, the plots of Hindu drama are often complex, imaginative, and melodramatic. Two of the greatest classics, *Shakuntala* and *The Little Clay Cart*, have been widely translated and are frequently performed in Europe and America. Both are highly romantic, perhaps naive, but at the same time they are full of a frank theatricality and make-believe that the Western theatre, especially under the influence of nineteenth- and twentieth-century realism, has often lacked.

Shakuntala is the story of a king who discovers and falls in love with a beautiful young maiden while hunting deer. Then, bewitched by an evil sorcerer, he forgets her and returns to his palace. He does not even recognize her but drives her away when the deserted girl, now pregnant with his child, appears at his court. But, as in all Hindu drama, the tale ends happily when the recovery of a magic ring restores the king's memory. After a journey to the celestial regions of Indra, the king, his lovely Shakuntala, and their manly little son are reunited in love and happiness. True, all this may be romantic melodrama, but a good production, with the aid of dancing and music, is also a thing of beauty— a sheer delight of unpretentious make-believe.

CHINESE THEATRE

Chinese drama, which began long before the time of Aeschylus and Sophocles, achieved its full development toward the close of the medieval period. Even more than in India, the theatre in China owes its fascination to the manner in which it is performed rather than to the literary merit of the scripts. Performances in the traditional Chinese theatre usually last for hours; audiences vary attention to the players with conversation, tea, and pleasant thoughts. The play is only a part of the total environment, and audiences pay attention with little more sense of responsibility than modern Americans pay to television. Costumes are almost invariably expensive and magnificent. Masks and makeup are wildly imaginative. Above all, from a Western point of view, stands the disarming theatricality of the staging. The property man, dressed in black or blue and therefore supposedly invisible, places chairs to rep-

FIGURE 2:7   Traditional costumes and characters from the Chinese mainland theatre.

resent mountains, straightens the folds in the hero's gown, tosses bits of paper to suggest a raging snowstorm, or drops a red ball to indicate that a head has been lopped off.

Chinese theatre more closely resembles dance and music than it does realistic drama or cinema. Music is used almost continuously, and the visual joy comes more from the infinite skill and beauty with which highly conventionalized pantomime is performed than from emotional conflict, ideas, or suspense. Wild and intricate sword battles are fought, although the swords never touch. Death scenes offer choice and enormously extended acting opportunities. Pantomimic riding of horses, rowing of boats, and racing of chariots provide some of the more delicious moments for the actors and for the audiences. No attempt is made to render these scenes realistically, but rather the enjoyment lies in the appreciation of the actors' skill in portraying these actions. Being a theatre of color, convention, and make-believe, it exerted a healthy influence on Western theatre—especially, as we shall see, on artists like Robert Edmond Jones and Thornton Wilder. Through its influence on such writers, the Chinese theatre helped break realism's stranglehold in both Europe and America.

JAPANESE THEATRE

While not as old as the Chinese theatre, the Japanese Nō theatre traces its origins back to the eighth century. Since reaching full development during the fourteenth century, it has remained essentially unchanged in both content and form. For the most part traditional schools of the Nō have preserved the costuming, staging, gesture, and intonation from generation to generation, passing these from fathers to sons (adopted, if not natural) on a hereditary basis and with an essentially religious devotion to tradition and accuracy. The underlying purpose of the Nō is not entertainment in the Western sense as much as a desire to preserve Japanese culture and to exploit the principal motives of Buddhist thought.[5]

It is not surprising that Western audiences find the Nō difficult to appreciate. The Honshu School of Nō that toured American universities

---

[5] I am indebted to Professor Earl Ernst, University of Hawaii, for this phrase and for many of my ideas about Japanese theatre.

FIGURE 2:8 *Kantan*, a Nō play at the University of Hawaii; directed and designed by Earle Ernst. (John Bonsey)

in 1966–1967 was probably appreciated more as a cultural curiosity than as theatre; yet even without the experience and background required to understand such an art, audiences were deeply impressed by the overall atmosphere, the color, the beauty, and the incredible discipline of the performers.

Everything about a Nō performance is slow, ceremonial, and dignified. Gestures and movement are steeped in a symbolism and significance largely lost on Western eyes; yet in this modern world, so madly searching for the new, it may be pleasing to find a small island of quiet stability filled with reverence for the old.

But if the Nō theatre lies beyond the appreciation of most Western observers, this is not true—or, at least, is less true—of the popular and often spectacular Kabuki theatre. On the surface the development of the Kabuki has much in common with the Elizabethan theatre. Both originated during the late sixteenth century, both performed on an open or thrust stage, both used men or boys to play women's roles, and both attracted a popular following. The differences, however, are also obvious. The Kabuki has had a continuous existence from its beginning to the present day, whereas the Elizabethan theatre was destroyed by the Puritans in 1642. Far more important is the fact that the Kabuki has produced nothing of great value in the way of playwriting. It is famous instead for its acting and production techniques, the plays themselves remaining unimportant as far as any freedom of thought or insight into human existence is concerned.

While the Kabuki may seem traditional in comparison to Western theatre, it has changed freely in comparison to the Nō. Its playhouse, at first a thrust stage closely resembling that of the Nō, has evolved until the present Kabuki-za in Tokyo resembles the typical proscenium theatre in America. The chief difference lies in its continued use of the *flower path*, a long narrow ramp extending from the edge of the stage to the back of the auditorium, thus providing for spectacular entrances and exits in the same way that similar ramps are used by models in some American fashion shows. The stage uses scenery, traps, and lavish effects; in fact, the revolving stage originated in Japan. Music, costuming, and especially the acting are the elements of importance, just as they are in the Nō theatre, but everything is larger and more spectacular. Masks

FIGURE 2:9   Javanese shadow puppets.

are not used by the actors, but faces are painted until they resemble masks. The action is no longer restricted to the formalized dignity of the Nō. In *Yoshitsune Sembonzakura*, for example, the defeated general commits suicide. We see him standing high on the brink of a great cliff overlooking the sea. He ceremoniously ties one end of a huge coil of rope around his waist and the other around a ship's anchor which he then hurls into the sea! Audiences are invariably spellbound as the coil spins away until it finally rips him from the edge of the cliff to disappear forever beneath the waves.

Since the Orient covers a vast, densely populated area, its forms of theatre are numerous, often mysterious, and not at all as simple or uncomplicated as this tiny introductory glimpse might imply. In Japan, for example, there is also the Bunraku, a fascinating theatre where dolls are manipulated like puppets; in Java we find the world-famous shadow puppets and the Javanese theatre that Antonin Artaud, guiding spirit of the modern theatre of cruelty, held up as the ideal. In recent times, of course, Western theatre and cinema have often corrupted or replaced the native forms.

All Oriental theatre, however, seems to have one thing in common: The emphasis is on the production rather than the play. Scripts serve largely as a skeleton for the visual and auditory display of the performers. Such thoughts or lessons as the scripts contain tend to stress loyalty and faith to support the status quo, not disturb it. Such a theatre can be beautiful in the way that dance, music, and painting are beautiful. Moreover, as already pointed out, this Oriental emphasis on skill and make-believe has also helped to free Western theatre from some of the more oppressive bonds of realism. As the world grows smaller and communication easier, the Oriental theatre seems destined to provide greater and greater influence on Western life.

CHAPTER 3

FROM MEDIEVAL DRAMA TO THE NINETEENTH CENTURY

THE MIDDLE AGES

The fifth century A.D. saw the final collapse of Rome and its Western Empire. As far as theatre is concerned, however, Rome's fall is a fact of slight importance, since theatre of any artistic merit had already been dead for centuries. Seneca, the last writer of importance, died in A.D. 65, and, as already pointed out, even he had not written for public presentation. Whatever stage shows were given soon degenerated into entertainments that featured obscenity and vulgarity. Consequently, when the Christian Church came into power, one of its first acts was to abolish all theatrical activity and to include actors in the same category as thieves, prostitutes, and other undesirables.

Rome fell, but not the Church. The latter assumed a power over the life of Europe that was to exert a fundamental guiding influence for the next thousand years. Certain aspects of this medieval Church were highly commendable. For example, almost the only kindness, learning, art, and beauty of this dark period were centered within the Church.

From another point of view, however, its influence was less fortunate. Many of its attitudes and practices originated not from the example or teaching of Christ, but as a reaction against anything Roman or Greek. Thus while the Greeks had emphasized the here rather than the hereafter, and the Romans had extended this to a philosophy of eat-drink-and-be-merry-for-tomorrow-you-die, the early Church pronounced the present a vale of tears, a trial to test us as we journey toward the eternity of a hereafter; the greater the suffering now, the greater the reward in heaven. The Greeks had admired and cultivated the human body; the Church covered it with robes as a thing of shame, if not evil. The Greeks had looked upon the expression of beauty through art as one of man's highest functions; the Church frowned upon this as pleasure and vanity. The Greeks had sought for the answers to the great mysteries of life and death; the Church insisted on faith in the established answers.

Whatever the causes, the fact remains that from the death of Seneca until the beginning of the so-called Middle Ages, playwriting was practically nonexistent. There were exceptions, of course. We know that the mimes and strolling players never entirely disappeared. We also know that in the tenth century, Roswitha, a nun of Saxony, wrote several pious comedies in the manner of Terence. But on the whole the Dark Ages, as far as playwriting was concerned, were dark indeed.

MYSTERY PLAYS

Curiously enough, the rebirth of drama is traced neither to strolling players nor to Roswitha, but to the very Church that had been so influential in the theatre's destruction. At some time during the tenth century, a tiny four-line playlet, introduced into the Church's Easter service, dramatized the Resurrection in the simplest possible terms; yet it must have scored a success, for soon Christmas and other holy days were also being embellished with dramatizations. Finally these short Biblical plays were moved outside the church and organized into groups known as *mystery cycles.* Based always on the Scriptures, their function remained fundamentally religious, yet in spite of religious and other restrictions we begin to see the playwright's creative faculties once more at work. Thus the story of Adam picks up new insight into human nature as Lucifer shrewdly plays upon Eve's vanity; the sacrifice of Isaac becomes more touching because of the boy's tender regard for his mother; while the story of Noah gains a delightful quality from the character of Noah's shrewish wife, who refuses to board the ark unless permitted to bring her local club of town gossips.

In England famous mystery cycles were developed at York, Wakefield, Coventry, and Chester. In Germany one can still see the Passion play at Oberammergau, which dates back to 1662 and is essentially a medieval mystery play that has survived to the present day.

MIRACLE PLAYS

Only a short step from the mystery play, which dealt with Biblical themes, is the *miracle play*, which depicted the lives of the saints. Apparently hundreds of these plays were written, though few have survived. These plays usually gave the playwright greater freedom than the mystery plays had done. Some depict exciting scenes of torture and martyrdom; others verge on secular romance. The religious purpose is sometimes preserved only by the device of introducing a saint or the Virgin at some point in an otherwise romantic adventure to perform a miracle and resolve the tangled situation, thus preserving the spiritual and moral function of the production.

MORALITY PLAYS

A third type of drama that developed during the medieval period was the *morality play*, the familiar *Everyman* being the outstanding example. We see Everyman, summoned by Death, appeal in vain to Fellowship, Cousin, Kindred, and Goods. Even Strength, Discretion, the Five Wits, Beauty, and Knowledge desert him as he reaches the grave. Only Good Deeds, frail but true, is willing to accompany him and plead for him before the judgment seat of God. On the surface such an allegorical form — the personification of virtues, vices, and other abstract qualities — seems stiff and unpromising, yet closer examination reveals that these morality plays are a step nearer to true drama than either the mysteries or miracles. The challenge to the imagination of the playwright was much greater, and his freedom in dealing with his material was comparatively unrestricted.

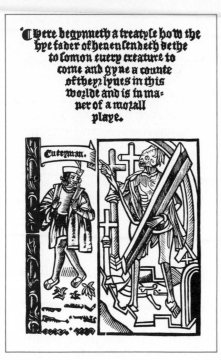

FIGURE 3:1   The title page of *Everyman*.

One other type of drama developed during the Middle Ages, or perhaps it had never entirely disappeared—the *farcical interlude.* Perhaps these interludes grew from the moralities, perhaps from the strolling players. In any event, they represent an important step in the history of playwriting, for in these the theatre once again emerged as entirely secular, once more devoted to the primary purpose of entertainment. Many excellent examples have survived. From France comes the famous *Pierre Pathelin.* Modern audiences still view with delight this story of the clever shyster, Pierre, who, among other adventures, manages to secure the acquittal of a sheep thief through the audacious prank of having his client answer "Baa" to every question of judge and prosecutor, only to be trapped by his own cleverness as the not-so-dumb client, in answer to Pierre's request for his fee, produces a final lusty "Baa."

Perhaps the best farces of all came from Germany, where Hans Sachs (1494–1576), the beloved poet-shoemaker of Nuremberg, turned out dozens of homely but cheerful examples of the genre. In *Der todte Mann,* for example, we see a harassed husband, no longer sure of his wife's affections, decide to test her by the naive device of lying down and pretending to be dead. We can be sure that he never attempts such deception again, for the shrewd wife, immediately seeing through his hoax, proceeds to torture him by rejoicing over the prospects of widowhood until he rises from the dead in consternation and anguish. Even though the wife finally confesses that she was only teasing, we sense that the distraught husband can never be quite sure. He has saddled himself with greater tortures of uncertainty than before. It ends with a jingle:

> You'll lose your mind, perhaps your life,
> By playing tricks on the shoemaker's wife![1]

England, too, had its farcical interludes, those by John Heywood (c. 1497 – c. 1580) being the most celebrated. In fact, it is but the slightest step from a play like Heywood's *Johan Johan* to plays like *Ralph Roister Doister* and *Gammer Gurton's Needle*, which mark the beginning of Renaissance playwriting in England — a beginning that was to culminate in the genius of Shakespeare.

THE RENAISSANCE

Early in the fourteenth century Dante, possibly sensing the coming of a dangerous new age, summed up the essence of medieval thought in *The Divine Comedy:* fear of punishment and hope for redemption. Already the old faith was beginning to crumble. People were beginning to question, to reexamine life and death. Whether the new age started with the invention of gunpowder or the printing press, with the establishment of universities or with the fall of Constantinople, which drove scholars and classic literature into Western Europe — whether it grew from a combination of these and other influences matters little. What does matter is that people once more became interested in people and in living. Once more they dared to believe, as the Greeks had believed long before them, that a healthy body was better than an unhealthy one, that a happy life was more desirable than an unhappy one, that the improvement of one's lot in this life was not a vanity but a virtue, that a person should be free to examine for himself, to question authority, to struggle with the restless

[1] Han Sachs, *The Shoemaker's Wife*, trans. David Thompson (New York: Harper & Row, 1955).

FIGURE 3:2 *The Second Shepherd's Play* at the University of Utah; directed by Charlene Bletson; scenery designed by Angie Riserbato; costumes by Wendy Stuart.

energy of a Faust—these qualities and others were all a part of the spirit known as *humanism* and are associated with the term *Renaissance.*

More specifically, of course, the Renaissance refers to the rebirth of interest in the civilization of Greece and Rome. Almost at once the Renaissance individual sensed that in classic ages the emphasis had been upon living rather than preparation for death. People began to rediscover, through books and ruins, the arts and sciences that classic human beings had cultivated to improve their lot.

Like all great movements, the Renaissance was infinitely complex and variegated. Evil frequently balanced or overshadowed the good. The newly found freedom to live was all too frequently interpreted as freedom to exploit, rape, murder, or oppress. In a sense the Renaissance is still in progress, and whether it will eventually end in the destruction or exaltation of humanity seems at this moment of history to hang in precarious balance.

But whether good or evil, the life of Western civilization since the dawn of the Renaissance has seldom been dull. Contrast it with the pace of life in civilizations that have crystallized under religious faith — Egyptian, Hindu, or medieval — and one can see the speed and chaos with which the Renaissance individual has moved.

ITALY

While the above discussion has viewed the Renaissance in its large and general sense as a spirit still very much alive, it is also customary to restrict the term to a much narrower span of years, and especially to Italy during the fourteenth, fifteenth, and sixteenth centuries, for it was here that the movement first developed. During this period Italy's accomplishments in painting, architecture, sculpture, and science were outstanding. By comparison, the results in theatre were disappointing. Much was achieved, but it does not compare with what had been accomplished in Greece and Rome or was soon to be accomplished in England, Spain, and France.

Largely responsible for Italy's weak showing in drama was the political climate of the area. There was no national unity and very little stability. Individual city-states were under the control of powerful and frequently despotic families. These privileged few sponsored art and learning, but in most cases there were not enough of them in any given city to make much of a playgoing audience. When a nation centers its cultural life in one city, as France centered its cultural life in Paris at the time of Molière, then a theatre of the elite may have vigor. Otherwise the theatre has flourished best where the spirit has been far more democratic than it was in Renaissance Italy.

This failure to produce great plays may also have been due to a contradiction between life and theory. Italian scholars in their enthusiasm had unearthed Aristotle as well as most of the extant Greek and Roman plays. With overzealous eagerness they proclaimed such principles as the three unities and applied them with a rigidity that practically outdid the medieval Church in intolerance. A rigid and highly restricted form was thus forced upon the would-be playwrights of an age that was bursting with color, energy, and imagination. This contradiction between life and theory was felt primarily in the field of tragedy. Scholars have always had a tendency to deal ponderously with tragedy, to fetter it with rules and regulations until free and honest expression becomes next to impossible; and this is what happened during the Italian Renaissance.

But though it produced no tragedies of great merit, the Italian Renaissance is still of vast importance in any history of the theatre. It reestablished the art of playwriting on somewhat the same plane as the Greeks and Romans had left it. It also saw the birth of opera, pastoral drama, and *commedia dell'arte.*

The *commedia* will be treated more fully in a later chapter on acting, since it was a theatre that centered on the actor, not the playwright. With only a scenario to guide them, these talented performers apparently improvised some of the most enjoyable entertainments ever seen. This was the popular theatre, the theatre of the people. The scenarios, many of which have been preserved, are usually quite trivial and ordinarily feature some variation of cuckoldry or the eternal triangle. The artistry and skill came from the players.

Opera, the most notable contribution of the period, was to some extent an accident, the result of a misinterpretation of Greek acting by a group of enthusiastic scholars who believed that Greek tragedies had been intoned and sung. It was not long until the enthusiasm of two of the group, Peri and Rinuccini, produced *Dafne* (1597), which is commonly regarded as the world's first opera. Not bound by the classic restrictions that had hampered and were to hamper tragedy, opera gained ground rapidly. The musical genius of Monteverdi had much to do with this. There was also the influence of scenic embellishment, which quickly associated itself with opera and, through its appeal to a Renaissance taste, aided opera in becoming the characteristic theatrical expression of Renaissance Italy.

But Italy's major contribution to the dramatic literature of the period lies in the field of comedy. For some reason scholars and critics concentrated their attention on tragedy, leaving comedy free; or perhaps there is something in the very nature of comedy that refuses to bow to rules and restrictions.

Of the many skillful comedies that were written, the best example is Niccolò Machiavelli's *La mandragola* (*The Mandrake*, c. 1520). The plot concerns Callimaco, a young man whose love has been inflamed by the beauty of Lucrezia, wife of the middle-aged and gullible Messer Nicia Calfucci. In order to be with her the young man has his assistant convince the husband that he, Callimaco, is a wonder-working doctor from Paris who can cure Lucrezia of her apparent sterility by having her take a potion of mandragola. The only problem is that the next man to lie with her must surely die. To avoid making himself the victim of such a catastrophe, the stupid husband decides to kidnap some worthless young drunk from the streets and place him with Lucrezia to absorb the fatal effects of the medicine. Lucrezia offers stout resistance to this evil plan, but when the arguments of her husband are reinforced by those of her mother, and even by those of her priest, she is finally forced to consent. Callimaco, of course, has arranged that he shall be the one who is kidnapped. Alone with Lucrezia he wins her affection by revealing his own love and her husband's stupidity. The play ends the next morning with the cuckolded husband showering praises upon Callimaco, who has now returned as the doctor. The unsuspecting cuckold even insists that Callimaco accept the key to the back door in order that he may come and go at will.

As the above plot indicates, Italian Renaissance comedy resembles Roman comedy, except that it is even more licentious. It is usually preoccupied with a young man and his love affairs, which consequently leads to a comedy of disguise, mistaken identity, and misrepresentation. The object of the young man's affection is almost always a married and essentially virtuous woman—one capable of putting up a good fight. These comedies are important because of their wit, their brilliance, and the insight they afford into their times.

ENGLAND: THE ELIZABETHAN AND JACOBEAN THEATRE

While the dramatic output of Renaissance Italy was somewhat disappointing, that of Renaissance England exceeded all expectations. Even without Shakespeare the period would have been an important one, but including his genius it may be claimed that London from about 1580 to 1642 contributed more great plays than any other city during a comparable period before or since, the only possible exception being Athens during the fifth century B.C.

There are certain parallels in the backgrounds of London and Athens during their respective heights. Both were young in spirit, boisterous, eager, filled with zest for living. Commerce and trade flourished; activity and excitement were in the air. Both cities experienced the exhilaration of finding themselves in positions of world power, London through the defeat of the Spanish Armada in 1588, and Athens through the defeat of Persia during the early years of the fifth century B.C. Both, in other words, provided the stimulation and widening horizons that great playwrights require.

Other forces were at work, of course. Some scholars trace much of the greatness of Shakespeare to a happy blending of two views of life, medieval and Renaissance. Happily, when these two met and merged, neither completely dominated the other. The medieval contributed scope, imagination, homely realism, and hearty laughter, while the Renaissance contributed the classic form with its sense of order, skillful plots, deft solutions, brilliant word play, and Senecan verse. Thus the best features of each tended to combine to produce the age of Elizabeth, one of the truly dazzling literary periods of all time.

Renaissance influence on playwriting was first felt in the colleges. As early as 1553 or 1554 Nicholas Udall, headmaster of Eton, using Plautus as his model, wrote *Ralph Roister Doister*. This fairly robust comedy substituted English for Latin types. At about the same time came *Gammer Gurton's Needle*, a rousing farce-comedy of uncertain authorship that is still performed. The latter was first acted in 1552 but not published until 1577.

In serious drama the Renaissance influence made its first appearance in *Gorboduc* (1562), by Thomas Sackville and Thomas Norton. This was a Senecan tragedy of blood and revenge that employed blank verse, the verse form later perfected and used with such success by both Marlowe and Shakespeare. Like *Ralph Roister Doister* and *Gammer Gurton's Needle*, however, it substituted English characters and an English setting for the Latin originals. From these beginnings Elizabethan drama grew, until by 1564, the year in which both Shakespeare and Marlowe were born, fully developed plays could already be seen.

EARLY ELIZABETHAN PLAYWRIGHTS

Shakespeare's immediate predecessors were for the most part brilliant young college men who had been caught up in the reckless, dangerous spirit of the age. In evaluating these men, not so much on their own merit as in terms of their influences, it is logical to begin with John Lyly, an Oxford graduate, poet, and playwright of high favor in the court of Queen Elizabeth. While unpopular today, Lyly, through his comedies and poetry, may have done more than any other early Elizabethan to add refinement, eloquence, and taste to the prevailing ruggedness of the English style. In fact, the term *euphuism*, commonly associated with high-flown diction and excessive elegance of style, is derived from Lyly's famous *Euphues, or The Anatomy of Wit*.

In vivid contrast to Lyly stands Thomas Kyd (c. 1557 – c. 1595). Seldom have two names been more delightfully descriptive, for in contrast to Lyly's refinement, Kyd fired his drama with native Elizabethan qualities of vigor, power, and imagination. Only one surviving play, *The Spanish Tragedy*, can be traced with certainty to his hand. This play, enormously popular during his day, still has qualities that merit its occasional revival. The plot is sensational. Hieronimo, the elderly marshal of Spain, awakened one night by cries from his arbor, hurries outside to find that his only son has been brutally murdered. The main action of the play follows the old man, at times on the brink of madness and always an object of pity, as he charts his way through intrigues and counterintrigues until he at last achieves revenge by the destruction of those responsible for the terrible crime. The play shows unmistakable Senecan influence in its ghosts, its theme of revenge, and its bloody deeds. Unlike Seneca, however, Kyd placed his scenes of blood and violence on stage in the best medieval tradition instead of having them related by a messenger. The murder of the son, the father's discovery of the body, the play within the play where the guilty ones are actually killed instead of meeting only a make-believe death, and the final scene where the old man, having been captured, bites out his tongue to avoid confession, are all scenes of violence that Kyd dared to portray to the last drop of blood.

In this brief account we must skip the contributions of the other "University Wits," with the exception of Christopher Marlowe

(1564–1593), who, save only for Shakespeare, ranks as the greatest tragic playwright England has produced. Both his life and his plays reflect his stormy revolutionary spirit. The son of a shoemaker, he worked his way to an M.A. from Cambridge. One great poem, four great tragedies, and some lesser works had come from his pen by the time of his death in a tavern brawl at the age of 29.

Marlowe's contribution to the theatre rests upon four plays: *Tamburlaine*, *Dr. Faustus*, *The Jew of Malta*, and *Edward II*. *Tamburlaine* is a heroic tragedy of such colossal proportions that it sometimes escapes the ridiculous only because of the originality, poetic skill, and impassioned sincerity of its author. *Dr. Faustus* brings a new kind of dignity to tragedy—not the dignity of a king or titled hero but that of a common man, the restless medieval scholar Faustus. It also combines what is essentially

FIGURE 3:3 Marlowe's *Edward II*. Mary Joan Negro, Norman Snow, and Peter Dvorsky in a production by the Acting Company; directed by Ellis Rabb.

best he could for his fellow actors and his audiences. He made no attempt to collect or publish these plays. He does not even mention them in his will, though he does mention his "second best bed." A country boy lacking a college education, it probably never seriously occurred to him that he had outdistanced his contemporaries in lasting literary value.

In common with almost all the great playwrights, Shakespeare knew his theatre, loved his theatre, and lived with his theatre; as a result, his plays play even better than they read. Nor are they limited in appeal to the select few. High school audiences have been known to laugh and applaud with more genuine enthusiasm for *The Taming of the Shrew*, *A Midsummer Night's Dream*, and *Much Ado About Nothing* than for any-

FIGURE 3:5 Shakespearean tragedy. (a) *Anthony and Cleopatra*. Keith Baxter and Maggie Smith in a Stratford, Ontario, production; directed by Robin Phillips (b) *Hamlet*. Richard Monette and Marti Maraden in a Stratford, Ontario, production; directed by Robin Phillips and William Hutt. (c) *King Lear*. Morris Carnovsky in the title role at the Goodman School of Drama; directed by Charles McGaw.

(a

(b)

(c)

thing the modern theatre has to offer. I have never seen a modern audience so deeply moved as during a performance of *King Lear*. Even in the movies, which have traditionally scorned Shakespeare as "highbrow," Sir Laurence Olivier's *Hamlet* and *Henry V* and Franco Zeffirelli's *Romeo and Juliet* have scored box-office successes.

The sources of Shakespeare's effectiveness have been variously analyzed. All would agree, however, that he tells a dramatic story with tremendous theatrical effectiveness. He also displays an insight into character that is truly remarkable. Even when intellectually unsympathetic toward a character, as in the case of Shylock, Shakespeare still is able to see life from the character's point of view and, almost in spite of himself, to give his Shylock motivation that makes him human — tragic as well as comic. Because of his skill in drawing character, Lady Macbeth is certainly more real to the average adult than Queen Elizabeth I. The "real" historical figures of Antony, Cleopatra, Enobarbus, and Octavius Caesar remain distant and blurred to most of us who read only history, but to those who have worked closely with Shakespeare's *Antony and Cleopatra* these characters suddenly acquire life, vividness, and conviction. One who reads, one who sees, and especially one who acts Shakespeare gains in wisdom and experience, for it is like living many lives, passing through many great crises in company with many great people — as though he or she had been there with Lear, Falstaff, Macbeth, Cleopatra, and so many others. While the excellence of Shakespeare's major characters is universally recognized, his genius is nowhere more apparent than in his vivid delineation of hundreds of so-called minor characters. In *King Lear* a captain is summoned by Edmond and handed a warrant for the death of Lear and Cordelia. He has one speech: "I cannot eat oats or draw a cart, but if it's a man's work I'll do it." Here is characterization in a single line. The captain stands before us more vividly than do characters of lesser writers, though they may hold the stage for a full two-and-a-half hours.

Shakespeare's uncanny ability to crawl into the skins of his characters, to understand, to empathize into their very souls is probably the chief source of his universality. Readers who can learn to tune in on his plays are often amazed by the feeling that they have finally found someone who understands, who expresses so many of their own ideas with masterful skill. Each generation tends to find new meanings — its own. Take *Hamlet*, for example. Actually, there are almost as many interpreta-

(a)

(b)

(c)

FIGURE 3:6
Shakespearean history, dark comedy, and fantasy. (a) *Julius Caesar*. Sam Tsoutsouvas as Brutus in a production at the Utah Shakespearean Festival. (b) *Measure for Measure*. Patricia Connolly and Nicholas Kepros in a Guthrie Theatre production; directed by Michael Langham; designed by Desmond Heeley. (c) *The Tempest*. Tom De Mastri and Ellis Rabb in an Old Globe Theatre production.

tions of *Hamlet* as there have been critics, but to cite only a handful: Romanticists tended to revel in the play's melancholy—brooding on death, ghosts, madness, skulls, and graves. Freudians found in it sterling examples of the subconscious—abnormal relationships with his mother, his father, and even his friend Horatio. Realists in the 1930s were intrigued by Hamlet's intelligence and the manner in which it short-circuited his actions, a problem related to their own world, in which intellectuals aware of complexities had been slow to react, thus leaving the world to the mercy of men like Hitler, Mussolini, and Stalin. Young rebels of the 1960s could also relate to Hamlet, for here was a youth confronting a corrupt and dishonest Establishment, something "rotten in the state of Denmark."

Nor is *Hamlet's* appeal limited to the fact that generation after generation has been able to relate to it and cherish it. The scope of its appeal has also been international. It has been translated into practically every major language and performed wherever a stage has been available.

Finally we must glance at Shakespeare the poet. Who else has ever expressed so many things so well? Take the music of Oberon's "I know a bank where the wild thyme blows . . . "; of Antony's "Sometime we see a cloud that's dragonish . . . "; of his final refrain, "I am dying, Egypt, dying . . . "; the heartbreaking simplicity of Lear's "Pray, do not mock me: I am a very foolish fond old man. . . . "Take the tragic mixture of weariness and bitterness in Macbeth's "To-morrow, and to-morrow, and to-morrow, creeps in this petty pace from day to day. . . . " Even such tiny snatches indicate a poet of extraordinary quality.

There are flaws in his work. He was often careless about details. His descriptions of offstage events sometimes verge on ridiculous bombast; his subplots sometimes clutter rather than help; some critics lament his lack of social criticism and satire; he is guilty of *Titus Andronicus* and a few other plays of questionable merit, but perhaps his very lack of perfection, along with his unconsciousness of greatness, increases our affection for him. For both Shakespeare and his characters are of this imperfect world—they are a part of each of us.

The final marvel is that he excelled in so many areas. A person selecting the world's greatest writers of tragedy might name Shakespeare, Sophocles, and Goethe. The greatest comedy writers might be Shakespeare, Molière, Aristophanes, and Shaw. The greatest writers of chronicle plays might be Shakespeare, Schiller, and Strindberg. Even in the field of romantic tragicomedy there is nothing by Beaumont and Fletcher or anyone else to equal *The Tempest.* Nor is Shakespeare's fame solely a matter of English pride. His plays have been translated into almost every language. They are performed wherever a stage is to be found, and they have made living a richer experience for millions.

BEN JONSON

As Christopher Marlowe with his tragedies is outstanding among those who preceded Shakespeare, so Ben Jonson (1572 – 1637) with his comedies is outstanding among those who followed. A big man, dashing, daring, Elizabethan, he fought duels with both the pen and the sword. His most colorful exploit with the latter weapon is reported to have occurred while fighting with the English volunteers. In the best theatrical tradition Jonson challenged the enemy to send forth a champion. Then, as both armies looked on, Ben slew his man and carried the armor home in triumph. His belligerent duels with the pen were almost as spectacular, and yet in spite of his blustering nature a certain good humor shines through. It is significant that he later collaborated in writing plays with some of the men with whom he had quarreled. It is also significant that he ended his days surrounded by a group of young admirers who called themselves "The Sons of Ben."

As to his plays, he wrote — or attempted to write — both tragedies and comedies. His tragedies, while highly regarded by Ben Jonson, find few admirers today. Perhaps they smell of Jonson's self-conscious attempt to write in the correct classic style, or perhaps Jonson, in spite of such lovely lyrics as "Drink to Me Only with Thine Eyes," simply did not have sufficient gift as a poet. In any event, even his best tragedy, *Sejanus,* makes one appreciate the remark, "Shakespeare came from heaven, Jonson from college."

In comedy, on the other hand, Jonson stands out as Shakespeare's only contemporary rival; in fact, in the area of satire Jonson is clearly superior. In characteristic academic fashion, Jonson had reasons and theories for almost everything he did. Consequently, he becomes an interesting and important figure in the history of dramatic criticism. The theory for which he is famous both as playwright and as critic is that of the *comedy of humors.* The concept of the humors is an outgrowth of medieval physiology which held that four elements, black bile, yellow bile, phlegm, and blood, according to their balance and proportion, determined a person's disposition. By the time of Jonson the term *humor* was in common usage much the same as the term *complex* was between World Wars I and II. Jonson conceived the idea that if all these humors were evenly balanced, a normal and noncomic personality would be the result, but if unbalanced—if the personality had too much of any one element—an eccentric and potentially comic personality would emerge. Jonson, of course, did not limit himself only to four basic humors, but he did try to find some quality or trait in almost every character that if sharply accentuated would render the character comic. While we may smile today at the physiological concept that was the root of the Jonsonian theory, we cannot deny that he came close to the discovery of a basic truth. Every satirist, from the professional cartoonist to the high school author of a satire on the faculty, knows the comic potentials of exaggerating traits or features already too prominent in his or her victim.

Jonson's first important comedy was entitled *Everyman in His Humour;* his second, *Everyman Out of His Humour.* Yet while these are vigorous and interesting, they cannot compare with his four masterpieces: *Volpone, The Alchemist, Epicoene,* and *Bartholomew Fair.* Jonson's skill in plot construction is well illustrated by *Epicoene; or, The Silent Woman.*[3] It concerns Morose, a testy old gentleman whose humor consists of a violent allergy to noise. The least sound, other than that of his own voice, throws him into a fit of rage. Being at odds with a young nephew, his only relative and consequently his heir, Morose determines to thwart the young rascal by marrying—provided that he can find a silent woman. Luck smiles upon him. He soon discovers a beautiful and extremely soft-spoken young lady. He proposes, she accepts, and he marries her, but the moment the ceremony is performed she finds her tongue! Soon the house is full of wedding guests, including an assortment of young suitors bent on turning Morose into a cuckold at the earliest possible opportunity. The act ends in a bedlam of noise and confusion.

In desperation Morose appeals to lawyers to have the marriage annulled, but the learned gentlemen of the bar only distress him further

---

[3] Dryden, in his *Essay on Dramatic Poesy,* discusses *Epicoene* as an example of this particular excellence of Jonson's.

with their endless discourses on legal technicalities. Although he submits to gross personal humiliation, he cannot escape from his bride or from the pandemonium she has created. At this point the erring nephew, Dauphine, arrives on the scene. He pretends to be shocked by his uncle's distress and promises to clear up the whole mess provided that Morose will sign over his fortune. At his wits' end, the old man consents, whereupon Dauphine reveals that the wife is a boy, Dauphine's own page, in disguise, a revelation that leaves the seductive suitors quite as disconcerted as the avaricious old man.

While *Epicoene* is perhaps Jonson's funniest play, his masterpiece is undoubtedly *Volpone; or, The Fox*. This was not written just to be amusing; it is an indictment of the viciousness of the human race. Written during the same period that Shakespeare was writing his great tragedies, its bitter theme suggests that both men may have been motivated by the decay and growing evil of life about them. Shakespeare lashed out with tragedy, Jonson with comedy. Euripides and Aristophanes had complemented each other in the same way 2000 years earlier.

Jonson centers the action of his masterpiece around a vicious, cynical, avaricious old man, Volpone, who with the help of his servant Mosca (the fly) conceives a brilliant swindle by pretending to be on his deathbed in order that money-mad self-seekers may be drawn into the trap of offering everything from gifts to the use of their wives in the hope of being named sole heir to Volpone's fortune. In this mad merry-go-round of corruption Volpone finally overreaches himself, and everyone suffers his just deserts.

THE JACOBEAN PERIOD

There were many other important playwrights in the period, but rather than briefly list all of them, our discussion will be limited only to those few who were leaders of some particular trend of the later Elizabethan or Jacobean period.

One such trend that came early and influenced Shakespeare's later plays grew from the work of Beaumont and Fletcher in the field of tragicomedy. This genre tended toward the romantic. It verged on the tragic but usually avoided death. Both Beaumont and Fletcher were cultured, well-bred gentlemen, and while both wrote some independent works, their most important contributions were made in collaboration. *Philaster; or Love Lies a-Bleeding* (1611) is perhaps their best play in the standard tragicomic style. In it they take over one of Shakespeare's favorite devices, disguising their heroine as a page boy. It is interesting to note, however, that Beaumont also gave the period its only important example of burlesque with his well-known *The Knight of the Burning Pestle* (1609).[4]

A few plays of the period deserve mention because they provide insight into the lives of the common people. Next to Shakespeare's *The Merry Wives of Windsor*, the best comedy in this respect is *The Shoemaker's Holiday* (1599), by Thomas Dekker. Here the delightful and very human adventures of a group of London shoemakers are mixed with the proud success story of their master, who rises to the exalted station of Lord Mayor.

As far as tragedy about common people is concerned, there is Thomas Heywood's *A Woman Killed with Kindness* (1603), in which a wife unfaithful to her husband is given no punishment save separation from the gentle spouse and from their children. Under such generous treatment she soon wastes away from remorse, finally to be forgiven on her deathbed amid many tears and much pathos. While not a great play, it does foreshadow the coming of bourgeois tragedy, which will be discussed later.

The final characteristic that merits attention in this period is the trend toward tragedies of horror, suspense, and death. Most of the best writing in the late years of the period belongs to this genre. Much of it contains great poetry; much of it is fascinating even if unpleasant. It is the sign, perhaps, of a dying age. Two examples of the trend are *The Changeling* (1623) by Thomas Middleton and *The Duchess of Malfi* (c.1618) by John Webster. The first is a gripping case study of a young woman who hires a middle-aged man to murder an undesirable suitor. We see her go from the first shock when the murderer claims her virtue as his reward through a strange mixture of fascination and loathing for his love, until at the end both she and the murderer are destroyed.

The study of evil in Webster's *The Duchess of Malfi* is made slightly less somber than in Middleton's *The Changeling* by the fact that the two leading characters are sympathetic. Having lost her husband, the Duch-

---

[4] Fletcher may have also collaborated with Beaumont in writing *The Knight of the Burning Pestle*.

FIGURE 3:7   Dekker's *The Shoemaker's Holiday*. Robin Gammell, Grace Keagy, Douglas Campbell, and James Lawless in a Guthrie Theatre production; directed by Douglas Campbell; designed by Dahl Delu.

ess is forbidden to marry by her brothers, the Cardinal and the Duke, who hope thereby to inherit her fortune. In spite of their threats she secretly marries her steward, a man of excellent character but lowly rank. Learning that their sister has deceived them, the Cardinal and the Duke hunt her down in the most relentless manner. At times the suspense and horror grow almost unbearable. Finally, after many brilliantly conceived and macabre scenes, the Duchess, her husband, her children, the Duke, and the Cardinal are all killed. According to T. S. Eliot, Webster could always see the skull beneath the face.

Plays continued to be written until 1642, but few bearing a date later than 1630 are of any importance. The decline of the great age was nearing its final stage. Consequently, there is little need to bemoan the fact that one of the first official acts of the Puritans, as they rose to power under Cromwell in 1642, was to close the theatres. Perhaps the very act of closure gave the English theatre a much-needed rest in preparation for its resurrection under the reign of the Merry Monarch, Charles II.

SPAIN: THE GOLDEN AGE

The coming of the Renaissance found Spain in control of most of Italy and much of Europe. Discovery and plunder of the New World had resulted in power and riches that established Spain (in its own estimation, at least) as the leading nation of the world. Its achievements in art and learning, however, are of a somewhat hollow and disappointing quality, probably because in Spain the Renaissance spirit met two stumbling blocks, the Inquisition and the defeat of the Armada. If any one characteristic of the Renaissance was important, it was freedom of thought—freedom to question, to probe, to reexamine life and life's values. While such freedom of thought met with natural opposition everywhere—and still does—it has never met with anything to equal the Spanish Inquisition. Freedom of thought in religion was effectively discouraged by means of the iron maiden, the rack, and the flaming stake. Freedom of political thought fared little better, and thus the Spanish nobility maintained its position of superiority through a highly artificial code of conduct and an insistence that this code be rigidly obeyed.

The effect upon playwriting is quite obvious. Religious plays, exciting romances, melodramas, and clever comedies could be written, but true greatness in literature comes only from those who dare to probe deeply and honestly into life. It may not be so serious if an author is required to conform only to a few general codes that harmonize with logic and common sense, but regrettably, many Spanish codes did not do this. As a result we can have a play like Calderón's famous *Physician of His Own Honor*, in which a husband who murders his wife because he suspects that she has stained his honor is exonerated by the king and given another woman as a bride, even though we know that the first wife was entirely innocent. Adherence to a code of honor that condones such "justice" is not characteristic of great writers. Fortunately, it is not characteristic of Spanish writing at its best, but unfortunately, it is characteristic of most Spanish playwriting during the period we are discussing.

This partial failure of the Renaissance in Spain had at least one advantage. If the Spanish playwright failed to gain freedom from state and church, he at least gained freedom from the restrictive rules of the literary critics who had stifled the life of serious drama in Italy. In general, while the major playwrights of Spain knew of the rules, they made little attempt to follow them.

The defeat of the Armada also encouraged the avoidance of deep thinking. It was easier and more pleasant to use drama as an escape — to build castles in Spain — than to face the reality of defeat. It was this Spanish tendency to live in a world of dreams, romance, and chivalry that Cervantes so effectively explored in his great satirical novel, *Don Quixote*.

There were many important playwrights during the period. Cervantes himself wrote a number of plays. There was also Juan Ruiz de Alarcón, who was born not in Spain but in Mexico. For our purposes, however, it seems best to concentrate on two playwrights who tower above their fellows: Lope de Vega and Calderón.

LOPE DE VEGA

Lope de Vega (1562 – 1635) is the more colorful and interesting. In fact, it seems doubtful whether any other playwright in history can match Lope in this regard. His personal life was sensational. He survived the sinking of the Armada, was exiled, was rescued, became a tempestuous lover, and finally, as a playwright, turned out a volume of work that staggers the imagination — somewhere between 1600 and 2200 plays, in addition to other literary works. No one in history seems to have written with such speed and facility. (Shakespeare, writing in England during the same years, turned out a total of 37 plays.) With such an overwhelming quantity to his credit it should not be surprising to learn that Lope's plays tend to have shortcomings; on the contrary, one is amazed to discover how much merit they possess. At times their poetry picks up a lyrical quality that is excellent; as far as scholars can determine, his characters and plots were usually original; finally, his sense of action and excitement shows a keen awareness of how to hold an audience's attention. Lope's influence on playwriting has been important not just in Spain but throughout the world. If for nothing else he deserves a reward of some sort for having cheerfully ignored the classic rules that proved so stifling in Italy.

But while he usually concerned himself with entertainment rather than with depth and experience, there are moments that surprise us — moments when a genuine spirit of freedom, justice, and independent thinking breaks through in opposition to the ruling codes of church and state. One such play is *Fuente Ovejuna (The Sheep Well)*, which deals with the rebellion of the peasants of the little village of Fuente Ovejuna against their aristocratic and corrupt commander. The play rises to genuine greatness in many scenes — for example, when Laurencia, a young girl who has just been ravished by the commander, stirs the timid town board into action:

> My face is bruised and bloody in this court of honest men. Some of you are fathers, some have daughters. Do your hearts sink within you . . . ? You are sheep, sheep! Oh well-named village of Fuente Ovejuna, the Sheep Well! Sheep, sheep, sheep.[5]

Even greater in dramatic potential is the scene where the judge, sent by the king to investigate the murder of the commander, meets a united village. Boys of ten, old men, and women are put to torture in a brutally determined effort to discover who killed the commander, but although all know the answer, not one will confess. The reply wrung from the tortured victims is always the same, "Fuente Ovejuna!"; in other words, the entire village killed him. Finally the king, filled with admiration for the courage and strength of the people, pardons their crime and takes Fuente Ovejuna under his own protection.

It seems strange that a man capable of such power should have written hundreds of plays devoid of any serious purpose. It is also strange, from a humanistic point of view, that this man could have stood by and watched a monk being burned at the stake for heresy. But perhaps in-

---

[5]*Fuente Ovejuna*, act 3, in *Four Plays by Lope de Vega*, ed. and trans. John Garrett Underhill (New York: Scribner, 1936).

consistency is as inherent a characteristic of his life and works as color and energy.

PEDRO CALDERÓN DE LA BARCA

The other highly regarded playwright of the age is Calderón (Pedro Calderón de la Barca, 1600–1681). While his output is feeble in comparison with Lope's, it nevertheless included 70 religious plays and 111 dramas. Considering that as an important figure of state and church his time was largely occupied with official duties, we can scarcely dismiss him as lazy.

Calderón's life, like that of Sophocles and in contrast to that of Lope, appears to have been serene and exemplary. He was a Spanish gentleman in the finest sense of the word. His plays excel Lope's in only one respect: The poetry is generally regarded as superior, or at least more polished. This does not mean that he was a painstaking craftsman. Some of his errors and anachronisms growing from hasty writing are quite as startling as those of his great predecessor. He has Herodias describe America, he places Jerusalem on the seacoast, and he locates the Danube between Russia and Sweden!

Calderón's best plays are probably *The Mayor of Zalamea* and *Life Is a Dream*. The first resembles *Fuente Ovejuna* in that the rugged honor of the Spanish peasant is once more pitted against the corruption of the nobility. *Life Is a Dream* is usually regarded as Calderón's masterpiece. King Basilio of Poland, having been warned by prophecy that his son Segismundo will do great evil if ever allowed to rule, is forced to imprison the child for life. With the approach of old age and death, the King relents and determines to allow his son a trial of one day in his rightful place. Accordingly the young prince is given a sleeping potion, dressed in royal robes, and brought to the palace. But his character proves to be so brutal and ungovernable that the old King is forced to order another sleeping potion, and Segismundo returns to prison. On waking, he is convinced that the royalty of yesterday was but a dream—or is the present a dream?—a problem that foreshadows Pirandello, an important playwright of the twentieth century.

Aside from the two plays outlined above, Calderón's work, like Lope's, was largely concerned with conventional themes of love and

hardships abounded, but they learned from these, and after 12 years emerged as the outstanding troupe in France. Then on October 24, 1658, came the great night when they appeared before Louis XIV and his court. Unfortunately, they decided to rise to the dignity of the occasion by performing one of Corneille's tragedies. The performance was a failure, but Molière, skilled as a showman and speaker, stepped before the curtain to beg that the company be permitted to present one of his own slight farces, *Le Docteur amoureux (The Lovesick Doctor)*. In the tradition of the best soap opera romance, the little farce scored a brilliant success, and Molière found himself and his company established in royal favor.

During his years of trouping the provinces, Molière had written several clever pieces, but his first important contribution to the world of dramatic literature, *Les Précieuses ridicules (The Affected Young Ladies*, 1659), came after his dramatic debut before the king. The plot is simple but delightful: Two gentlemen, rejected by two affected young ladies, take revenge by disguising their clever servants as supergentlemen, who spend a mad half-hour completely unmasking the insincerity and shallowness of the silly girls and their whole affected cult. Like Aristophanes, Molière had used material immediately at hand. While he had not designated them by name, everyone knew that the barbs were aimed at a certain Madame de Rambouillet and her group. The *précieuses* ladies were outraged, but Molière enjoyed royal protection. Here was comedy once more returning to its highest function: rich in wit and entertainment while serving as a satirical lash against social follies.

In his two most serious plays, *Tartuffe* and *Le Misanthrope*, and even in lighter pieces like *L'Avare (The Miser)*, Molière's satiric purpose is driven home with an intensity that almost, but never quite, loses its comic value. *Tartuffe* (1664) was such a stinging attack upon religious hypocrisy that not even Louis XIV dared protect it, and the play was withheld from public presentation. *Le Misanthrope* (1666), like so many of Molière's plays, reveals his philosophy that extremes are bad, that wisdom is to be found in the neighborhood of the golden mean, and that honest acceptance of the facts and follies of life is the only sane course a person can follow to escape being ridiculous.

Probably nothing in the life and works of Molière does more to humanize the man and win our admiration than his last comedy. Knowing that death was not far away, he rose gloriously and ironically to the occasion and penned *Le Malade imaginaire (The Imaginary Invalid*, 1673).

FIGURE 3:8 Molière's *The Miser*. Hume Cronyn and Zoë Caldwell in a Guthrie Theatre production; directed by Douglas Campbell; costumes by Tanya Moiseiwitsch.

His old antagonism toward the hypocrisy and pseudoscientific jargon of the medical profession is given free rein, and learned doctors receive a thorough beating, along with frugality and other human weaknesses. It is one of the most entertaining and popular of all his plays. Courageous and theatrical to the last, Molière himself played the leading role. During the fourth performance he collapsed. Four hours later he was dead.

PLAYWRIGHTS OF THE EIGHTEENTH CENTURY

While Molière, Racine, and Corneille are the giants of French theatre, even an introduction to plays and playwrights cannot entirely ignore three figures of the next century, Voltaire, Diderot, and Beaumarchais. Voltaire (1694–1778) claims attention because the great philosopher was keenly interested in theatre and wrote some fairly successful, if somewhat bizarre, plays. Denis Diderot (1713–1784), the famous Encyclopedist, made an attempt to break the stranglehold of pseudoclassicism by acclaiming a new type of drama—the drama of people. He wrote two plays, *Le Père de famille* and *Le Fils naturel*, to illustrate his principles. While not particularly moving plays, they do contain elements that foreshadow Ibsen and realism.

Beaumarchais's claim to greatness rests on two lively, uninhibited comedies, *Le Barbier de Seville* (*The Barber of Seville*, 1775) and *Le Mariage de Figaro* (*The Marriage of Figaro*, 1784). Some of their fame, of course, belongs to Rossini and Mozart, who transformed them into delightful operas. While primarily enjoyable as entertainment, they also contain much satirical criticism, particularly in the character of Figaro, who appears in both plays. Had not most of Beaumarchais's life and energy been devoted to the French Revolution, he might have become a formidable rival to Molière himself.

FROM THE ENGLISH RESTORATION TO THE EIGHTEENTH CENTURY

Wearied by the stern, colorless quality of life under Cromwell and the Puritans, England finally invited Charles II, "the Merry Monarch," to return from France and ascend the throne left vacant by the execution of his father 11 years earlier. With the crowning of Charles II (1660) came the return of the English court, made up largely of a nobility that, like Charles himself, had spent most of the years of the Commonwealth in France. Consequently it should surprise no one to learn that playwriting, along with other arts and pleasures, was also restored but that it took its style and standards from French rather than from English tradition.

Though there was of course some blending of the two, the style for the most part resembled Molière far more closely than it did Shakespeare.

Contrasts between the Elizabethan and Restoration theatres are numerous and striking. The Elizabethan theatre had been a theatre of the people and included all classes, from the lowest groundlings to Elizabeth herself. The Restoration theatre, on the other hand, was a pleasure of the court alone. At the height of the Elizabethan era numerous playhouses had been in profitable operation at the same time. During the Restoration only two small theatres were licensed, and even these had difficulty in attracting patrons. Consequently, it should be remembered that Restoration playwrights, instead of writing for or about the English people, were concerned only with representing and pleasing a few members of the highly select and highly sophisticated upper class. This Restoration audience was perhaps the most thoroughly aristocratic audience the theatre has ever known, even exceeding the aristocracy of its model, the French court of Louis XIV. In France Molière had been able to mix bourgeois and aristocratic elements, whereas in England Restoration playwrights simply ignored the commoners or used them (including the clergy and professionals) as servants. As in France, however, what mattered was intelligence and good taste. Life was a game of wits, not something to be reformed. Verbal skill and style were the virtues; the sins were to be dull, to be clumsy, or to get caught. Let the commoners resort to animal violence; let the fops make fools of themselves; let the clergy and Puritans fume about morality; the Restoration aristocrats, the only ones (in their estimation) who mattered, would accept life as it was without illusions, extracting whatever enjoyment they could with disarming, amoral good taste and high spirits. Their dress was elegant, their weapons (for the most part) words, and although their critics have long assailed the immorality of this small, select society, it was clearly one of the most civilized the world has ever known.

COMEDY

It is not surprising that such a society should have failed miserably in its attempt to write tragedy. In comedy, however, the results were excellent. Dorimant, a character in *The Man of Mode*, sets the keynote when he says, ''Next to the coming to a good understanding with a new mistress,

I love a quarrel with an old one." Some of the Restoration's comic success may have been due to the fact that the playwrights were men of
ample intellectual capacity who were also leaders in affairs of state. Sir
George Etherege (c. 1635–c. 1691), the first important Restoration playwright, is an excellent example, for he was a favorite of Charles II, handsome, dashing, an able diplomat, and a skillful lover. Playwriting to him
was not a profession but an amusement. He bothered to write only three
plays, the best being his last, *The Man of Mode; or, Sir Fopling Flutter*, the
title itself indicating the tone of the play.

FIGURE 3:9 Wycherley's *The Country Wife*. A Hilberry Repertory Theatre
production; directed by Richard Spear.

FIGURE 3:10 Congreve's *The Way of the World*. A Guthrie Theatre production;
directed by Douglas Campbell; designed by Tanya Moiseiwitsch.

The foregoing comments about Etherege also apply, with slight
modification, to William Wycherley (1640–1716), whose *The Country
Wife* has been enormously enjoyed by audiences of our own day and
whose *The Plain Dealer*, based on Molière's *Le Misanthrope*, is greatly
admired by critics. However, it was with William Congreve (c.
1670–1729) that Restoration comedy reached its polished perfection. His
greatest play, *The Way of the World*, appeared at the exact turn of the century—1700. The plot, though clever and complicated, is not the item of
importance. To understand Restoration comedy one must turn to the
dialogue. Note the skill with which the beautiful Mrs. Millamant com-

bats one of Mirabell's rare attempts to become serious and perhaps a bit sentimental:

MRS. M.   Ha! ha! ha! What would you give, that you could help loving me?

MIRABELL   I would give something that you did not know I could not help it.

MRS. M.   Come, don't look grave, then. . . . Prithee, don't look with that violent and inflexible wise face, like Solomon at the dividing of the child in an old tapestry hanging.

MIRABELL   You are merry, madam, but I would persuade you for a moment to be serious.

MRS. M.   What, with that face? No, if you keep your countenance, 'tis impossible I should hold mine.[6]

Although *The Way of the World* marked the apex of high comedy, forces were already working toward its destruction. Excesses of the aristocrats of the Restoration had resulted in the Bill of Rights of 1689. Money and the power that went with it were shifting into the hands of the sturdy and industrious merchant class. The problems of common people, viewed by earlier writers as objects for laughter, were beginning to be taken seriously. As early as 1698 high comedy had come under bitter attack when Jeremy Collier, a church official, shook the theatrical world with his publication of *A Short View of the Immorality and Profaneness of the English Stage.*

But the greatest opposition to high comedy came from the theatre itself, where a new genre, sentimental comedy, began to take over. Perhaps the most vivid foretaste of things to come occurred in 1696 with the production of Colley Cibber's new play entitled *Love's Last Shift.* The plot begins like the typical Restoration comedy. Loveless, a Restoration rake, marries a beautiful and virtuous young girl, Amanda, only to tire of her and desert her in favor of a wild life in France. As the play begins he has returned to England, dissipated, penniless, and asking only for one last fling. In trying to arrange a meeting with some lady of easy virtue, his servant quite by accident makes contact with Amanda, the faithful wife. Seeing a chance to reclaim her erring husband, Amanda consents to a meeting. So Loveless meets her, does not recognize her, vows

---

[6] William Congreve, *The Way of the World*, act 2, sc. 2.

he has never known such love, such beauty, such ecstasy. At this point Amanda reveals her identity.

So far the plot might be that of any true Restoration comedy; had it continued in the high comedy vein the worthless rake of a husband would probably have been mortified to find the divine creature his lawful wife. He would probably have stormed from the house, making a fool of himself as well as of the virtuous Amanda who had thought she could reclaim him. But instead of this, Amanda's revelation of her identity catches the soul of Loveless up in an orgy of repentance; Amanda weeps tears of joy, Loveless practically weeps tears of joy, and, most astonishing of all, audiences wept tears of joy! Here was sentimental comedy, the happy tearful ending—"life as it should be."

For a while the writers of high comedy fought back. Sir John Vanbrugh wrote a brilliant answer to Cibber's sentimental ending with the play *The Relapse*, which pictures Amanda trying to live with her "reformed" husband, who is once more on the prowl only six months after his "conversion"; but in spite of Vanbrugh's efforts and the efforts of others like him, sentimental comedy quickly became the predominant form.

While Colley Cibber may claim credit for having written the first important sentimental comedy, he is not really one of the leaders in the movement. His sentimental ending was probably nothing but a happy, unpremeditated accident. With Sir Richard Steele (1672–1729) this was not the case. This famous and beloved essayist became the ardent champion of the sentimental genre in theory as well as in practice. His own comedies, *The Conscious Lovers* and *The Tender Husband*, are among the best of their type. They advance the belief that people are fundamentally good at heart. Unlike the satirical comedies of Aristophanes, Jonson, Molière, and Congreve, who either cared nothing about reforming society or, if they did, had sought to do so by making vice ridiculous, Steele's comedies sought to reform society by making virtue attractive. They aimed to arouse not scornful laughter but kindly laughter and tears. Relationships between parent and child, nature and humanity, and church and goodness were pictured as ideal. Above all, virtue was always rewarded, vice detected, and happiness eventually triumphant.

A complete account of the eighteenth-century sentimental movement is far more complicated and extensive than the above discussion would indicate. It can be traced in the theatre of other lands as well as in other phases of the life and literature of England. The conflict between the sentimental and the satirical view of life is still with us. Moreover, the problem is complicated by the fact that sentimental comedy and satirical comedy have had a tendency to merge. This is apparent toward the end of the century in the work of Oliver Goldsmith (1728–1774), one of the two outstanding playwrights of his day. By nature and emotion he was sentimental (Irish, lovable, and tenderhearted), but by intellect and in theory he was the champion of satirical comedy. Maintaining that laughter had been all but banished from the stage, he set about the task of restoring the comic muse by writing *The Goodnatured Man* and *She Stoops to Conquer*. The latter play, while imperfect, is one of the most popular English comedies between Shakespeare and Shaw, enjoying a long and successful history both with the reading public and on the stage.

Closer to true satirical comedy are the plays of Richard Brinsley Sheridan (1751–1816). His first comedy, *The Rivals*, gives us such famous characters as Lydia Languish, Sir Lucius O'Trigger, the blundering Bob Acres, and Mrs. Malaprop, whose passion for the use of polite language saturates her speeches with such famous malapropisms as "the pineapple of politeness" and "like an allegory on the banks of the Nile."

Sheridan's second play, *The School for Scandal*, is clearly an English masterpiece. It is a comedy of manners, a satire of the follies of the fashionable social circle of Sheridan's day. Against a background of scandal, gossip, and intrigue, Sheridan spins a complicated plot, which among other things involves the affairs of a vivacious young wife, Lady Teazle, who has married an old husband, Sir Peter. There is nothing unusual about such a situation, but there is about the brilliance of the wit with which they quarrel.

SIR PETER T.   Very well, ma'am, very well; so a husband is to have no influence, no authority?

LADY T.   Authority! No, to be sure; if you wanted authority over me, you should have adopted me, and not married me: I am sure you were old enough.

SIR PETER T.   Oons! madam; if you had been born to this, I shouldn't wonder at your talking thus; but you forget what your situation was when I married you.

FIGURE 3:11 Sheridan's *The Rivals*. A Missouri Repertory Theatre production; directed by John O'Shaughnessy; designed by Mort Walker.

LADY T.   No, no, I don't; 't was a very disagreeable one, or I should never have married you.

SIR PETER T.   This, madam, was your situation; and what have I done for you? I have made you a woman of fashion, of fortune, of rank; in short, I have made you my wife.

LADY T.   Well, then, and there is but one thing more you can make me to add to the obligation, and that is —

SIR PETER T.   My widow, I suppose?

LADY T.   Hem! hem!

. . .

LADY T.   For my part, I should think you would like to have your wife thought a woman of taste.

SIR PETER T.   Ay, there again; taste; Zounds! madam, you had no taste when you married me!

LADY T.   That's very true indeed, Sir Peter. . . . [7]

[7] Richard B. Sheridan, *The School for Scandal*, act 2, sc. 1.

In spite of his early success as a playwright, before he was 30 Sheridan withdrew from the impractical world of playwriting to devote himself to the practical world of politics. One may note with regret that only a handful of historians know of his work as a member of Parliament, while hardly anyone with so much as a secondary school education has failed to hear of *The School for Scandal* or *The Rivals*.

OTHER COMIC FORMS

Having traced the major course of comedy through the Restoration to the close of the eighteenth century, we should now note that the period was also famous for having originated, or at least developed, a number of new comic forms. Most notable perhaps was ballad opera, where lyrics were interspersed with dialogue much as they are in modern musical comedy, although unlike musical comedy, they were sung to old tunes. John Gay's *The Beggar's Opera* (1728), a devastating satire on politics, morals, and Italian opera, is the outstanding example of the genre. It set a new record in London for length of run, but because of its satire it helped to stimulate the passage of the famous licensing act of 1737, which opened the way for rigid censorship of all plays.

Another genre worthy of notice is burlesque, of which there are at least three examples of importance: *The Rehearsal* (1671), by the Duke of Buckingham, *Tom Thumb* (1730), by Henry Fielding, and *The Critic* (1779), by Sheridan. Of the three, *Tom Thumb* (published in 1731 as *The Tragedy of Tragedies*) is the most fantastic and had the most telling results. It dealt a deathblow to heroic tragedy, as tiny Tom conquered giants in battle and the passionate Princess Huncamunca in love. This is one play for which reading the script is probably more enjoyable than seeing it performed on the stage, for the copious footnotes are half the fun. For example, after Tom has cried, "Oh happy, happy, happy, happy, Thumb!" a footnote solemnly informs us that Tom is exactly one-fourth happier than Masinissa, a well-known character in the tragedy *Sophonisba*, who was only "happy, happy, happy!"[8]

In addition to ballad opera and burlesque, farce enjoyed a vogue during the period. Most of these farces were short and were used as cur-

---

[8] Henry Fielding, *The Tragedy of Tragedies*, act 1, sc. 3.

tain raisers or afterpieces. They are not of world-shaking importance, but they did serve to keep the spirit of laughter alive and healthy at a time when comedy was becoming more and more lachrymose. Some of the best of these short farces were written by the great actor David Garrick.

TRAGEDY

Turning from the comic to the tragic muse, we find both parallels and contrasts. The greatest contrast lies in the fact that whereas comedy reached a high degree of excellence during the Restoration, tragedy reached a preposterous degree of bombast. Heroic tragedy, as it is now labeled, exhibits most of the worst qualities of Seneca. Extravagant situations, unbelievable heroes, and impossible deeds were mixed with a rigid adherence to classic rules, a strict sense of decorum, and a verse form of rhymed couplets, which had been borrowed from the French. But just as comedy evolved in subject matter from the life of the aristocrats to that of the common people, so tragedy moved from the heroic to the bourgeois. In fact, just as *Love's Last Shift* tended to establish or at least to crystallize a new genre—sentimental comedy—so *George Barnwell; or, The London Merchant* established a new genre—bourgeois tragedy. Written by George Lillo and produced in 1731, the plot, based on an old ballad, features an innocent young boy of 18 who falls under the spell of an evil woman, Millwood. Under her influence this young apprentice plays false to his noble old employer, Thorowgood, his loyal friend, Trueman, and his innocent sweetheart, Maria. Finally he is driven to the murder of his kind and thoughtful uncle. The last act shows his pitiful repentance and march to the gallows.

Several qualities establish the thoroughly bourgeois character of this tragedy. It is written in prose, it exalts the merchant class, and it presents no character of genteel or noble birth. The central character is weak and pathetic, but not tragic. George Barnwell has no strength of character. If Millwood says, "Come hither," George comes; if she asks him to steal from his employer, he steals; if she suggests that he murder his uncle, he murders his uncle. Contrast George with a King Lear or an Oedipus and one sees why critics maintain that the play is not tragic. To be tragic, an element of strength, significance, and greatness of character must blend with the pity and terror.

As in the case of sentimental comedy, the trend toward bourgeois tragedy was not confined to England alone. In France, as we have already noted, both Voltaire and Diderot were identified with the movement, but it was in Germany that the bourgeois genre first gained the strength to command genuine respect.

GERMANY: THE ROMANTIC SPIRIT

The shifting tide from the aristocratic and classic toward the bourgeois and sentimental in both life and literature had progressed smoothly during the early and middle years of the eighteenth century. However, as the period drew to a close, signs of turbulence and unrest became evident. In America the new spirit of liberty and equality broke the hold of King George III. In France, a few years later, it burst out in the storming of the Bastille. But even where revolution and physical violence were held in check, the minds and hearts of people were stirred with a new excitement—a new hope for freedom and equality.

In literature this new spirit led to a movement known as *romanticism.* Inspiration, not rules; variety, not unity; and freedom, not restriction were among its characteristics. There was also a love of nature, a worship of the "noble savage," and a strange quality of nostalgic sadness that found its way into much of the literary work of the day.

In the theatre, Germany, through the work of Lessing, Goethe, and Schiller, carried the romantic spirit to its greatest heights. Germany had been slow in its theatrical development. A good beginning had been made during the sixteenth century by Hans Sachs, but then came the devastation of the Thirty Years' War, and a century of progress was lost. During the years when England with Shakespeare, Spain with Lope de Vega, and France with Molière were giving the world plays rivaled only by those of ancient Athens, the best Germany had to offer was a crude, vulgar farce featuring such characters as Hans Wurst and Pickleherring.

The awakening began with the efforts of Johann Gottsched and Karoline Neuber. Working sometimes as partners and sometimes as enemies, they waged a war against the crude vulgarity of the popular German stage. Unfortunately the remedy that both proposed was almost worse than the disease itself, since both crusaded for the dull and lifeless decorum of French pseudoclassicism. But in spite of such shortcomings they did manage to rid the stage of Hans Wurst, and they did pave the way for the great period that was to follow.

GOTTHOLD LESSING

Working in Karoline Neuber's company during its last years was a young man named Gotthold Ephraim Lessing (1729–1781), who was destined to become the first great playwright in Germany, though his influence and contributions as a critic probably overshadow his work as a playwright. With a clearness of insight that had been lacking in both Neuber and Gottsched, Lessing saw that while the classic form had been excellent for the Greeks, it could not be applied to the restless spirit of eighteenth-century Germany. Dramatic effectiveness, not rules, became his basis of judgment; nor were Seneca or his French imitators to be the recommended models, but rather Shakespeare with his freedom and imagination. Lessing also saw merit in the attempt of George Lillo and his followers to relate drama to the life of the common people. Such views were skillfully stated in his *Hamburgische Dramaturgie*, a periodical which, though it lasted less than two years, ranks second only to Aristotle's *The Poetics* as a landmark of dramatic criticism. Almost single-handedly he turned the German theatre from the sterile path of pseudoclassicism to the stimulating freedom of Shakespeare.

Lessing's plays *Emilia Galotti* and *Miss Sara Sampson* are bourgeois tragedies far superior to anything either France or England had yet contributed in that genre. *Minna von Barnhelm* still remains one of the finest German comedies, while *Nathan der Weise (Nathan the Wise)*, although not one of the world's greatest plays, is probably one of the world's greatest pleas for religious tolerance. If Lessing's poetry and dramatic skill had equaled his thesis, this last play would rank as one of the masterpieces of all time. Partly through the device of having a Christian, a Muslim, and a Jew discover that they are blood relations, but largely through the character and wisdom of Nathan, Lessing drives home his message.

The old Jew represents the best in all religions. While technically adhering to the faith of his Hebrew fathers, he has equal respect for all other faiths. According to his famous parable of the ring, only by the test of years, only by observing which one brings the greatest good to mankind, can we determine which, if any, is the "true" religion.

JOHANN WOLFGANG VON GOETHE

Lessing's tendency to allow ideas to overshadow his skill as a playwright is also apparent in the works of his great contemporary, Johann Wolfgang von Goethe (1749–1832). Few names in history command greater respect, for Goethe, like Leonardo da Vinci, nearly mastered the whole of contemporary knowledge in both art and science. The theatre may well be proud of the fact that such an intellectual giant chose to cast so much of his work in the dramatic form, even though the result does not always meet the demands of practical stage production.

His masterpiece is, of course, *Faust*. Into it went much of a lifetime's search for truth, for the essence of good and evil, for the meaning of humanity's restless striving for knowledge. But those who understand Goethe insist that he would have been outraged could he have seen what modern audiences extract from his masterpiece, usually identified in the popular mind by the "Soldier's Chorus" from Gounod's opera, which, in common with most stage productions, limits itself to the pathetic story of Gretchen. Taken alone, this first half of *Faust* is practically meaningless. The film *Faust and the Devil*, for example, featured beautiful romantic scenery and beautiful singing of Gounod's music, but the intellectual essence of the story seemed to be the childishly simple tale of a man who, having sold his soul to the devil, seduces a beautiful girl, kills her brother, deserts her, and returns in time to see her tried for infanticide and burned at the stake. Now what is the meaning of such a story? Do not sell your soul to the devil? Is one really likely to face the problem in quite such a direct and obvious way? And what of Gretchen? The moral is apparently to beware of strange, handsome men; but with the cards so stacked against her, Gretchen could not possibly have resisted. Her piety and resistance were admirable; had they been any stronger, she could scarcely have avoided being frigidly unattractive. We are at a loss to find any meaning in seeing beauty and innocence tortured inhumanly for no reason at all. Or is the moral one of social protest against the fantastic cruelty and lust for punishment on the part of the medieval Church and medieval townspeople? In that case Mephistopheles becomes the only admirable character, for he persecutes these innately evil, ignorant, and superstitious beings whenever possible.

Obviously Goethe had other ideas when he wrote his great dramatic poem. It would be futile to attempt here an analysis of this complex masterpiece, but it is at least possible to state its main outlines, for Faust has much of Goethe in him, much of Renaissance man, much of every person who ever sought honestly and deeply for the meaning of life. Unable to satisfy his hunger for knowledge or happiness through human means, Faust wagers with Mephistopheles that nothing the devil can provide will satisfy this hunger. In the first major search for satisfaction Mephistopheles leads Faust into the realm of sensual pleasure. This brings tragedy and suffering both to himself and to Gretchen. His next search leads him into the realm of the aesthetic, but even this finally vanishes into nothingness. Finally his quest leads him to the service of humanity, and in draining the swamps to bring a better life to others, he himself finds his moment of satisfaction and, via the direct intervention of God, his salvation—salvation because of the very struggle, the endless, restless quest for knowledge, that had brought so much of both good and evil into the world.

FRIEDRICH VON SCHILLER

While no match for Goethe as a thinker, the third outstanding playwright of the period, Johann Christoph Friedrich von Schiller (1759–1805) excelled him as a man of the theatre. Schiller's plays have dramatic fire, excitement, and lyric qualities that have never ceased to win favor with both actors and audiences. A true son of the romantic spirit, his first play, *The Robbers*, written when he was only 22, breathes a passionate spirit of freedom as it traces the tragic adventures of Charles von Moor, who under the sting of treachery becomes leader of a band of robbers. He and his band fight valiantly against injustice, but in the end his lawlessness brings death to his own father as well as to the girl he loves. Entangled in meshes from which there is no escape, he leaves the band and gives himself up to certain death.

Schiller's greatest plays are generally considered to be his historical tragedies. Not since Shakespeare had anyone made the material of history so effective on the stage. Such plays as *Wilhelm Tell* and *Maria Stuart* probably gained much of their popularity from the fact that the title roles offered excellent histrionic opportunities to great stars of the nineteenth century. His greatest work from a literary standpoint, however, is *Wallenstein*, a trilogy of three plays greatly admired by critics but infrequently seen on the stage.

Were we following a strictly chronological pattern, this discussion would have to include a few eighteenth- and nineteenth-century playwrights from Russia, America, and other countries. For our purposes, however, it seems best to consider these in the following chapters.

CHAPTER 4

ENTERTAINMENT AND ESTABLISHED FAITH

Thus far we have been able to follow the development of playwriting year by year and nation by nation, but as we approach the twentieth century the pace of life in the theatre, like that of civilization in general, grows in both volume and complexity until a simple chronology of events becomes tedious and confusing. More plays were published between 1900 and 1975 than during all the preceding centuries combined. Movements and countermovements became international in scope; a theatrical hit in New York, London, Paris, or Moscow usually was produced throughout most of the Western world within one or two years. Instability and contradictions were everywhere; college professors and scholars struggled to establish rational principles that might serve as foundation stones for the evaluation and understanding of drama, but by the mid-twentieth century even these had crumbled, until today each individual can speak only for himself or herself — not in the egotistical sense but in the lonely sense. As Saroyan's old man in *The Time of Your Life* keeps repeating, "No foundation. All the way down the line."

But in spite of the bulk and chaos of present-day playwriting, three major divisions can be discerned:

1. The theatre of entertainment　Whether we like it or not, most people go to the theatre to be entertained—to escape from their daily problems into a world of romance, excitement, and adventure. Not many years ago it was fashionable for scholars to look with scorn upon such objectives; today they are no longer so dogmatic. Enough is wrong with our real world so that all of us need occasionally to relax and escape if we are to preserve our sanity. But even so, two charges against the theatre of entertainment still have validity: (1) It seldom says anything that makes one any wiser and (2) there is so much of it, especially since the arrival of television. Moreover, the theatre of entertainment is primarily the theatre of the Establishment. It works best in a society in which faith in some religion or philosophy is firm and the people are essentially satisfied with the status quo. The theatre of entertainment includes melodrama, farce, romantic comedy, and most musical plays. And it is, of course, the basic product of our mass media: motion pictures, radio, and television.

2. The theatre of realism　Some people go to the theatre for mental stimulation and new ideas. They want to attend plays that have something to say—plays with wit or new insight into the real problems of real people. Generally speaking, both those who write and those who enjoy such plays have strong faith in people and in their ability to improve through the intellectual control of life—through rational, objective, and scientific understanding. Although still very much alive, the heyday for this type of play extended from the last quarter of the nineteenth century, with writers like Ibsen, to the middle of the twentieth, with writers like Arthur Miller.

3. The theatre of disillusionment, protest, and the search for alternatives　This is a general classification covering expressionism, existentialism, despair, cruelty, and absurdity. It springs from disillusionment. It has little faith in present-day religions, in rational ideas, or in conventional values. It sees today's god of science as having achieved unprecedented violence and ugliness plus the very real possibility of human annihilation. It is a frustrated outcry: cursing, sobbing, or laughing at the human condition.

While the above divisions are obviously imperfect, they should at least guard against the folly of trying to appreciate or evaluate all drama from any one point of view. For example, *Charley's Aunt*, one of the most entertaining plays ever written, was vulgar trash to the realists; many of the plays by Shaw and Ibsen are old-fashioned nonsense to the absurdists; while many modern plays, like *The Homecoming*, are incomprehensible obscenity to the "right-thinking" masses. Dividing modern drama into three areas should increase our ability to appreciate and understand each type of drama on its own terms. In this chapter we will discuss the theatre of entertainment.

MELODRAMA

The nineteenth century is sometimes referred to as the age of melodrama. Although this is not strictly true, the fact remains that melodrama was the dominant and most characteristic form until the end of the century, when Zola, Ibsen, Shaw, and others marshaled the great realistic revolt. Melodrama's plots, while disregarding probability, were often masterpieces of suspense and excitement; its characters, lacking the complexity of reality, were crystal-clear types — the noble hero, the lovely heroine, the dastardly villain, the pert ingenue; it thrived on the spectacular — lavish scenery, mechanical wonders, and atmospheric music; and its ending was invariably happy — evil discovered and virtue rewarded.

As already implied, critics and teachers operating under the influence of realism scorned and ridiculed melodrama unmercifully; in fact, no melodramatic villain was ever painted with blacker hue. They ignored the deft theatrical skill with which many melodramas were constructed; they ignored the fact that melodrama enabled millions of dull, careworn theatre-goers to escape into a world of romantic adventure; and they especially ignored the fact that melodrama was admirably fitted to the age for which it was written, for the nineteenth century, in England especially, was (with numerous exceptions of course) essentially an age of faith: "God's in his heaven — All's right with the world."

Faith also extended to white superiority, which was a foregone conclusion; to wealth and power, which were highly respected; and to human destiny, where the perfectability of man stood just around the corner. Even if justice misfired in this life, which it often did, all knew that it would be meted out to the last quiver of the scales in the hereafter. In matters of decorum and propriety England's Queen Victoria set the almost perfect example, and because of her the period is known as the Victorian age.

As far as the popular theatre was concerned, its conservative, middle-class audience had little interest in new or disturbing ideas. The fundamental questions of existence were already comfortably answered. The audience desired only that its basic assumptions be reinforced and that it be allowed to escape from everyday existence (not always so pleasant as everyone pretended) into the romantic world of make-believe — into life as it should be. The answer was obviously melodrama — with a smattering of farce or romance plus an occasional classic or opera to add variety and cultural respectability.

But the dubious distinction of perfecting melodrama belongs not to England but to Germany and France, where August Friedrich Ferdinand von Kotzebue (1761–1819) and Guilbert de Pixérécourt (1773–1844) developed the genre to its full maturity. Between them they turned out over 300 thrillers, which were soon translated, adapted, mutilated, or just plain stolen by writers all over the Western world.[1]

The new form was quick to take root in America. Playwriting, in spite of Puritan opposition, had already gained a foothold on the new continent, the most notable examples being our first tragedy, *The Prince of Parthia* (1767), by Thomas Godfrey, and our first comedy, *The Contrast* (1767), by Royall Tyler. But the natural theatrical diet for the hard-working, empire-building American pioneers was melodrama, for they came to the theatre to be entertained, not perplexed. Plays by Kotzebue and Pixérécourt were soon discovered and "adapted" even by such distinguished men as "the father of the American theatre," William Dunlap. An early American dictionary even defined a playwright as "one who adapts from the French." But it would be easy to overstress such borrowing, for American melodrama soon developed roots of its own. Augustin Daly (1838–1899), one of the most successful theatrical managers of the century, turned out a thriller in *Under the Gaslight* that made European models look pale, as honest Snorky, lashed to the railroad tracks by black-hearted Byke, was left in the path of onrushing terror: the deafening thunder and blinding gaslight of the midnight express! Daly outdid even this trick in *The Red Scarf* by lashing an actor to the carriage of a

[1]The first international copyright law, which protected authors against unauthorized reproduction of their works in other nations, was not passed until 1887.

FIGURE 4:1 Melodrama! Honest Snorkey is lashed to the rails in *Under the Gaslight*. A Minnesota Showboat production; designed by Wendell Josal.

sawmill, then slowly propelling the victim toward the screaming teeth of a huge circular saw!

But even Daly's success with melodrama could not match that of *Uncle Tom's Cabin*. There were several dramatizations of Harriet Beecher Stowe's famous novel, but the one that captured America was the work of George L. Aiken. From its first appearance in 1852 until well into the twentieth century, it established an amazing record of popular success. It was played as rousing abolitionist propaganda, a tear-jerker, a comedy, a musical, an animal show, a scenic spectacle, and a burlesque. From America's largest cities to its frontier hamlets, from its finest theatres to its tents and dime museums, *Uncle Tom's Cabin* demonstrated its amazing power to attract an audience. The novelties and effects employed to keep the show alive were fabulous. At times the bloodhounds received more publicity than the actors. The river of ice over which Eliza flees with her baby, Little Eva's ascent into heaven, and other "scenic wonders" were exploited to the last ounce of spectacle. Tiny companies with as few as three players performed the entire script; other companies expanded until they included such items as jubilee singers and brass bands. During the 1880s a few even advertised themselves as "double" companies with two Evas, two Toms, two Topsies, and so on. Although from a critical standpoint *Uncle Tom's Cabin* leaves much to be desired, its success on the stage was colossal.

Most prolific and probably the best writer of American melodrama was Dion Boucicault (c. 1820–1890). Boucicault's career began in his native Ireland; then he moved to London, where he wrote a remarkable comedy entitled *London Assurance*, which was very successfully revived in London in 1972. In 1853 he moved to America, where he finished the remainder of his long and successful career as an actor, playwright, and manager. Best of his many American melodramas is *The Octoroon*, a play that foreshadowed the future by touching on the racial problem. But although his treatment of Zoe, the beautiful octoroon, is ahead of its time, the play as a whole belongs to its age, for it also features a dastardly villain, a true-hearted Yankee, and a noble Indian savage. There is a solution to a murder by means of a new-fangled invention, the camera, and an abundance of scenic spectacle climaxed by a steamship explosion.

Another play that flirts with a serious problem but does so in a sentimental and melodramatic manner is *Hazel Kirke* (1880). Its author, Steele MacKaye, like Daly and Boucicault before him and Belasco after him, was an all-around man of the theatre—manager, director, playwright, and inventor. The setting for *Hazel Kirke* is England. Young Lord Carringford has been saved from death by the rugged old miller, Dunstan Kirke. He is nursed back to health by the miller's beautiful daughter, Hazel, who is already pledged in marriage to a likable middle-aged gentleman, Squire Rodney. Discovering that Hazel has fallen in love with the young lord, Dunstan flies into a rage, disinherits her, and drives her from his home. Not daring to let his aristocratic mother know of his love for a commoner, Carringford marries Hazel in secret, but unknown to him his servant has arranged an illegal ceremony. In a climactic scene reminiscent of a similar scene in *Camille*, Lady Carringford, old and ill, visits Hazel, begs for the freedom of her son, and finally reveals that the marriage was a sham. With a tragic shame that only a nineteenth-century heroine could muster, Hazel rushes away from Carringford to hide from all who know her.

Back at the mill Dunstan has gone blind, but his bitterness toward Hazel is still intense. Chancing to appear at the window, Hazel, whose wanderings have led her home, hears his angry words, sobs out her tragic farewell speech, and throws herself into the river. Dunstan hears the cries for help, tries to save her, but is helpless. Since the play is a melodrama, Lord Carringford arrives in the nick of time, saves Hazel, and all ends happily. *Hazel Kirke* may not be great literature, but in its day and for its audience it was great theatre. It set a box office record of 486 consecutive performances. One final note: It seems to be one of the first melodramas on record with no villain (which may be an advantage or disadvantage, depending upon one's point of view).

FIGURE 4:2 *Uncle Tom's Cabin.* Eliza crossing the river on ice in a spectacular 1901 production.

Toward the end of the century the mantle for showmanship—the practical gift of giving the public what it wanted—descended upon David Belasco (1854–1931). Born in San Francisco, Belasco was destined to scale the heights in almost every phase of the popular theatre, and we shall meet him again as a director, scenic designer, and lighting artist. As a playwright he was for the most part an adapter and collaborator, but the results were invariably successful with play-goers. He was sentimental and melodramatic, but, like Boucicault, he was also effective. One of his most sensational situations occurs in the second act of *The Girl of the Golden West*. The scene is the girl's cabin in the mountains. Her sweetheart lies wounded and hidden in the loft as a posse enters to search for him. Unable to find him, the men leave except for Jack Rance, sheriff and gambler, who pauses in the doorway for a last word just as blood splashes on the table! His eyes go to the blood-stained ceiling. She knows; he knows! In desperation she makes a gambling offer. They will play poker. If she wins, Rance goes away. If Rance wins, he gets his man and the girl besides. Audiences scarcely able to breathe saw the game that followed. Now the sheriff thumps down his last and deciding hand, "Three kings!" But wait! The girl shows hers. "Three aces and a pair!" Audiences were so wildly partisan that they forgave her, even though they had just seen her pluck the winning hand from the top of her stocking!

Melodrama was widespread during the nineteenth century, but it seems unnecessary to trace it further except in France and England, where evolution and exceptions to the general trend were taking place. In France during the early years of the century, the work of Pixérécourt went almost unnoticed in literary circles, where a battle was being waged between the forces of neoclassicism and the aristocratic relative of melodrama, romanticism. Neoclassicism, with its rules and regulations, had dominated French tragedy ever since the time of Racine. Outwardly the break was sharp and revolutionary. The groundwork had been laid with the translation of Shakespeare's plays during the 1820s. The decisive battle, however, was waged and won by Victor Hugo with his romantic tragedy *Hernani*, which appeared in 1830. For weeks the theatre was a scene of excitement and uproar as the classicists tried to boo the play down and romanticists tried to cheer it on. It was the battle of *Le Cid* all over again except in far more volcanic proportions, and this time the romanticists and Hugo scored a decisive triumph. Romanticism is not necessarily superior to neoclassicism; no French romantic playwright ever equaled the profound and near-perfect achievements of the classic Racine. Nevertheless, Hugo's victory meant new freedom and vitality to the French stage, and in 1830 both qualities were sorely needed.

But while the French neoclassicists fought to stem the tide of romanticism, they paid little attention to romanticism's lowbrow offspring, melodrama, which, first under Pixérécourt and later under Eugene Scribe, was capturing the masses. Skilled in theatrical know-how and equipped, like Belasco, with an instinct for commercial success, Eugene Scribe (1791–1861) set about the business of play making. Through his keen sense of audience analysis he perfected a formula for the manufacturing of plays that almost placed playwriting on an assembly-line basis. Once his formula was perfected some 400 "well-made plays" poured off the line to bring him fortune, if not undisputed fame.

At the same time we can notice an evolution taking place. Scribe's characters and situations are no longer the simple, direct, black-and-white characters and situations of earlier nineteenth-century melodrama. His plays more closely resemble the pseudoprofound and sentimental soap operas of twentieth-century radio and television. In fact, his formula for playwriting calls for meticulous care in such elements as preparation, reversal, and suspense. And while everything else about the melodramatic approach was soon to be ridiculed by the realists, they tended to adopt the form and technique of the "well-made play" in its entirety.

In England as in France the trend toward popular melodrama went essentially unnoticed by the literary elite. As a matter of fact, most of the great Victorian poets and novelists ignored the theatre entirely. Perhaps the English stage had not recovered its moral respectability since the attack by Jeremy Collier; perhaps the essential cheapness of melodrama drove them away; perhaps the commercialism of the stage was responsible, which, judging success only in terms of the box office, inevitably encouraged sensation rather than merit. In any event, the art of playwriting was not held in high esteem. That at least part of the difficulty lay in the cheapness of the stage may be concluded by the fact that though Shelley, Byron, Tennyson, and Browning were all attracted to the theatre and unable entirely to resist the temptation to write plays, they wrote for the reading public only. Their plays are called *closet dramas*, for they were never seriously intended for performance.

If writers of melodrama went too far to entertain their audiences, these writers of closet drama went too far in the opposite direction. Their plays remain dramatic poems rather than pieces for production upon the stage. This avoidance of the stage is particularly regrettable in the cases of Robert Browning and Charles Dickens. Browning shows a keen sense of the dramatic. Had he been privileged to work with a real theatre and for a discriminating audience, as were Sophocles, Shakespeare, and Molière, his contribution to dramatic literature might have been outstanding. Charles Dickens is even more interesting. He loved the stage and even spent much time acting in amateur theatricals. His sharp sense of character and his flair for the dramatic all seem ideally suited for a career in the theatre, but for some reason he avoided the dramatic form, except for one or two immature pieces.

An exception among the established Victorian authors was Edward George Bulwer-Lytton (1803 – 1873), who wrote several successful plays, including *The Lady of Lyons*, considered by Victorians to be the greatest romantic drama of all time. Take, for example, the flowing rhetoric at the end of Act 4:

> PAULINE [*the once-haughty beauty of Lyons*]   And you would have a wife enjoy luxury while a husband toils! Claude, take me; thou canst not give me wealth, titles, station—but thou canst give me a true heart. I will work for thee, tend thee, bear with thee, and never, never shall these lips reproach thee for the past.
>
> DAMAS [*the rugged old soldier*]   I'll be hanged if I am not going to blubber.
>
> CLAUDE [*the gardener's son*]   This is the heaviest blow of all! What a heart I have wronged! . . . Pauline!—angel of love and mercy!—your memory shall lead me back to virtue! . . . [*applause*] Place me wherever a foe is most dreaded,—wherever France most needs a life! . . . If I live, the name of him thou hast once loved shall not rest dishonoured; if I fall amidst the carnage and the roar of battle, my soul will fly back to thee, and love shall share with death my last sigh!—More—more would I speak to thee!—to pray!—to bless! But no; . . . Farewell![2]

Melodrama has lived on with popularity and commercial prosperity, even though its outward style has changed. True, nothing seems more old-fashioned to present-day audiences than melodramas like *The Lady*

---

[2] Edward George Bulwer-Lytton, *The Lady of Lyons*, act 4, from *The Works of Edward Bulwer-Lytton* (New York: Collier, 1901), vol. 29.

of Lyons, but this is partly because actors usually play them for laughs with tongue-in-cheek. Played sincerely and with less grandiloquent language, these same audiences might have difficulty in distinguishing between nineteenth-century melodrama and the everyday diet of soap operas and westerns that they enjoy on television. Even the theatre's most sophisticated patrons still weep for *Madame Butterfly* and thrill to the charm of *The Girl of the Golden West* when presented as operas.

Generally speaking, however, the basic ingredients of melodrama are now clothed in different styles. The 1920s brought the vogue for murder mysteries. One of the first and one of the best of these was *The Bat* (1920), by Mary Roberts Rinehart and Avery Hopwood. It featured suspense, thrills, comic relief, dim lights, shadows, hidden chambers, sliding doors; and above all, it tortured the audience with the mystery of "Who done it?" until the final moment of Act 3, when the one person above suspicion turned out to be the killer.

During the 1930s and 1940s another style of melodrama, the psychological thriller, became popular. One of the earliest and best in this category was Emlyn Williams's *Night Must Fall*, the central character of which is Danny, a charming, boyish, psychopathic killer who carries the head of one of his victims in a hatbox. Alfred Hitchcock has developed this type of psychological suspense to perfection in films. Films, as a matter of fact, have generally surpassed the stage not only in psychological suspense but also in sentimental romance, as well as in the raw power of violence. Moreover, films, both in theatres and on television, have captured the great mass audience that asks for little more than entertainment and escape. Like Molière's Monsieur Jourdain, who was amazed to learn that he had been speaking prose all his life, most Americans would probably be surprised to learn that they had been quite seriously enjoying melodramas for most of theirs.

FARCE AND COMEDY

But melodrama is not the only form of drama concerned primarily with entertainment and escape. Comedy and farce have also done their share in relaxing the masses and helping them to forget daily cares.

It was in farce that the comic muse of the nineteenth century broke

FIGURE 4:3 *An Italian Straw Hat.* Paul Ballantyne, Lance Davis, Tovah Feld-shuh, and Peter Goetz in a Guthrie Theatre production; directed by David Feldshuh.

FIGURE 4:4 *A Flea in Her Ear.* A Wayne State University production; directed by Richard Spear; setting by William Rowe.

forth most clearly and successfully. Several of the best are French, among them *An Italian Straw Hat*, *A Flea in Her Ear*, and *Hotel Paradiso*. Outrageous and fast-paced, these farces if skillfully presented can still be hilariously funny, and all three of the above have scored recent successes in England and America. Russia gave the world some fine one-act farces by a young playwright named Anton Chekhov; these included *The Boor* and *The Marriage Proposal*. England contributed a masterpiece of light farcical nonsense in *Charley's Aunt* (1892), which, especially during the half-century when realism was in vogue, was ridiculed by critics,

FIGURE 4:7
Company pro
vate audience

Musical com
to the world
Each of its l
old as the th
opera, burle
ple credit *Th
with the dis
lieve that *T*
shows like t
town (1890)
(1904), conti

FIGURE 4:5 *Charley's Aunt*. A Minnesota Showboat production; scenery by Wendell Josal; costumes by Hertha Schulze.

FIGURE 4:8   *Show Boat*. Zelle Daniels and Robert Peterson in a University of Utah production; scenery by Ron Crosby; costumes by Sue Young.

E
there
as 18
icule
turn
Room
naug
when
Amer
bring
polisl
singl
litera
produ
one v
of Mo
actors
their
wrote
achie
they

T
You,
with
have
vorite

B
comp
ly as
cludir
C. Ho
Beare
Mami
mon'
exten
and s
relaxi

clearly recognizable form, the Broadway musical comedy, had evolved.

Perhaps the first real classic of the form was *Show Boat* (Jerome Kern and Oscar Hammerstein), which first appeared in New York in 1927. Songs like "Only Make-Believe," "Why Do I Love You?" and especially "Old Man River" probably account for much of its incredible success and for its numerous revivals.

Perhaps the first outstanding achievement as far as wit and satire are concerned, was the Pulitzer Prize-winner *Of Thee I Sing*, which appeared in 1931. The book was written by George S. Kaufman and Morrie Ryskind, the music and lyrics by George and Ira Gershwin. The plot follows J. P. Wintergreen as he rides triumphantly into the White House on a program of "Love!"—not dignified love of humanity, but young, romantic love. Even at the play's climax, when the new president is about to be impeached, disaster is averted by the discovery that our hero is about to become a father, and the chorus bursts into the swelling refrain, "Posterity is just around the corner!"

The maturity of musical comedy as a comic form was strikingly illustrated by the success of *My Fair Lady*. On first impulse the thought of turning one of George Bernard Shaw's finest comedies, *Pygmalion*, into a Broadway musical seemed almost sacrilegious, but so skillfully did the authors, Alan Jay Lerner and Frederick Loewe, perform the transformation that even the dour literary purists were silenced. Shaw's dialogue and ideas were preserved to a remarkable degree. At the same time, the addition of such musical hits as "On the Street Where You Live" and "I Could Have Danced All Night," plus lavish staging and the skillful directing of Moss Hart, resulted in a production that broke almost every record in the books. It cost hundreds of thousands, but it has made millions. Countless Americans who knew next to nothing about Shaw laughed at his wit and cheered him to the echo because of *My Fair Lady*.

FIGURE 4:9   A scene from *My Fair Lady*, which ran for a record-breaking six-and-one-half years on Broadway.

FIGURE 4:10 *The Threepenny Opera.* Ruth Kobart, Ray Reinhardt, and Deborah May in an American Conservatory Theatre production; directed by Andrei Serban.

But *My Fair Lady* was not the first or the only musical to be based on an already successful play. *Oklahoma!* (Rodgers and Hammerstein) was based on *Green Grow the Lilacs*, by Lynn Riggs; *Carousel* (Rodgers and Hammerstein) on Molnar's *Liliom; Take Me Along* (Stein, Russell, and Merrill) on O'Neill's *Ah, Wilderness!; Hello, Dolly!*, the smash success of the 1960s, on Wilder's *The Matchmaker; West Side Story* (Bernstein and Laurents) on *Romeo and Juliet;* and there are many other examples.

Among other outstanding musicals we find Irving Berlin's *Annie Get Your Gun.* Berlin, another of the old pros of Broadway showmanship, included such songs (and ideas!) as "You Can't Get a Man with a Gun" and "There's No Business Like Show Business" in his story about Annie Oakley and her discovery that in order to win a man, she had to lose a shooting match. *Finian's Rainbow* (Harburg and Saidy) is an incredible mixture of Irish folklore and American racial problems. Among other things, the plot is concerned with a bigoted Southern senator who learns the meaning of brotherhood only after Celtic fairy magic transforms the senator's skin from white to black. The popularity of these and other musicals is indicated by the fact that although it now costs far more to produce a musical than it does to produce a standard legitimate play, people who have money to invest are becoming more and more inclined to gamble on the musical. Whether we like it or not, there is something about this genre that reflects America as nothing else does. And while we think of musicals as primarily dedicated to entertainment, they have sometimes outdistanced the more ponderous realists in ideas, criticism, and satire. Bertolt Brecht's *The Threepenny Opera*, a witty and unmerciful satire of modern business and morals, ran for a record 2611 performances off Broadway at the Theatre de Lys. *Fiddler on the Roof* (Bock and Stein), which treats the problem of Jews in old Russia with an amazing blend of humor and humanity, broke almost every known record of commercial success. *Hair* and *A Chorus Line* will be discussed later.

CHAPTER 5

REALISM AND FAITH IN HUMANITY

From the last quarter of the nineteenth century to the close of the Second World War, realism dominated the theatre. It, of course, never enjoyed unanimous approval; there were always rebels and dissenters. Yet realism was the major force, not only in acting, scenic design, and playwriting but also in critical thinking. Artists who opposed the dominant trend were still greatly influenced by it, since realism provided a form and a set of principles against which they could react.

The dominance of realism is not surprising when one recognizes its relationship to the rational ideals of the age of science—a science that has produced marvels in our control and understanding of the world about us, even though it has not fared well in dealing with our emotional and spiritual nature. In a sense the rational attitude from which modern science grew may be traced to the Renaissance, for it springs naturally from people's determination to rely upon themselves. Although it does not pretend to answer the ultimate riddle of existence, nor does it deny the possibility of higher powers, it does insist that a scientist rely upon natural and rational explanations, though these be painful and complicated, rather than upon supernatural, emotional, or mystic explanations, though these be pleasant and simple. It follows, then, that scientific evidence is essentially that which can be experienced through one of the five senses (sight, sound, taste, touch, or smell) and preferably that which can be demonstrated experimentally, so that even doubters must confront the evidence.

The early realists of the theatre accepted the scientific attitude with enthusiasm. As they saw it, the evils and shortcomings of Victorian life stemmed from obsolete morals, habits, and organized religions. It seemed to them that an objective, scientific attitude, relying on logic, evidence, common sense, and understanding, could cure all. As a result their battle cry became not art for art's sake, but art for truth's sake. "True to life" became the measuring stick for everything from playwriting to stage lighting (David Belasco once discarded an expensive sunset for *The Girl of the Golden West*, not because it lacked beauty but because it was "not Californian.")

In playwriting Émile Zola (1840–1902) became the first great champion of realism, or naturalism, explaining his theories in terms that were clear and uncompromising. (Naturalism is the most extreme form of realism and differs from realism primarily by going further toward the "slice of life" and in allowing less selection and rearrangement of life's material. In practice it usually dealt with painful or tragic problems.) According to Zola the stage was to become a laboratory for the study of life—a laboratory where the motives and the behavior of human beings could be viewed with complete objectivity, a place where case studies could be laid before an audience with the scientific detachment of the lecture hall but with greater vividness and clarity, a place where a "bleeding slice of life" might be held up for study and analysis. Romantic illusions were to be abolished; life was to be seen naked and as it actually was, sparing neither pain nor ugliness. His revolt against romanticism was just as extreme as the romantic Victor Hugo's revolt had been against neoclassicism. In Zola's *Thérèse Raquin*, an unpleasant study of crime which appeared in 1873, Thérèse and her lover drown her husband and then, wracked by remorse and guilt, commit suicide. As might be expected, nineteenth-century audiences rejected the play, apparently agreeing with the French critic Sarcey, who wrote, "This fellow Zola makes me a little sick."

HENRIK IBSEN

Although it was Zola who first and most clearly stated the creed of realism in its naturalistic extreme, it remained for others to give the genre stature as dramatic literature. The first, and one of the greatest, of these was Henrik Ibsen (1828–1906), who came not from the theatrical capitals of France, Germany, or England but from the hitherto unproductive soil of Norway.

A sensitive child, his early years were filled with struggle and disillusionment. He lived largely within himself, made few friends, and gradually developed a spirit of rebellion against society—a spirit very obvious in his earliest plays and still a motivating force in those of his maturity. As with most seriously introverted types, he was unlucky, displaying a chronic tendency toward bad breaks. A glaring exception to this tendency came in 1851 when the violinist Ole Bull offered him a position on the staff of the new Norwegian National Theatre in Bergen. Ibsen, literally on the verge of starvation, eagerly accepted.

For five years his duties as stage manager provided the same type of invaluable contact with the theatre that Shakespeare, Molière, and other great playwrights had enjoyed. In addition to this practical all-around experience, his contract required that he produce one play of his own on January 2 of each year. While none of the plays that he wrote to satisfy this requirement achieved greatness, they did provide training of the most valuable type.

Ibsen's comparatively happy Bergen years were followed by six less fortunate years in Christiania (now Oslo), but toward the end of that period he wrote two important plays, *Love's Comedy* and *The Pretenders*. The first, with its unorthodox view of love and marriage, created such a storm of criticism that Ibsen apparently resolved to leave Norway at the first opportunity. The second play, *The Pretenders* (1863), scored a genuine success, but it came too late. Ibsen's mind was made up, and in April 1864, he left Norway to spend the most productive years of his life in the less austere climates of Italy and Germany.

Ibsen, like Schiller and Shakespeare, devoted much of his early energy to writing historical plays, the best ones, like *The Pretenders*, being sagas of his native land. Next came his poetic dramas, *Brand* and *Peer Gynt*, which to some critics represent Ibsen at his best. Both were moti-

Figure 5:1 *A Doll's House.* Liv Ullmann and Barton Heyman in a New York Shakespeare Festival production; directed by Tormod Skagestad.

vated by Ibsen's indignation over the weakness of the Norwegian national character. *Brand* is the somber tragedy of a priest whose blind, uncompromising devotion to God brings more intense suffering to those about him "than the most talented sinner could possible have done with twice his opportunities."[1] He sacrifices everything—mother, child, wife—for

[1]George Bernard Shaw, *The Quintessence of Ibsenism* (New York: Brentano's, 1904), p. 51.

a God and a congregation who finally drive him into the mountains, where he dies in an avalanche that thunders, "He is the God of love!"

Peer Gynt stands in many ways in vivid contrast to the somber *Brand*. It is a wild, fantastic poem, sometimes bitter, sometimes gay, sometimes skirting the tragic. Peer, in contrast to Brand, goes "round about." He always compromises—or runs away. The play rambles almost as much as *Faust*, yet the overall effect is one of greatness. The characters are unusually vivid, while scenes like the death of Ase, Peer's mother, rank among the greatest in literature.

But while many regard *Peer Gynt* as Ibsen's masterpiece, none can deny that his fame in the history of the theatre rests primarily on another group of plays—his realistic, or thesis, dramas. The first of these to command world attention was *A Doll's House* (1879). During its course of action we see Nora, the central character, change from a seemingly delicate, impractical "doll" wife into a woman who walks quietly but firmly out of her house, closing the door on what contemporaries regarded as a wife's duty to her children and husband. No wonder that the play is now regarded as a milestone on the long road to an awareness of women's rights.

When *A Doll's House* stirred a moral protest reminiscent of *Love's Comedy*, Ibsen struck back at his critics with *Ghosts*. Here Mrs. Alving, the central character, unlike Nora, remains loyal to all the moral codes. Though married to Captain Alving, whose dissipation and excessive appetites make their marriage miserable, she stands by him and especially by his memory after his death. To protect her son from the father's contamination she sends the boy to Paris. She rears her husband's illegitimate daughter almost as though the child were her own. To sustain the myth of the Captain's nobility and goodness, she uses all his money to build an orphanage. But in spite of all this devotion to her duty, the orphanage burns to the ground, the illegitimate child deserts her, and the son, having inherited syphilis from his father, turns into a babbling idiot as the play ends. These are her reward for blind loyalty to duty!

If *A Doll's House* aroused a shower of criticism, *Ghosts* created a tornado. Critics became almost incoherent with rage. They babbled about "loathsome sores" and "reeking cesspools"; they described it as sickly, indecent, and fetid.[2]

[2]Ibid., pp. 3, 4.

But Ibsen continued to fight back. In answer to the violent attack upon *Ghosts* he wrote *An Enemy of the People*, which cries out the thesis that the majority is always wrong. A typical community has just completed the construction of new municipal baths and looks forward to a healthy and profitable tourist trade. Before the baths can be opened, however, Dr. Stockmann makes the shocking discovery that the baths are dangerously impure. With enthusiasm the idealistic young doctor reveals his discovery to the city authorities, expecting with almost childish naiveté to receive thanks for his public service. Instead the news touches off a frantic drive to suppress the truth. Stockmann's determined efforts to publish the facts he has discovered earn him the title of "an enemy of the people." His home, his family, and his life are endangered by an angry mob of the city's most respectable citizens, who are far more devoted to self-interest than to truth.

The next and the last of Ibsen's thesis plays, *The Wild Duck*, shows an admirable maturity of wisdom, for he now turned against his own overly zealous followers, who had begun to cry, "Strip away falsehood at all costs; the naked truth will make us free." This play is concerned with the sincere but blundering work of Gregers Werle, one of these new disciples of truth. Coming into the Ekdal household, which is living a comfortable middle-class existence in a world of illusion, Gregers clumsily shatters the home's foundation with the revelation that the sensitive young daughter, Hedvig, is not the child of the husband but of another man. He expects thereby to establish the marriage on a foundation of truth and beauty, but instead of reconciliation the truth brings disaster. The husband plunges into an orgy of self-pity; the wife is merely annoyed by her husband's adolescent antics. They are too weak to live by anything other than their illusions, and we could simply laugh at all of them were it not that the sensitive young Hedvig, believing that she is somehow responsible, kills herself.

After *The Wild Duck*, Ibsen apparently lost interest in reforming society. His later plays are more symbolic and more psychological. In this period came two of his best works, *Hedda Gabler* and *Rosmersholm*. By now the storms of protest had died away. Shaw and others had come to his defense, and through his declining years Ibsen must have found a measure of respect and contentment which were entirely foreign to him throughout most of his life.

Ibsen's contributions are many. He gave us a host of convincing and genuine characters: not black or white like those of melodrama but challenging, complex characters, with the many-sided characteristics of real people. He handled dialogue in a realistic prose that was far advanced in conversational quality and naturalness. Through his skill as a dramatist he made ideas become exciting and entertaining. Finally, he is usually considered the first to construct great dramas from the problems of the common people. With Henrik Ibsen both realism and bourgeois tragedy came of age.

THE SPIRIT OF REALISM IN ENGLAND: BERNARD SHAW AND OTHERS

In England the spirit of realism had been explored even before Zola and Ibsen pointed the way. As early as 1865, Tom Robertson's play *Society*, which dabbled pleasantly with social problems, was produced at a small, intimate theater in a new-style, realistic box setting. A few years later Pinero and other popular writers began to feel the influence of the new, thought-provoking realism and began trying to make adjustments in their own writing that would take advantage of the trend, but the playwright who responded most naturally and effectively was George Bernard Shaw (1856–1950). To the Victorians Shaw was a shocking disbeliever, to good churchgoers he was a heretic, and to conservative politicians he was a subversive; yet while Shaw may have had little faith in a conventional God or a conventional religion, his faith in humanity—or rather in humanity's potential—was colossal.

In wit, cleverness, and brilliance of ideas, Shaw is without a peer. Only Aristophanes catches something of the same quality of breathtaking surprise and delightful originality. No one was ever quite comfortable in Shaw's presence. He seems to have taken irrepressible delight in doing the unexpected, often at the expense of consistency, and, as a playwright, sometimes at the expense of structure and characterization. Yet had he been less contradictory, less of a paradox, he could never have been so interesting. His favorite device was to build up some pompous notion and then explode it for the joy of seeing his audience jump. For example, in *Man and Superman* a conventionally respectable Victorian family learns that the daughter, Violet, is pregnant. They react,

(a)

(b)

FIGURE 5:2 Three plays by Shaw. *(a) Saint Joan.* A Stratford, Ontario, production with Frank Maraden, Mervyn Blake, and Pat Galloway; directed by William Hutt; designed by Maxine Graham. *(b) The Devil's Disciple.* A Wayne State University production; directed by Richard Spear; designed by Russell Smith. *(c) Arms and the Man.* A production on the Minnesota Showboat. Scenery designed by Wendell Josal; costumes by Mary Qualey.

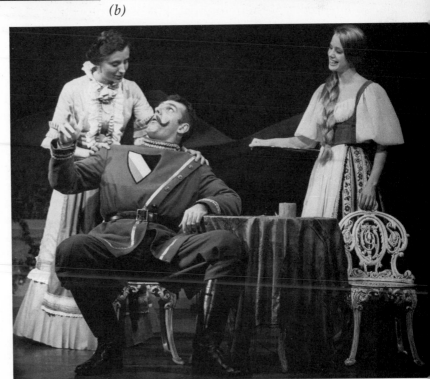

(c)

as expected, with varying degrees of mortification, indignation, and shock. Finally a freethinking cousin, Tanner, whom we quickly recognize as a mouthpiece for Shaw, unable to stand their hypocrisy any longer, launches into an eloquent defense of the erring girl and especially the innocent unborn child. But now comes the surprise, for Violet explodes with moral indignation, not against those who had abused her but against Tanner who has just defended her. She had been secretly but respectably married all the time. In fact, she is one of the most narrowly respectable of the lot, much to the discomfort of Tanner and of those in the audience who had smugly assumed that they understood everything about Shaw.

He was, or so he always maintained, a great opponent of art for art's sake. Art, according to Shaw, should have utility. To him a play was simply a more effective means of distributing ideas than either the speaker's platform or Socialist pamphlets, and yet his plays promise to live on long after the problems about which they were written have lost most of their interest. His first important play, *Arms and the Man*, is a good example. His basic idea that heroic notions about war are ridiculous is no longer exciting, shocking, or novel. Had he been only a common writer, the play would now be dead. Instead it remains one of the most persistently popular plays in England and America. It is the skill with which he handles the theme that makes it live. Even though the art may not have been placed there for art's sake, the fact remains that it is there, and in abundance.

While Shaw gives us characters and character development plus the other elements of good drama, it is in the conflict of ideas that he excels. No one has explored life's problems with greater sharpness and penetration; his ideas alone are enough to keep one alert and satisfied, even when he stops the show in order to bombard his audience with them, as he does in the following speech in *Man and Superman*. The scene is hell; the devil and Don Juan are engaged in discussion.

DEVIL   Have you walked up and down upon the earth lately? I have; and I have examined Man's wonderful inventions. And I tell you that in the arts of life man invents nothing; but in the arts of death he outdoes Nature herself, and produces by chemistry and machinery all the slaughter of plague, pestilence and famine. The peasant I tempt to-day eats and drinks what was eaten and drunk by the peasants of ten thousand years ago; and the house he lives in has not altered as much in a thousand centuries as the fashion of a lady's bonnet in a score of weeks. But when he goes out to slay, he carries a marvel of mechanism that lets loose at the touch of his finger all the hidden molecular energies, and leaves the javelin, the arrow, the blow-pipe of his fathers far behind. In the arts of peace Man is a bungler. I have seen his cotton factories and the like, with machinery that a greedy dog could have invented if it had wanted money instead of food. I know his clumsy typewriters and bungling locomotives and tedious bicycles: they are toys compared to the Maxim gun, the submarine torpedo boat. There is nothing in Man's industrial machinery but his greed and sloth: his heart is in his weapons. This marvelous force of Life of which you boast is a force of Death: Man measures his strength by his destructiveness. What is his religion? An excuse for hating me. What is his law? An excuse for hanging you. What is his morality? Gentility! An excuse for consuming without producing. What is his art? An excuse for gloating over pictures of slaughter. What are his politics? Either the worship of a despot because a despot can kill, or parliamentary cock-fighting. I spent an evening lately in a certain celebrated legislature, and heard the pot lecturing the kettle for its blackness, and ministers answering questions. When I left I chalked up on the door the old nursery saying "Ask no questions and you will be told no lies." I bought a sixpenny family magazine, and found it full of pictures of young men shooting and stabbing one another. I saw a man die: he was a London bricklayer's laborer with seven children. He left seventeen pounds club money; and his wife spent it all on his funeral and went into the workhouse with the children next day. She would not have spent sevenpence on her children's schooling: the law had to force her to let them be taught gratuitously; but on death she spent all she had. Their imagination glows, their energies rise up at the idea of death, these people: they love it; and the more horrible it is the more they enjoy it. Hell is a place far above their comprehension: they derive their notion of it from two of the greatest fools that ever lived, an Italian and an Englishman. The Italian described it as a place of mud, frost, filth, fire, and venomous serpents: all torture. This ass, when he was not lying about me, was maundering about some woman whom he saw once in the street. The Englishman described me as being expelled from Heaven by cannons and gunpowder; and to this day every Briton believes that the whole of his silly story is in the Bible. What else he says I do not know; for it is all in a long poem which neither I nor anyone else ever succeeded in wading through. It is the same in everything. The highest form of literature is the tragedy, a play in which everybody is murdered at the end. In the old chronicles you read of earthquakes and pestilences, and are told that these shewed the power and majesty of God and the littleness of Man. Nowadays the chronicles describe battles. In a battle two bodies of men shoot at one another with bullets and explosive shells until one body runs away, when the others chase the fugitives on horseback and cut them to pieces as they fly. And this, the chronicle concludes, shews the greatness and majesty of empires, and the littleness of the vanquished. Over such battles the people run about the streets yelling with delight, and egg their Governments on to spend hundreds of millions of money in the slaughter, whilst the strongest Ministers dare not spend an extra penny in the pound against the poverty and pestilence through which they themselves daily walk. I could give you a thousand instances; but they all come to the same thing: the power that governs the earth is not the power of Life but of Death; and the inner need that has nerved Life to the effort of organizing itself into the human being is not the need for higher life but for a more efficient engine of destruction. The plague, the famine, the earthquake, the tempest were too spasmodic in their action; the tiger and crocodile were too easily satiated and not cruel enough: something more constantly, more ruthlessly, more ingeniously destructive was needed; and that something was Man, the inventor of the rack, the stake, the gallows, and the electrocutor; of the sword and gun; above all, of justice, duty, patriotism and all the other isms by which even those who are clever enough to be humanely disposed are persuaded to become the most destructive of all the destroyers.[3]

The above was published in 1903!

Shaw's ability to deal fairly and honestly with all his characters is amazing. In *Saint Joan*, for example, a play that many regard as his masterpiece, Shaw follows the authentic court records of Joan of Arc's trial with amazing accuracy; dramatic liberties are few, and yet the drama that results is one that only he could have written. Joan emerges with halo untarnished and natural-born genius intact. No longer a melodramatic heroine or a pathetic martyr, she has acquired a sense of humor and other life-giving qualities that make her one of the most appealing characters in modern literature.

Shaw's genius is even more apparent in dealing with those who burned her. He portrays them as neither villains nor tools of the devil

---

[3]Bernard Shaw, *Man and Superman*, act 3. Reprinted by permission of The Society of Authors on behalf of the Bernard Shaw Estate.

but as men of faith and sincerity, devoted to the Church, to their country, and to the truth—as they saw the truth. In other words, Shaw is dealing with one of the great human ironies: Saints like Joan are destroyed not by evil people, but by those of insufficient vision, devoted to the truth but incapable of understanding a new or profound truth.

With the death of Shaw in 1950, the world lost one of its greatest thinkers, playwrights, and humanitarians. One wonders when we shall see his like again.

IRELAND

If there is such a thing as national dramatic ability, no nationality appears to have more of it than the Irish. Take the Irish blood from the theatres of England and America, and the loss would be staggering. A quick check of the playwrights considered thus far reveals that Sheridan, Goldsmith, Wilde, Shaw, and Boucicault were all of Celtic origin, while in America we shall discover many others, including Eugene O'Neill.

Evidence could be multiplied, but this is unnecessary. The interesting fact is that while Ireland has contributed more than its share to dramatic literature, most of the plays have been written in exile, so to speak, for until the twentieth century Ireland with its chronic poverty, its powerful church, and its absence of theatres offered little encouragement to playwrights.

A change in this state of affairs came about as a result of deliberate effort and planning on the part of a small group of artists who set out to preserve Irish culture. The leaders, as far as the theatre was concerned, were William Butler Yeats and Lady Gregory, whose struggles finally led to the establishment of the world-famous Abbey Theatre. Both Yeats and Lady Gregory themselves made worthwhile contributions as playwrights—the former through his poetry, the latter through her keen sense of the comic. Both caught the native Irish flavor, the lilt of the language, the feel of the land, and the qualities of the common people. However, it was John Millington Synge (1871–1909) who first gave the Irish theatre plays of worldwide importance. Yeats, with his usual luck, or intuition, had discovered Synge in Paris—"an Irishman wasting his time trying to be French"—and had persuaded the young man to return to Ireland and the Irish. For the next three years Synge lived with the people of the bleak Aran Islands, in the belief that to find meaning in drama and poetry one should turn not to urban civilization but to people who know the meaning of harvest, springtime, life, and death. The experience would have been rewarding if nothing more had come of it than his *Riders to the Sea*. Some maintain that this short play is the greatest example of modern tragedy. Technically it is written in prose, but a prose far more beautiful and moving than most poetry. This tragedy of an old woman who has lost a husband and six sons could easily have become sentimental or merely pathetic; Synge has avoided both pitfalls. There is depth and honesty in lines like the following:

> They're all gone now, and there isn't anything more the sea can do to me. . . . I'll have no call now to be up crying and praying when the wind breaks from the south, and you can hear the surf is in the east, and the surf is in the west, making a great stir with the two noises, and they hitting one on the other. . . . It isn't that I haven't prayed for you, Bartley, to the Almighty God. It isn't that I haven't said prayers in the dark night till you wouldn't know what I'd be saying; but it's a great rest I'll have now, and it's time surely.[4]

Of Synge's full-length plays, *The Playboy of the Western World* is most famous. Some of its reputation may be traced to the fact that it stirred violent protests from certain Irish groups both in Ireland and in America. To a neutral observer it is difficult to understand what was so objectionable, for this is a delightful comedy, and while it sparkles with satire it is never cruel, nor is it a satire of the Irish alone. It begins as young Christy Mahon, desperate and exhausted, arrives at the public house of a small Irish village and admits that he has killed his tyrannical old father. Instead of being shocked, the inhabitants of the village, particularly Pegeen and the other young girls, react with romantic awe and admiration. Christy is soon the town hero. His confidence swells with the attention, and in a local athletic meet he wins every prize. At the height of the excitement Christy's father, his head well bandaged from the not quite mortal blow, arrives to even scores with his son. Another fight develops and Christy "kills" his father again, this time before the genu-

---

[4]John Millington Synge, *Riders to the Sea* in *Complete Plays of John M. Synge* (New York: Random House, 1960).

FIGURE 5:3 Synge's *The Playboy of the Western World*. A Utah State University production; directed by Floyd Morgan; scenery by Sid Perkes.

inely horrified eyes of the villagers. They obviously require aesthetic distance in their killings, for they now turn on Christy as a criminal rather than a hero. While they are in the very process of bringing him to swift and stern justice, the tough old father revives for a second time. But the old man has learned his lesson; a new respect for Christy has dawned; a new relationship between father and son is established, and together they walk out of the village leaving Pegeen and her friends to mourn their loss—the loss of "the only playboy of the Western World."

Synge died in 1909. The Abbey Theatre continued to encourage native writers, and a number of good plays, particularly several by Lennox Robinson, were written; but no real rival to Synge appeared until Sean O'Casey (1884–1964). Where Synge had captured the essence of comedy and tragedy among rural folk, O'Casey caught this essence among city dwellers. Born in the slums, he knew only too well the bitterness of poverty and underprivilege. His education was acquired by hard work, reading, and observation. He bought books even when it meant going hungry to do so. He was a fighter and a humanitarian.

His first play, *The Shadow of a Gunman*, staged by the Abbey Playhouse in 1923, showed promise; his next, *Juno and the Paycock*, removed all doubt. It is one of the great plays of the twentieth century. Juno is a portrait of a woman not unlike O'Casey's own mother, whose magnificent strength of character seems to be the only hope of a disintegrating, poverty-stricken family. Juno's husband, Captain Boyle, is a romantic boaster who will do anything to escape work or responsibility, her boy Johnny is a sensitive cripple of the revolution, and her lovely daughter Mary is still young and weak. Mary becomes pregnant and is deserted by her schoolmaster lover. The furniture that Captain Boyle acquired on the strength of an expected inheritance is carted away, and finally Johnny, suspected of being an informer by his revolutionary companions, is executed. Although such events are presented with relentless realism, the play escapes being sordid or depressing because of O'Casey's rich use of humor and language and his dramatic skill. In fact, among twentieth-century playwrights there are few who can match his power over language, his burning passion, or his deep sense of the tragic.

CENTRAL EUROPE

Germany's contribution to realism has been manifold. A quarter of a century before Ibsen wrote *A Doll's House*, Friedrich Hebbel (1813–1863) and others had written plays that clearly anticipated the realistic genre. At least five years before *A Doll's House*, the Duke of Saxe-Meiningen with his "amateurs" introduced sweeping reforms in staging, acting, and directing, all of which tended toward greater verisimilitude. Only a decade after *A Doll's House*, Otto Brahm established his Freie Bühne, a theatre devoted primarily to the production of realistic and naturalistic plays.

Outstanding among naturalistic playwrights are Gerhart Hauptmann (1862–1946) and Arthur Schnitzler (1862–1931). One of Hauptmann's first plays, *The Weavers*, dramatizes a historical event, the revolt of the Silesian weavers. Its first scene pictures a long line of weavers on payday. One complains and is fired, a sick child faints, tales of unbearable hardship are related. As the play progresses we finally see these miserable and seemingly helpless beings rise against their employers, whom they consider responsible for their suffering. The force of the mass uprising wrecks factories, mills, and the home of the factory owner. Such a plot might easily amount to leftist propaganda and nothing more, but Hauptmann has tempered it with just the right blend of human sympathy and naturalistic objectivity. As in Lope de Vega's *The Sheep Well*, a group rather than an individual becomes the protagonist. In *The Weavers*, drama of the masses came of age.

Arthur Schnitzler was a product of old Vienna, and love rather than social problems became his chief concern. A successful physician by profession, he still found time to write many plays, both comedies and tragedies. *Liebelei (Light o'Love)* reveals his skill as a writer and stimulates our admiration for a playwright who could make such a moving tragedy out of such slight material. Christine, a sensitive girl of the middle class, falls deeply in love with Fritz, an aristocratic young student who, already embroiled in a dangerous love affair with a married woman, is scarcely aware of Christine's existence. Although Fritz means all the world to her, no one even troubles to tell her when he is challenged to a duel. He has already been buried before she learns what has happened. Out of such material Schnitzler weaves a play that is not only moving but also has depth. In other plays, notably *Anatol* (translated by Granville-Barker as *The Affairs of Anatol*) and *Reigen* (made into the outstanding French film *La Ronde* by Max Opuls in 1950), he works in a lighter vein, intriguing us with satires on love. But while his outlook is critical, it is also melancholy. He regrets life's lack of fulfillment yet accepts it with philosophic calm and is more intrigued by the joys we miss than the errors we commit.

Turning from the basically naturalistic theatre of Hauptmann and Schnitzler, we come to the Hungarian playwright Ferenc Molnár (1878–1952). A popular success in his own eyes and in the eyes of the world, his plays have little of the depth or social protest so characteristic of his age. Some of the best of them, *The Play's the Thing* and *The Guardsman*, are sophisticated comedies, brilliantly written, highly entertaining, and mildly satirical. In *The Guardsman* an actor grows suspicious of his actress wife. To test her he disguises himself as a romantic Russian guardsman and tries to seduce her. His consternation as he almost succeeds, his pompous indignation as he returns to confront her with her near infidelity, and his final confusion when she maintains that she knew him all the time and was only teasing—all this and much more makes *The Guardsman* rare entertainment.

In *Liliom* Molnár gives us a play of a vastly different quality, which has the beauty, compassion, and understanding of a great poem. Liliom, a carnival barker, is an unforgettable mixture of the braggart and the dreamer, of tenderness and brutality, of the strange good and evil in humankind. A failure when first produced, it later became a play of world importance and was made into a successful musical, *Carousel*, by Richard Rodgers and Oscar Hammerstein II.

RUSSIA

Neither Oriental nor Occidental, well acquainted with the earth and with suffering, Russia has often been a ponderous, awkward, brutal giant lagging behind most other countries in cultural development. Yet in an artistic sense she has commanded respect because of her deep sensitivity, imagination, and hunger for the ideal. Song, poetry, and drama come naturally to the Russian people, although their troubled history has seldom allowed these impulses to grow to fulfillment. According to Gogol, "English drama reverberates with a beautiful and wise knowledge of life; French drama glitters and shines and flits away; German drama has a meaning unattainable to any one else; Russian drama, however, is torn from the heart itself."[5]

Russian drama, which now supposedly belongs to the proletariat, began with the czars. Peter the Great invited foreign actors with foreign plays to visit his court; Catherine the Great encouraged the drama, especially native drama, and even wrote several plays herself. Many others also made contributions, but the first writer to command serious attention was Alexander Pushkin (1799–1837), who in 1825 wrote his great

[5]Quoted by H. W. L. Dana in "Russia," *A History of Modern Drama,* ed. Barrett H. Clark and George Freedley (Englewood Cliffs, N. J.: Prentice-Hall, 1947), p. 370.

FIGURE 5:4 Gogol's *The Government Inspector*. Bernard Behrends, Paul Ballantyne, Jeff Chandler, Peter Goetz, Sheriden Thomas, and Barbara Bryne in a Guthrie Theatre production; directed by Michael Langham; designed by John Jensen; costumes by Tanya Moiseiwitsch.

historical tragedy, *Boris Godunov*. Although not well known to Americans except in the operatic version by Mussorgsky, this play is a landmark in the history of Russian drama, both because it was written by Russia's greatest poet and because it was patterned after Shakespeare. Thus Pushkin occupies much the same position in Russian drama that Lessing does in German drama. Both took Shakespeare as a model, and while Pushkin's tragedy does not equal those of the English master, it is a richly imaginative work.

NIKOLAI GOGOL

Eleven years after *Boris* came Russia's first comedy of world importance, *The Government Inspector*, by Nikolai Gogol (1809–1852). This is a brilliant exposé of provincial graft and political corruption in old Russia. The town's mayor robs the shopkeepers, the police sergeant is always drunk, the hospital superintendent feeds his patients on a diet of cabbage, the judge raises geese in the courtyard, and the postmaster opens all letters. Panic strikes these guilt-ridden grafters when it is rumored that they are about to be investigated. To their horror they soon discover that a mysterious stranger from Moscow is already at the local hotel. The audience is next introduced to the stranger, Khlestakov, an unimportant little government clerk with no power whatever except for his own natural endowment of shrewd wit and the uninhibited flexibility of his code of honor. As the mayor and other local officials swoop in upon him, Khlestakov quickly sizes up the situation, senses that they have mistaken him for the government inspector, and proceeds to play his cards to the limit. He is showered with attention. The mayor's wife and daughter offer their affections. One after another the crooked officials ply him with bribes. At last, loaded with booty, he leaves the town just as the postmaster arrives at the mayor's house with a letter that he has intercepted from Khlestakov to a friend. In a hushed room filled with the culprits, the letter revealing exactly what Khlestakov thinks of each of them is read aloud. Before they can recover from the shock of the letter, they are frozen into a final tableau of horror by the sudden arrival of the real government inspector.

ANTON CHEKHOV

The Russian skill for picturing life as it is but should not be is seen in more subdued and sensitive tones in the work of Russia's greatest playwright, Anton Pavlovich Chekhov (1860–1904). Most critics regard Chekhov as the supreme naturalist; yet even in translation his plays have a prevailing atmosphere, a quality of mood and longing, that is almost poetic. Their naturalism shows up in a lack of contrived situation, a lack of violence, and a lack of the sensational. Very little happens, "life rusts away," laughter and tears merge, hopes and dreams fade unrealized; yet with the right kind of acting these plays hold audiences spellbound. The secret of their spell is hard to describe, but certainly one important element is characterization. So genuine and vivid do his characters appear that even common crises in their lives become dramatic and important, just as common crises in our own lives or within our own families seem to us dramatic and important.

FIGURE 5:5   Chekhov's *The Cherry Orchard*. The Moscow Art Theatre production which played in New York in 1968.

The Cherry Orchard is generally regarded as Chekhov's masterpiece. An ancestral estate is to be sold at auction, but there is no last-minute rescue by a hero, no purchase of the estate by a villain. *The Cherry Orchard* is a symbolic, nostalgic story of the futility of the old Russian nobility and their inability to cope with the modern world, but they are treated with sympathy and understanding. Madam Ranevsky, with her kindness, extravagance, and gracious ways, endears herself to us from the start. On the other hand, she is helpless and useless when it comes to practical problems in the new world of business and progress. The best she can do on the eve of the auction is to give one more lovely party. And so Lopahin, the newly rich businessman, buys the cherry orchard—Lopahin, whose father had been a peasant on the estate, who had never forgotten Madam Ranevsky's kindness to him as a ragged boy with a bleeding face. The play lives because of the vividness and compassion with which Chekhov has drawn his characters. It is not necessary to have murders, mistaken identity, intrigue, and other theatrical para-phernalia. These characters become our intimate acquaintances; consequently, even trivial events become moving.

Almost equal to *The Cherry Orchard* in both quality and fame are Chekhov's *Uncle Vanya*, *The Sea Gull*, and *The Three Sisters*. All have much the same qualities: the quiet tragedy, the wistful yearning, the living characters. To capture and portray these qualities, however, requires acting of a highly sensitive and convincing order. The declamatory, theatrical style that was in vogue when Chekhov first began to write was highly inappropriate, and largely because of this his first plays were unsuccessful. The failure of *The Sea Gull* in its first production was a particularly bitter blow, and Chekhov threatened to write no more for the theatre. Then two years later a Russian playwright, Nemirovich-Danchenko, and an amateur actor, Constantin Stanislavsky, organized the Moscow Art Theatre. Among the plays offered during their first season was *The Sea Gull*, which opened December 17, 1897. Almost overnight both Chekhov and the Moscow Art Theatre became famous. Seldom has there been a more fortunate combination of playwriting and production. The deep *psychological naturalism* of the Stanislavsky system of acting provided a perfect means of expression for Chekhov's naturalism. When the author was too ill with tuberculosis to come to Moscow for the production of his *Uncle Vanya*, the Art Theatre took the play to him at Yalta. A special opening performance of *The Cherry Orchard* was arranged in order that Chekhov might see the play on what proved to be his last birthday. To this day the emblem of a sea gull is the official insignia of one of the world's most famous producing groups—the Moscow Art Theatre.

MAXIM GORKI

When the Moscow Art Theatre visited Yalta in 1900, Chekhov introduced them to a powerful and fascinating young author who had made his way up from the depths of poverty, suffering, and even imprisonment. His name was Maxim Gorki (Maxim the Bitter, 1868–1936). It was soon decided that Gorki should write a play depicting the lives of the submerged and broken failures he knew so well. One of the results was *The Lower Depths*. In a cellar below Moscow we meet the outcasts

FIGURE 5:6 Chekhov's *The Three Sisters*. An Idaho State University production; directed by Don Alkoffer; designed by John Gerth.

of society. A woman lies dying in childbirth, yet she is scarcely noticed. There is also the baron and his streetwalker, the actor, the young thief, the receiver of stolen goods, and the bitter old philosopher, Satine. Into the midst of these derelicts comes a pilgrim, Louka. Under the spell of his wisdom and humanity we soon begin to discover that in spite of their hopeless exteriors, these people of the lower depths all have a dream of goodness; each is bitter that life should be as it is. Under his spell they begin to change and to gain new hope, but Gorki is too tough-minded and naturalistic to permit a happy ending. A quarrel flares up, the proprietor of the hovel is accidentally killed by the young thief, and Louka disappears as mysteriously as he had arrived. Without him the characters slump back into dispair, save for powerful, brutally unsentimental Satine:

> The old man's no humbug! What's the truth? Man! Man—that's the truth! He understood man—you don't! You're all as dumb as stones! I understand the old man—yes! He lied—but lied out of sheer pity for you. . . . I know what lying means! The weakling and the one who is a parasite through his

very weakness — they both need lies — lies are their support, their shield, their armor! But the man who is strong, who is his own master, who is free and does not have to suck his neighbors' blood — he needs no lies! To lie — it's the creed of slaves and masters of slaves! Truth is the religion of the free man![6]

DEVELOPMENT OF THE AMERICAN THEATRE

In tracing the origins of drama in the Americas, Spaniards can point with pride to the fact that as early as 1603 daily theatrical performances were being given in Mexico City. The French likewise might boast of performances of plays in their early Canadian settlements, for both the French and the Spanish transplanted theatrical culture to their new colonies as early as possible, just as they transplanted other elements of their national life.

But with the English it was different. Puritans and Quakers were deeply opposed to the theatre, and even as late as 1792 a production of *She Stoops to Conquer* had to be advertised in the Boston Gazette as "A moral lecture in five parts in which the disadvantages of a neglected education will be strikingly described."[7] Even today the American theatre is regarded by many with a faint air of suspicion and hostility foreign to the other arts.

During the early years the chief exceptions to this prevailing hostility were found in the South. Virginia and Carolina, both largely Episcopalian, displayed comparatively tolerant and kindly attitudes toward all forms of culture, and it is in these states that much of the American theatre's early history is to be found. The earliest record of a theatrical performance in the Colonies goes back to 1665 when *Ye Bare and Ye Cubb* was performed in Virginia, and although those responsible for the production were hailed into court, they were promptly acquitted. There are many other scattered theatrical records of historical interest, many of

---

[6]Maxim Gorki, *The Lower Depths*, trans. Jennie Covan, in *The Moscow Art Series of Russian Plays*, ed. Oliver M. Saylor (New York: Brentano's, 1922).

[7]For a reproduction of this advertisement, see Oral Sumner Coad and Edward Mims, Jr., "The American Stage," in *The Pageant of America Series* (New Haven: Yale University Press, 1928), p. 39.

them in connection with early college productions, but certainly the outstanding theatrical event of the pre-Revolutionary period was the arrival in 1752 of Lewis Hallam with a company of 15 professional actors from England. They opened on September 15 in Williamsburg, Virginia, with *The Merchant of Venice,* and, during the years that followed, survived, built theatres, and brought plays to the Colonies. It would be hard to overestimate their influence on our early theatrical history.

Hallam died while on a trip to Jamaica, but his widow and her second husband, David Douglas, carried on. The plays the company produced were standard English pieces, including *King Lear*, *Hamlet*, *Othello*, *The London Merchant*, *The Conscious Lovers*, and *The Beggar's Opera.* The first American play to be performed by this company was *The Prince of Parthia* (1767), by Thomas Godfrey. Its fame rests almost entirely on its claim to being the first American play ever to be performed by a professional company. How good or how bad it is depends on one's point of view. Considered as our first play, it is not bad at all, being closely akin to the English heroic tragedies of the Restoration. Considered on its own merits, however, it is a rather uninspired heroic tragedy on a foreign theme, without the slightest suggestion of anything like a new idea or fresh point of view from a new world.

Comedy fared better. Prior to and during the Revolutionary War, Mercy Warren and others wrote a number of original satires on the British, and in 1787 Royall Tyler wrote *The Contrast,* the first American comedy to win professional production. Tyler's inspiration came from having seen a few plays, including a production of *The School for Scandal*, at the John Street Theatre in New York. He set to work and, with all the confidence of young America, proceeded in the space of three weeks to dash off a comedy of his own. The surprising thing is not that the result was imperfect but rather that an imaginative production of the old piece can still delight an audience. The title indicates both the theme and the plot. The sophisticated dandy, Dimple, provides a vivid character contrast to honest, plain-dealing Colonel Manly; Dimple's servant, Jessamy, is employed as a contrast to the American Yankee, Jonathan, while Charlotte is used as a contrast to the sentimental Maria. Some of the scenes have a dash of real wit and cleverness, while Jonathan holds the distinction of being the apparent original of a long line of stage Yankees, who have been responsible for much native American humor.

Tyler's play with its American setting and American theme is also a contrast to Godfrey's *The Prince of Parthia* with its foreign setting and foreign theme. In fact, until recently it was customary for teachers to divide nineteenth-century American drama into two divisions: plays on an American theme and plays on a foreign theme.

Among the best examples of plays on a foreign theme are *Charles the Second*, a comedy by John Howard Payne and Washington Irving; *Francesca da Rimini*, a tragedy by George Henry Boker; and *Hazel Kirke*. Among the best examples of plays on an American theme are André, a tragedy of the American Revolution by William Dunlap; *Fashion;* and *The Octoroon*. According to Arthur Hobson Quinn, the movement toward American realism began with Augustin Daly, but while Daly may have stimulated the movement the real beginning is much more apparent in the works of Bronson Howard (1842–1908).[8] Though not a genius, Howard was a well-educated writer who devoted himself to the task of playwriting with more than customary skill and honesty. His most interesting play is *Shenandoah*, probably the best play of the nineteenth century on the subject of the Civil War. Although written largely in the "well-made" style of its day, it nevertheless reveals some insight into the tangled loyalties of war.

Still closer to the serious realism of the thesis plays of Ibsen is the work of James A. Herne (1839–1901). Like Belasco, MacKaye, Boucicault, and Daly, Herne was a successful actor-manager. Consequently, it is not surprising to find that he wrote plays like *Hearts of Oak* and *Shore Acres* that were theatrical successes. On the other hand, it is surprising to find that in writing his most important play, *Margaret Flemming* (1890), he cared little for popular success but rather focused on trying to say something about the double standard. Bits of naturalism, such as nursing a baby on stage, were both realistic and shocking. Herne's objective, as he himself so well phrased it, was to use "art for truth's sake."[9]

During the early years of the twentieth century American playwriting was dominated by Clyde Fitch (1865–1909). "The great Mr. Fitch" was often referred to as the dean of American playwriting and in 1901 had four smash hits playing on Broadway. Fitch, along with George Ade, Augustus Thomas, Percy MacKaye, and many others, did much to

[8]Arthur Hobson Quinn, *A History of the American Drama from the Civil War to the Present Day*, vol. 1 (New York: Harper & Row, 1927), p. 1.
[9]James A. Herne, "Art for Truth's Sake in the Drama," *Arena*, February 1897.

keep the theatre alive and prosperous during the first two decades of this century. At the same time they paved the way for the great period that was to follow, for from approximately 1920 to 1960, American playwriting was generally conceded to have assumed world leadership.

THE IMPORTANCE OF AMERICAN REALISM

Among the many influences behind America's rise to a position of world importance in playwriting were the general factors in national life that had already made America a world power in such other areas as industry, invention, wealth, and military might. America's contribution in the other fine arts became significant much earlier than it did in playwriting, possibly because of the theatre's strangling commercialism, possibly because of its overzealous desire to please everyone in every audience, or possibly because of America's general lack of mental and emotional maturity. This last deficiency was more apparent in theatre, which is a group art, than in the more individual arts like poetry or painting, where a select few could set the standards. It has always been difficult for the theatre to rise much above the general level of its audience.

But American playwriting of the 1920s owed debts to factors other than the nation's general prosperity and growing importance. It owed a debt to the work of a group of realistic writers, including William Dean Howells, Hamlin Garland, Henry James, and James A. Herne, who even before the close of the nineteenth century had started a movement toward noncommercial literary drama. It owed a particular debt to George Pierce Baker, professor of playwriting at Harvard and later at Yale, whose instruction provided guidance and inspiration for many an outstanding young playwright, including Eugene O'Neill. Finally, it owed a debt to three independent producing organizations: the Neighborhood Playhouse, the Washington Square Players, and the Provincetown Players. These organizations had much in common: all began in 1915, all started as nonprofessional and noncommercial organizations, and all were housed in tiny theatres seating fewer than 300. (Houses seating fewer than 300 people avoid most of the union entanglements and licensing problems of larger theatres.) The Neighborhood Playhouse, backed by the wealth of the Lewisohn family, was a beautiful and well-equipped little theatre which introduced many excellent and unusual plays, including *The Dybbuk* and *The Little Clay Cart*. It is now the home of the well-known Neighborhood Playhouse School of the Theatre. The Washington Square Players evolved into the powerful Theatre Guild, which, under the leadership of Lawrence Langner and Theresa Helburn, had a great influence on raising the standards of American theatre. Although both professional and commercial, the guild was concerned with long-range objectives and with theatre as an art. In general it produced plays of originality or established literary merit. It also organized subscription audiences in major cities across the country, thus striving for a measure of stability and permanence.

The Provincetown Players, made up of young writers and artists who spent their summers on Cape Cod, began by founding the Wharf Theatre in Provincetown. Later they moved to New York, where they gained renown primarily because they were the first to produce the plays of Eugene O'Neill.

To understand the contribution of these independent art theatres we should place them against the background of their times. The first two decades of the twentieth century had seen a titanic struggle between the Theatrical Syndicate and the Shubert Brothers for control of the American commercial theatre. These decades had also seen the stagehands' union and finally Actors' Equity battle to positions of power. Yet while these forces struggled against one another, the prize over which they fought was disintegrating. The popular audience was being lured away by an inexpensive and entertaining new form of theatre, the movies, until by the beginning of World War I the chance of securing a monopoly over a big-money theatrical industry was gone. However, there still remained a high-quality though limited audience, which was being bolstered by an increasing interest in theatre on the part of American schools and universities. On the whole the old managers and the new unions underestimated the growing competition of the movies on the one hand and the modest but potential possibilities of a new art-conscious audience on the other.

But though the independent art theatres under the inspiration of men like Lawrence Langner, Robert Edmond Jones, Kenneth Macgowan, and Lee Simonson led the way in this new surge of activity that was to make New York the theatrical capital of the world, it would be unjust to give the impression that the old Broadway commercial theatre was a villain or a millstone around the neck of progress. Probably no theatre in the history of the world has had so many things wrong with it, for Broadway is shot through with money-mad commercialism and union featherbedding. It is helplessly at the mercy of four or five critics and addicted to the extravagant waste of single-shot productions, which sometimes hit but usually miss. Yet somehow, out of all the chaos and waste, Broadway continues to come up with great plays and great productions. Perhaps the overwhelming pressure to succeed sometimes forces that extra ounce of effort that makes the difference between great art and mediocre art as well as between success and failure. Perhaps Elmer Rice, after a lifetime on Broadway, has hit upon the answer:

> Two conditions are largely responsible for the undeniable vitality of the Broadway theatre. The first is that it operates in a free and democratic society, and is unhampered by censorship and governmental control. The dramatist is free to write as he chooses, the producer to present what pleases him. Secondly, the theatre is small business, not big business. Its entrepreneurs are individuals whose exercise of personal taste in the selection of plays, and whose concentration upon particular productions, are in striking contrast to the prescribed standards and mechanized procedures of big business. Consequently, the plays that are offered to the public represent a wide variety in taste and quality, ranging from the often horrendous to the occasionally magnificent.[10]

But Broadway and the early experimental groups such as the Provincetown Players are not the only producing units that influence playwriting. Off-Broadway theatres, summer theatres, community theatres, educational theatres, children's theatres, and regional professional theatres have made, or are beginning to make, their contributions. The off-Broadway theatre was really an extension of the work begun by such groups as the Provincetown Players, although off-Broadway's importance as a force in New York professional theatre did not become widespread until the early 1950s. Among factors that led to its popularity were the old abuses and limitations of Broadway—limitations that left many talented writers and directors as well as thousands of actors with no opportunity for expression. Rather than wait indefinitely for a chance on the Great White Way, some of these theatre artists moved into old

[10]Elmer Rice, *The Living Theatre* (New York: Harper & Row, 1959), p. 288.

warehouses, churches, or nightclubs and began to produce plays that cost hundreds of dollars instead of hundreds of thousands of dollars. Some of the productions that resulted were awful, but others were outstanding. The phenomenal run of *The Threepenny Opera* (Brecht) at the Theatre de Lys has already been mentioned. *The Iceman Cometh* (O'Neill) at the Circle in the Square scored a solid success, whereas the original production on Broadway had failed. In his tiny Fourth Street Theatre, David Ross turned out beautiful productions of Chekhov, while at the Phoenix Theatre, Norris Houghton and T. Edward Hambleton proved that limited runs of excellent plays could attract a loyal following. Some of the enthusiasm for off-Broadway was undoubtedly due, as we shall see later, to the intimacy and informality of its tiny playhouses. These provided audiences with a new sense of sharing—a sense of joining with the actors in a living experience.

But off-Broadway also developed its own limitations. Being a showcase for talent, most of its best artists are soon lured away by lucrative offers from Hollywood, Broadway, or television. Moreover, the sensible economy of its early years remained economical only as long as there were no profits. As soon as off-Broadway became a "success" it found itself beset with many of the same commercial ills that plagued Broadway. This gave rise to the off-off-Broadway theatres in cafes and churches. All this led to confusion, but there was also a great virtue: playwrights with unusual, offbeat, and new ideas had a far better chance to be heard.

EUGENE O'NEILL

Turning from the factors behind America's creative burst of playwriting to the plays themselves, we are soon struck by the powerful contribution of tragedy. Perhaps this trend toward the tragic was set by the brooding and gloomy nature of our first great playwright, Eugene Gladstone O'Neill (1888–1953). Son of the famous actor James O'Neill, Eugene had ample opportunity to secure early theatrical experience and education. On the other hand, life as a great actor's son had its problems, its trials, and its loneliness. Anyone doubting this need only read one of his last and greatest plays, the autobiographical *Long Day's Journey into Night*, produced after his death.

O'Neill was deeply influenced by the sea stories of Joseph Conrad and the expressionism of August Strindberg. He shipped to sea deliberately searching for ideas and stories; these experiences provided the basis for his first group of plays, mostly one-act stories of the sea. Many of these early plays, *The Long Voyage Home*, *Ile*, *In the Zone*, and *The Moon of the Caribbees*, show vivid promise of what was to come. In 1920 came the production of his first full-length success, *Beyond the Horizon*. This is a story of two New England brothers and a girl. Robert Mayo, the dreamer, yearning for travel and adventure, is trapped into staying on the farm, while his brother, Andrew, who wanted to stay home, is driven to sea. The play may be overwritten and too long, it may be depressing rather than truly tragic, but at the same time it provided the American theatre with a new standard of emotional and intellectual maturity. It explored some of life's frustrations with new irony and insight, and it rated well above any previous American effort. It won its author his first Pulitzer Prize and almost overnight established him as America's newest and most promising playwright.

During the next decade and a half many plays came from his pen. Looking at them as a whole, we are struck by O'Neill's restless search for new devices and new forms of expression. *The Emperor Jones* and *The Hairy Ape* stand out as America's first successful attempts at expressionism; *The Great God Brown* makes intermittent use of masks in order to contrast our real selves with the external selves we present to others; *Strange Interlude* returns to a free use of soliloquies and asides. (Its playing time was so long that it was necessary to begin its performance at 5:30 P.M., pause one-and-one-half hours midway into the show for dinner, and then return for the second half, which lasted until after eleven.) Even *Mourning Becomes Electra*, which many consider his masterpiece, shows the same restless tendency to experiment. It is an extremely long trilogy based on Greek tragedy but set in New England during the Civil War, with Freudian psychology very evident in its tragic motivation.

But although O'Neill attracted attention as an innovator, his real reputation has always rested on his power as a realistic playwright. Those who objected to his plays usually objected on moral grounds. They found his characters and situations genuine enough but sordid and unpleasant. He was too brutally honest about the problems and frustrations of very imperfect people. *Desire Under the Elms*, for example, was concerned with a powerful and very realistic struggle between three

FIGURE 5:7 O'Neill's *Desire Under the Elms*. A Utah State University production; directed by Vosco Call; designed by Floyd Morgan.

unpleasant but very genuine members of a New England family who were torn between lust for land and a lust for love. Then in 1932 those who objected to O'Neill's subject matter received a surprise with the Broadway production of *Ah, Wilderness!* Here was a nostalgic comedy about an essentially normal American family, a comedy with a happy, rather sentimental ending. It was a play that proved that O'Neill could write popular comedy as well or better than the best of the old pros on Broadway, if he cared to do so.

During the 1940s O'Neill's star seemed to wane. Some critics maintained that his plays were overwritten and overrated. Perhaps all playwrights face a critical period when their works appear to lose their luster. If so, O'Neill seems to have survived his crisis, for the years following his death in 1953 saw a great revival of interest in his work. José Quintero's off-Broadway production of *The Iceman Cometh* succeeded where the original Broadway production had failed; *Ah, Wilderness!* was transformed into a musical hit, *Take Me Along;* while three posthumous productions, *Long Day's Journey into Night, A Moon for the Misbegotten,* and *A Touch of the Poet,* received enthusiastic acclaim.

Long Day's Journey into Night, which won the Pulitzer Prize in 1957, is considered by many to be his greatest play; certainly it is the most nakedly autobiographical. In his own words, it is "a play of old sorrows

FIGURE 5:8 O'Neill's *Ah Wilderness!* at the Williamstown Theatre Festival; directed by Edward Berkeley; designed by Santo Loquasto.

written in tears and blood," enabling him "to face my dead at last."[11] O'Neill's family is disguised slightly as the Tyrone family, but they are all there: James (the famous actor and the father), an amazing portrait of a man hounded by an irrational fear of poverty; Mary (O'Neill's mother), a haunting portrait of a woman escaping into a narcotic dream world; Jimmy (O'Neill's own brother, James, Jr.), an alcoholic confusion of insight, affection, bitterness, and debauchery; and Edmund, the sensitive young Eugene O'Neill himself. During this journey into night we see the family torn by love and hate, understanding and misunderstanding, laughter and tears. John Henry Raleigh called it the "finest play . . . ever written on this continent,"[12] and there are many who would agree.

THORNTON WILDER

The dramatic fame of Thornton Wilder (1897–1975) rests primarily upon three full-length plays, *Our Town*, *The Skin of Our Teeth*, and *The Matchmaker*. *Our Town* has been a favorite among both professionals and amateurs, not only in America but throughout the world. Its absence of conventional scenery and its use of the character of the stage manager to established rapport directly with the audience places Wilder among the innovators. But the play has qualities beyond novelty. Like O'Neill's *Ah Wilderness!* it is an honest and revealing portrait of small-town American life. Its three acts are concerned with daily life, marriage, and death, and its theme is summed up in Emily's cry, "Oh, earth, you're too wonderful for anybody to realize you." *Our Town*, which won the Pulitzer Prize in 1937, has been criticized as sentimental, but American life is sentimental; Emily, George, and the others give us far more genuine insight into what most of the early twentieth-century Americans were really like than do studies of neurotics, psychotics, gangsters, or cowboys. It is a play of rare beauty and appeal.

In *The Skin of Our Teeth*, which won Wilder his third Pulitzer Prize (his first was in fiction, for *The Bridge of San Luis Rey*), his innovations are even more startling and enjoyable than in *Our Town*. Sabina, the

[11] From the dedication to his wife, Carlotta Monterey O'Neill, in *Long Day's Journey into Night* (New Haven: Yale University Press, 1956).
[12] *Partisan Review*, fall 1959, p. 573.

maid, frequently interrupts the play to speak her mind to the audience. Our realistic notions of time and place suffer outrageously as Wilder skillfully scrambles events of the Ice Age, the Biblical flood, and modern warfare to drive home his optimistic thesis that humankind is always squeezing through one crisis after another by "the skin of our teeth."

Wilder's third play to score a Broadway success was *The Matchmaker*, which was a rewriting of his earlier *The Merchant of Yonkers*. Tyrone Guthrie directed it, and Ruth Gordon starred as the unforgettable Mrs. Levi. As far as the script is concerned, its chief improvement over *The Merchant of Yonkers* is Wilder's addition of several delightful soliloquies — moments when characters frankly turn to the audience and confide bits of homemade wisdom and philosophy:

MRS. LEVI *(Now addressing the audience, she holds up the purse, crosses to below pouffe and sits.)* Money, money, money — it's like the sun we walk under: it can kill and can cure. Horace Vandergelder's never tired of saying most people in the world are fools, and in a way he's right, isn't he? Himself, Irene, Cornelius, myself! But there comes a moment in everybody's life when he must decide whether he'll live among human beings or not — a fool among fools or a fool alone. As for me, I've decided to live among them. *(Crosses and sits down Right end of sofa L.)* I wasn't always so. After my husband's death I retired into myself. Yes, in the evenings, I'd put out the cat and I'd lock the door and make myself a little rum toddy; and before I went to bed I'd say a little prayer thanking God that I was independent — that no one else's life was mixed up with mine. And when ten o'clock sounded from Trinity Church Tower I fell off to sleep and I was a perfectly contented woman. And one night, after two years of this, an oak leaf fell out of my Bible. I had placed it there on the day my husband asked me to marry him: a perfectly good oak leaf — but without color and without life. And suddenly — I realized that for a long time I had not shed one tear; nor had I been for one moment outrageously happy; nor had I been filled with the wonderful hope that something or other would turn out well. I saw that I was like that oak leaf and on that night I decided to rejoin the human race. On that night, I heard many hours struck off from Trinity Church Tower. You and I have known lots of people who've decided — like Horace Vandergelder — like myself for a long time — not to live among human beings. Yes, they move out among them — they talk to them, they even get married to them; but at heart they have decided not to have anything to do with the human race. If you accept human

FIGURE 5:9 Wilder's *The Matchmaker*. Karen Landry, Peter Goetz, Helen Carey, John Pielmeier, Barbara Bryne, and Tony Mockus in a Guthrie Theatre production; directed by Michael Langham; designed by Desmond Heeley.

beings and are willing to live among them, you acknowledge that every man has a right to his own mistakes. *(Rises to down Centre.)* Yes, we're all fools and we're all in danger of creating a good deal of havoc in the world with our folly; but the one way to keep us from harm is to fill our lives with the four or five human pleasures which are our right in the world; and *that takes a little money.* Not much, but a little. The difference between a little money and an enormous amount of money is very slight and that, also, can shatter the world. Money—pardon the expression—money is like manure; it's not worth a thing unless it's spread around encouraging young things to grow. *(Sits on pouffe Centre.)* Anyway, that's the opinion of the second Mrs. Horace Vandergelder.[13]

[13] Thornton Wilder, *The Matchmaker* (New York: Samuel French, 1955), act 4, pp. 109–110.

PLAYS OF SOCIAL PROTEST

The social and economic collapse of the Great Depression generated a search for new values that found vigorous expression in the theatre. This was not altogether a new movement. Elmer Rice, Maxwell Anderson, and others had voiced grave doubts about our economy and the American dream prior to the crash in 1929, although their most searching inquiries came later. Clifford Odets (1906–1963) was the first of the young Depression playwrights to gain prominence. He won fame in 1935 with *Waiting for Lefty*, a one-act play that grew out of a bitter taxicab strike in New York. The audience finds itself not in the atmosphere of a conventional theatre but in the tension of a labor hall. Characters rise from the audience to voice both grievances and appeals. The tension mounts until news comes that their leader, Lefty, has been murdered by hired assassins. When played during the Depression, audiences joined actors in the cry, "Strike, strike, strike!" which concludes the play.

Another socially conscious playwright who rose to prominence during the Depression is Lillian Hellman (b. 1905). Her first great success, *The Children's Hour*, deals with an unpleasant and malicious little schoolgirl who drives one teacher to suicide and ruins the life of another. Two later plays, *The Little Foxes* and *Another Part of the Forest*, are concerned with the utterly ruthless and predatory nature of a Southern capitalistic clan, the Hubbards. *Toys in the Attic*, which studies the effect of sudden wealth on members of a family, won the New York Drama Critics' Circle award for 1960.

John Steinbeck (1902–1968) was another playwright of the Depression. His greatest play, *Of Mice and Men*, goes far beyond the social and economic criticism found in his *Grapes of Wrath*. It delves into the loneliness and hopelessness of men who wander from one Western ranch to another. Lenny, the giant moron, probably has the lowest IQ of any major character in serious drama, yet his simplicity and childish appeal coupled with the rugged loyalty and understanding of his one friend, George, result in a human drama that is poignant if not profound.

In 1939 William Saroyan (b. 1908) made an effective entrance into the world of playwriting with *My Heart's in the Highlands*. It proclaims the doctrine that the little people of the earth are good and beautiful, and does so with poetry and skill. His next play, *The Time of Your Life*, says the same thing with sensitivity and dramatic ingenuity. Since then his variations on this theme have tended to grow monotonous. His work has also been marred by a lack of discipline; he is in the habit of writing a full-length play in approximately one week. But in spite of such defects he is a playwright with unusual compassion and natural talent.

TENNESSEE WILLIAMS

Like Eugene O'Neill, we could quite logically consider Tennessee Williams (b. 1914) among the playwrights of disillusionment and despair dealt with in Chapter 6. Like O'Neill he is obsessed by the suffering and psychological ills of our age. Yet behind his pessimism there is hope— an implication that life need not be as sick and sordid as it often is. Conventional-minded Americans have bitterly complained that his plays give an unfair and psychopathic view of American life, and there can be no doubt that Williams deals primarily with the mental and emotion-

FIGURE 5:10   Williams's *The Glass Menagerie*. Anthony Ross, Laurette Taylor, and Eddie Dowling in the original production which opened in Chicago on December 26, 1944; directed by Margo Jones and Eddie Dowling.

FIGURE 5:11 The family group from Williams's *Cat on a Hot Tin Roof* at the Guthrie Theatre; directed by Stephen Kanee; scenery by John Conklin; costumes by Jack Edwards.

al ills of our civilization. On the other hand, though he deals with these brutally, he handles them with honesty and skill. Moreover, in the psychoses and neuroses of his characters he finds great drama and sometimes great illumination. It is interesting, however, that his three best plays are probably the three that the Establishment finds least objectionable. *The Glass Menagerie* is a play of memory. "Being a memory play it is dimly lighted, it is sentimental, it is not realistic."[14] The three main characters are among the most vivid portraits in modern drama: Laura, the fragile sister, crippled outside and inside, afraid of reality, escaping into a dream world of old phonograph records and delicate glass ani-

[14] Tennessee Williams, *The Glass Menagerie* (New York: New Directions, 1966), act 1.

mals; Amanda, her mother, nagging but pathetic, desperately maintaining the ridiculous airs and outward trappings of Southern gentility in the face of a reality of failure and poverty; Tom, the wanderer and the play's narrator, who relives it all through an attitude that is a mixture of futility, sadness, and compassion.

The next play Williams wrote, *Summer and Smoke*, failed on Broadway, but his third play, *A Streetcar Named Desire* (produced professionally before *Summer and Smoke*), was an immediate success. The action centers on a woman, Blanche Du Bois. Still clinging desperately to remnants of Southern pride, worth, and culture, Blanche has arrived at "the end of the line." Her efforts to find a haven fail, partly because her pride drives her to assume irritating airs of grandeur, partly because of the crude animal natures of those pitted against her. At last she takes refuge in the only haven that remains: insanity.

In general it might be said that the preoccupation with violence and sex in the plays of Tennessee Williams reaches a climax in his drama *Orpheus Descending* and in the movie *Baby Doll*, which was based on some of his early one-act plays. Like O'Neill, Williams is widely known and produced abroad. A 1974 survey of productions in American colleges and universities found him more frequently produced than any other playwright except Shakespeare. His place in the world of playwriting seems assured.

ARTHUR MILLER

While Williams has been probing the mental and emotional ills of our life, one of his contemporaries, Arthur Miller (b. 1915), has been probing into the social and psychological forces that destroy people. Miller recognizes that people can be the victims of ills from without as well as from within. Because he has written plays concerning the environmental ills of our society, Miller, like Williams, aroused storms of protest, but whereas Williams outraged the moralists, Miller outraged the politicians.

In Miller's first success, *All My Sons*, Joe Keller, a likable and successful businessman, has saved his factory during the Second World War by allowing a small shipment of cracked engine blocks to slip by

FIGURE 5:12 Miller's *Death of a Salesman*. William McKereghan as Willie Loman in a Milwaukee Repertory Theatre production; directed by Nagel Jackson.

without being reported. These blocks, rushed into early fighting planes, cost the lives of several young fliers, including Keller's own son. After the war his second son forces him to face up to the enormity of his crime. Tragic irony lies in the fact that an act performed to save his business for the sake of his sons has killed one and alienated the other. Rather than face prison, Joe kills himself.

All My Sons, although a success, was soon overshadowed by Miller's next play, *Death of a Salesman*, which stands high in the field of modern tragedy. This is the story of an ordinary, middle-aged American salesman, Willy Loman, who is almost as lacking in nobility as George Barnwell. Yet Willy somehow achieves a measure of tragic greatness, perhaps through Miller's skill as a dramatist, perhaps through numbers, for in this common man Miller captured the tragic essence of the millions of common men who worship the modern "bitch goddess Success." Willy is a victim of glittering but shabby ideals; he knows all the formulas—the hearty smile, good fellowship, popularity, athletic prowess, influence. But by the time the play opens, these formulas have been worn threadbare, and the relentless facts of his failures have begun to close in on him. In one flashback after another, we relive the sorrows and mistakes into which his shabby ideals have plunged him, and in the end this common man, who might have been a successful father and an excellent carpenter, is driven to suicide.

FIGURE 5:13 Lawrence and Lee's *Inherit the Wind*. Booth Colman and Fred Thompson in a Meadow Brook Theatre production; directed by Charles Nolte.

FIGURE 5:14
Gibson's *The Miracle Worker*. A Gustavus Adolphus College production directed by Mrs. Evan Anderson.

Death of a Salesman was followed by *The Crucible*, Miller's answer to the Joseph McCarthy witch hunts for Communists, and *A View from the Bridge*, a powerful character study of a Sicilian laborer. For the next several years his powers as a playwright seemed to lay dormant; then came *After the Fall*, *Incident at Vichy*, and *The Price*, each dealing in one way or another with problems of guilt and responsibility. A 1973 production of *The Creation of the World and Other Business* failed on Broadway but was a glowing success when rewritten and repeated at the University of Michigan in 1974.

OTHER AMERICAN PLAYWRIGHTS

A number of other successful writers deserve attention: William Inge with *Come Back Little Sheba*, *The Dark at the Top of the Stairs*, and the Pulitzer Prize-winner *Picnic*; Robert Anderson with *Tea and Sympathy*, *All Summer Long*, and *Silent Night, Lonely Night*; Jerome Lawrence and Robert E. Lee with *Inherit the Wind*, *Auntie Mame*, and *The Night Thoreau*

Spent in Jail; William Gibson with *Two for the Seesaw* and *The Miracle Worker;* Paul Green with his regional dramas, including *The House of Connelly*, his outdoor dramas, including *The Lost Colony*, and his superb antiwar satire, *Johnny Johnson*. These writers, like most of the other American writers we have studied, were in no sense dedicated realists. Instead they tended rather to be eclectic; that is, they were not concerned with one particular style but simply with turning out plays that would say something effectively.

During the second half of the twentieth century trends in playwriting have been hard to follow. Much of the work will be discussed in the following chapter, even though realism, through it all, has been far from dead. In fact, as the rebellions and disruptions of the 1960s have declined, the essentially realistic theatre seems to be the one to have benefited. It has been shaken out of old ruts, given a new breath of freedom, and, one hopes, invigorated.

CHAPTER 6

DISILLUSIONMENT, PROTEST, AND THE SEARCH FOR ALTERNATIVES

Algernon's remark in *The Importance of Being Earnest*, "The truth is never pure and rarely simple," is especially apt as we consider much that has happened to playwriting during the twentieth century. Exceptions to the prevailing form of realism can, of course, be found from the very beginning, but the major attacks on realism came after the Second World War. Some of these attacks, as we shall see, were deep-seated and fundamental, attacking the very foundations of rationalism upon which realism, as well as modern science, rests. We shall begin, however, by examining attacks directed not so much against realism's philosophic foundation as against its restrictive use of realistic prose — the language of common, everyday life.

MODERN POETIC DRAMA

Probably the most famous crusader in the effort to reunite poetry and drama was T. S. Eliot. His *Murder in the Cathedral*, which deals with the martyrdom of Thomas à Becket, is considered by many to be the greatest

With his flair for the comic, the tragic, and the poetic, it is hard to estimate what Lorca might have accomplished had not Franco's bullets cut short one of the most promising careers of the twentieth century.

EXPRESSIONISM

A second form of revolt against the outward form of realism came to be known as *expressionism*. It is perhaps seen more clearly in staging than in playwriting and will be considered again in the chapter on scenic design. Although normally classified as a revolt against realism, expressionism in playwriting might more correctly be regarded as an evolution beyond realism. Thus, as we shall see, most of the expressionistic writers began as realistic or naturalistic writers; then, finding naturalism too inhibiting, they moved quite easily beyond it into expressionism.

Their revolt was simply against the outward form of naturalism which allowed no more expression on stage than it did in life. They cried out for frankly theatrical expression—for a style that came to be known as *presentational* theatre rather than *representational* theatre. Distortion, raw sound, violent color, dramatic lighting, fragmented speech, and soliloquies were among the techniques employed in the attempt to reveal people's inner essence.

One of the first to turn to expressionism was Strindberg, who will be considered later. Two other writers who, like Strindberg, moved from naturalism to expressionism were Leonid Andreyev (1871–1919), a Russian, and Frank Wedekind (1864–1918), a German. Andreyev, even in his comparatively conventional and popular *He Who Gets Slapped*, is obsessed with gloom and suffering. The main character, He, joins a circus where he endures beatings by other clowns rather than the more painful beatings "out there." Finally, out of mercy and pity, he strangles the girl he loves rather than let her be contaminated by the ugliness of a greedy baron and life. In *The Life of Man*, Andreyev's pessimism and bitterness carry him deeply into the unreal world of expressionism. Unlike Gorki, who cries, "Man! Man— that's the truth!" Andreyev pictures humanity as hopeless. We follow Man from his birth in pain and darkness through his pathetic rise to success, witness grotesque discord even in his moment of triumph, then see him sink into failure and finally back

FIGURE 6:2 Andreyev's *He Who Gets Slapped*. Myron Johnson, Bain Boehlke, and Carl Beck in a production by the Children's Theatre Company; directed by John Clarke Donahue.

into the void of darkness and death. Throughout the entire play a chorus of old women cackles and comments like a flock of insane harpies.

Wedekind's greatest play, *Spring's Awakening*, is essentially naturalistic, although the neurotic intensity with which he examines sex and the awakening of young love is only a short step away from the distortion of expressionism. Several of his later plays plunge into a nightmare world of sexual imaginings and violence that carry us far beyond naturalism into the realm of the subconscious.

But it was not until shortly before the First World War, and especially during the pain and disillusionment that followed it, that German expressionism emerged as an independent and clearly recognized movement. The outstanding playwrights of this period were Ernst Toller (1893–1939) and Georg Kaiser (1878–1945). Toller was an idealist devoted to communism but unalterably opposed to revolution or violence, a position that brought attacks from both right and left. His own struggle resembles the struggle of his heroine in *Man and the Masses*, which first appeared in 1921. Sonia, a woman of the upper class, leads the masses in a strike for peace. Her determination to avoid mob violence and bloodshed is contested by the Nameless One (mob spirit), whose plea for animal action and violence prevails, destroying the very peace for which the masses had revolted. In the end Sonia is imprisoned and sentenced to death. Kaiser is best known in America for *From Morn to Midnight*, which in a series of distorted and twisted scenes follows a petty bank clerk and thief as his dreams of happiness are thwarted and shattered by one experience after another.

Expressionism also took root in Czechoslovakia, especially in the work of Karel Capek (1890–1938). In *The Insect Comedy*, which Capek wrote in collaboration with his brother Josef, a drunken tramp in a forest sees the insect world magnified into a bitter, but also very funny, satire on humanity. Throughout the first act the butterflies flirt and love. Throughout the second the beetles hoard their filthy wealth (piles of manure). Throughout the third act we view life's crowning stupidity, war. First the red ants and then the yellow ants score victories, urged on by an ever-increasing tempo and cries of, "Kill all the women and embryos!" Finally, as the gloating and victorious yellow commander stands supreme over all, bloated with victory, the huge boot of the tramp comes crashing down, and we hear the bitter verdict, "Stupid little insect!"

America's best example of expressionism is probably *The Adding Machine* (1923), by Elmer Rice. The central character is Mr. Zero, one of the millions who stumble through a drab existence as cogs in an inhuman industrial machine. When Zero finds himself replaced by an adding machine he becomes unbalanced, kills his employer, and is executed for the crime. Adrift in the afterworld, he is too narrow-minded to recognize happiness when it is offered to him in the Elysian Fields, and he becomes an adding machine operator in heaven. Eventually he is forced to return to earth to begin the torture of living all over again.

EPIC THEATRE: BERTOLT BRECHT

During the 1950s and 1960s the most exciting theatre in the world was no longer the Moscow Art Theatre, the Old Vic, the Theatre Française, or the American Theatre Guild, but the Berliner Ensemble—the theatre of Bertolt Brecht. Prior to the establishment of this theatre, Brecht

(1898–1956) had been a controversial figure, but he was practically unknown in America in spite of efforts by Eric Bentley, Mordecai Gorelik, and others to arouse interest in his work. He came to the United States in 1941; in 1947 he was summoned before the House Un-American Activities Committee. He freely admitted his Communist sympathies, though he had never been a member of the Party, and voluntarily left the country. Permission to return to his native city of Augsburg in the American Zone of Germany was denied, and he finally settled in East Berlin, where his theatre, the Berliner Ensemble, was organized. The stark, hard-hitting productions that followed soon excited attention on both sides of the Iron Curtain. He died in 1956, but the company carried on under the leadership of his widow, Helene Weigel.

Although Brecht, like Shaw, Ibsen, and other realists, was an ardent crusader for humanity, he despised the realistic form — especially the form of the "well-made" play. Brecht was a reformer determined to make audiences think — determined to drive home his points by any and every theatrical device at his disposal. He detested romantic and sentimental emotions, demanding that audiences remain awake and critical, not hypnotized by pretty stories or wish fulfillment. This antagonism to emotion and his emphasis on the intellectual were widely misinterpreted. Somehow the assumption grew that he wanted his plays to be dull and unemotional. In fact, it may well be that Brecht's worst enemy was Brecht himself, for the words he used to express his theatrical theory obviously did not mean to others what he intended them to mean. He called for intellect, not emotion; for direct presentation, not illusion; for distance (the alienation effect), not empathy. But whereas all this theory seemed to say that ideas and intellect should replace excitement and emotion, his productions tended to indicate that far from banishing emotion and excitement, he was a master at exploiting them. Finally it became apparent that when Brecht called for the elimination of "emotions" he was thinking of the sentimental emotions — the romantic, maudlin love themes of popular "well-made" plays and operas. Brecht's antagonism was also aroused whenever emotion was employed merely for its own sake. On the other hand, when emotions were used to stir thought, to teach, or to provoke action, not only did he use them but he also employed every other theatrical device in the book. The important thing to remember, then, is that Brecht did not mean for the theatre to be a dry, didactic stage lecture. It is like a lecture only if we think of a lecture by an old-fashioned inspirational speaker who employed lantern slides, hand props, song, jokes, and tear-jerking stories to drive home his message. Brecht presents didactic theatre at its exciting best. Fortunately, his flair for the theatrical is supported by a keen mind, a deep compassion for humanity, a lyric sense of poetry, and incisive language.

Although Brecht's plays have enjoyed many highly successful productions in college and university theatres, it was not until the mid-1960s that they began to capture audiences in American professional theatres (with the obvious exception of *The Threepenny Opera*). In fact, it came as somewhat of a shock to most observers when *The Caucasian Chalk Circle* emerged as the hit of the Guthrie Theatre's 1965 season. Since then *The Caucasian Chalk Circle* and other plays by Brecht have scored numerous professional successes. Perhaps the public is finally learning to appreciate Brecht, or perhaps directors and actors are finally beginning to recognize and exploit the naked theatricality and hard-hitting power of his plays.

One of his best known plays is *Mother Courage (Mutter Courage und ihre Kinder)*. The action takes place in Europe during the terrible devastation of the Thirty Years' War. The play opens with Mother Courage and her children singing as they follow the armies with their canteen wagon (their source of income) drawn by her two strong sons. But as war drags on, the sons are killed, one by the Protestants, the other by the Catholics. Kattren, her daughter, is shot while warning helpless villagers of a surprise attack. Our last view is of a wretched old woman, bereft of all except life and her wagon, doggedly struggling to carry on in a hopelessly evil world. Brecht, although comparatively unknown in America before 1950, is now considered a major influence, for although few playwrights have tried slavishly to imitate his epic theatre form, many of its features—direct appeals to the audience, skeletal staging, and the use of music and visual aids—have become commonplace.

DISILLUSIONMENT, DESPAIR, AND ABSURDITY

As already mentioned, the serious opposition to realism came not from those who simply objected to some feature of its outward form but from the disillusioned, alienated victims of modern civilization who came to question the whole rational foundation upon which realism, like so much of modern life, was based. Disillusionment, despair, and alienation are, of course, not new. We have already encountered them in the plays of Euripides, plus outrageous comedy and absurdity in the plays of Aristophanes, as the Greek Golden Age sank to its destruction and death. We sensed something similar in the plays of Middleton, Tourneur, and Webster as the Elizabethan (Jacobean) period fell into decay. We found doubt concerning the nature of reality even in the balanced and stable mind of Calderón as Spain's Golden Age crumbled. But none of these equaled the disillusionment and chaos of the twentieth century, especially in Europe following the First and Second World Wars, and in America during the war in Southeast Asia.

To try to explain all the causes of our present dilemma would be an absurdity in itself, but we can at least point out some of the more obvious factors. As already noted, the realists and scientists of the nineteenth century, although generally skeptical about conventional religion, were nevertheless staunch believers: believers in humanism, truth, rational understanding, and the perfectability of the individual. Theirs was a world of tangible problems: poverty, disease, false ideas, false values. It never occurred to them that the problems they were bent on attacking and destroying were the very things that gave their own lives such purpose, meaning, and excitement; that an existence without tangible problems can become the greatest problem of all—empty, void, terrifying, and absurd. Our ancestors enjoyed many illusions: I could be happy if only I had a warm coat, if only I had enough food, if only my dying child could be cured, if only I could build myself a home, if only I had a new spouse. But the modern victim of despair has the new coat, too much food, a healthy child, a fine home, a new spouse, plus a sports car, a speedboat, a good job, and a nice boss, yet life is a void, a nightmare, and an absurdity to him. Marilyn Monroe may have been the perfect example: a woman with money, sex appeal, fame—all the external trappings of American success—who found existence too painful to be endured.

What is the answer? Perhaps human beings were never intended to be so "free" or "civilized." Maybe they need contact with the earth, fresh air, clear water, independence, and space. Even rats become psychotic when they are too crowded in their cages. Maybe human beings need the old tangible problems: the search for food, shelter, and simple comforts. It may even be that the happiness that they pursue is mainly the moment of relief that they feel when a problem is solved or a danger avoided. Perhaps without problems and dangers there can be no happiness. As Mark Twain said, "It's a good thing for a dog to have fleas; keeps his mind off being a dog."

Perhaps the utopia in which the scientific realists believed could have been realized had it not been for war, that ultimate in violence, evil, and inhumanity, which has steadily grown more violent, evil, and inhumane as the twentieth century has "advanced."

In America there have been the other problems—assassinations, sex scandals, riots, and Watergate—ripping away at the shreds of our innocence. Even our almost miraculous achievements in science have tended to backfire. In a quest to free ourselves from fear and ignorance, human beings have explored the earth from the top of Everest to the Mindanao Deep, have walked on the moon, unlocked the secrets of the atom, learned to replace hearts and kidneys, and are verging on the creation of living matter itself. But instead of confidence and security, this probing of life, the universe, and the dark mystery of existence has only increased human confusion. Our world, once the center of creation with sun, stars, and moon revolving around us under the guiding hand of God, has shrunk to a tiny satellite of a minor solar system in the incomprehensible vastness of space. We reach out in fear and loneliness, but our space probes and telescopes reveal no sign of life, our most penetrating electronic signals stir no friendly answer, nothing to indicate intelligence or awareness out there.

In a feverish effort to regain a sense of purpose and direction, we build automobiles, refrigerators, skyscrapers, and superhighways. We buy insurance on everything; we seek advice from social workers, experts, and psychiatrists; but all the science, the gadgets, and the modern wonders fail to give us the sense of power and direction that we once gained from our old-time religion. The human race, by and large, is frightened, confused, and lost as never before, and as this has happened many have become disillusioned and finally overwhelmed by a sense of absurdity. All this is reflected in our modern painting, our modern music, and especially in our theatre.

But although this generation may be the first to have experienced disillusionment and despair on such a massive scale, these qualities, as already suggested, have been present to some extent in all ages and have frequently found expression in the theatre.

AUGUST STRINDBERG

Beginning with the immediate ancestors of disillusionment and absurdity we quickly come face to face with a giant. During the second quarter of the twentieth century, critics and teachers under the spell of realism saw Henrik Ibsen as a mighty mountain on the lonely plain of Scandinavian literature. Now we realize that August Strindberg (1849–1912), his Swedish contemporary, may have been even mightier. Until the close of World War I, Strindberg's influence was comparatively minor, but since then the position of the two writers has tended to reverse itself. Although Strindberg has never commanded a popular following, his influence among critics, playwrights, and poets has been enormous.

While Ibsen had difficulties in adjusting to life, his sufferings were minor compared with those of Strindberg. An unwanted child, nervous and hypersensitive, Strindberg grew up in a large family that could satisfy neither his hunger for food nor his greater hunger for love. Minor events and personal slights that normal children would scarcely have noticed were tortures to him. He described himself as being born without an epidermis, with raw nerve endings exposed mercilessly to the brutal stimuli of life. His deep yearning for love and companionship resulted in three marriages, but his sensitivity and temperament doomed all three to failure. For a while he hovered on the brink of insanity and actually spent some time in a mental institution. Writing was his salvation. In autobiographies, novels, poems, and plays he poured out a feverish mass of work. He stands at the opposite end of the universe from a man like Eugene Scribe, who manufactured plays as impartially as if they had been nuts and bolts, for most of Strindberg's plays are torn from his own experience—some of them almost nakedly autobiographical.

Although Strindberg wrote several important historical plays, like *The Saga of the Folkungs,* and a few naturalistic plays, like *The Father,* his chief claim to fame rests on his expressionistic plays, especially *The Dream Play, The Dance of Death,* and *The Ghost Sonata.* In *The Dream Play,* he explains that he "tried to imitate the seemingly logical form of a dream. Anything may happen; everything is possible and probable. . . . On an insignificant pattern of reality, imagination designs and

FIGURE 6:3 Strindberg's *The Dream Play*. Peter Graves as the officer in a 1948 production at the University of Minnesota.

embroiders novel patterns: a medley of memories, experiences, free fancies, absurdities, and improvisations."[2]

As the play opens we see the daughter of the god Indra falling down, down through space. Caught in the murky atmosphere and gravity of earth, she cries out for help but is told to go down and learn why people complain so much. From this prologue the play moves with eerie unpredictability from one almost autobiographical fragment of human suffering or grotesque humor to another. Now we join the Officer inside the castle, with his painful memories of childhood; now we are outside the opera house where a young singer has just failed her audition; now we move to the Lawyer's office where the air is heavy with the

[2] August Strindberg, preface to *The Dream Play*, in *Eight Famous Plays*, trans. Edwin Bjorkman and N. Ericksen (New York: Scribner, 1953).

crimes and quarrels of humanity. As the Daughter drifts from one scene to the next, we hear the refrain, "Life is evil! Men are pitiful creatures!"

It is unnecessary to explain Strindberg to a playwright, artist, or poet. To explain him to the rest of us, the following words may help. Never has a great mind laid itself more nakedly and vividly before us. One does not read Strindberg for entertainment in the popular sense of the word, but for experience. Moreover, there is a poetic, sensitive, and imaginative quality in his prose that raises it far above the level of that of the ordinary playwright. Take the following from *The Saga of the Folkungs*. King Magnus is speaking:

MAGNUS   It is autumn!—Outside and in! *(Listens.)*

BLANCHE   What do you hear, dear?

MAGNUS   I am listening to the singing of the wind in the doorcrack over there. It sounds like the moaning of sick men, or the crying of children over their lost toys—have you noticed the strange way they cry then? —And why does the wind complain in the autumn only? Isn't the air the same that blows in summer? *(Listens.)* Listen!—I should like to put words to its tones of lament.

BLANCHE   What does it sing of—that melancholy north wind?

MAGNUS   It sings of youth and vanished love; sings so that I can see it— see the blue lake, with the white castle amid oaks and lindens, suspended over roses and lilies. I see the wedding folk, cheering my youth's bride, to whom I gave my first love. . . . And one day, a long time after, she comes and lays in my arms a little creature dressed in white; and I feel as though an angel had come down from heaven; for when I gaze into his eyes I become changed from an ordinary sinful mortal to a very good one—or so it seems to me. Yet it was only my son, Erik!—Those were the days of happiness, of rejoicing. And then came the end!—He had me bound with cords. . . .[3]

A deep sense of despair runs through almost all of Strindberg's work. He shows none of the confidence and optimism of the early realists, who were sure that science and reason could chart a path through even the ugliest and most difficult human jungles. He still hungered for God and for meaning, but God did not answer. The best Strindberg could find was a reasonable degree of resignation, acceptance, and compassion.

---

[3] August Strindberg, *The Saga of the Folkungs*, act 5, in *Master Olof and Other Plays*, trans. C. D. Lecock (New York: J. Cape and H. Smith, 1931).

PIRANDELLO

Of all the ancestors of the theatre of despair and absurdity, the closest was the Italian playwright Luigi Pirandello (1867–1936). This is at first surprising, for sunny Italy is the home of the Catholic Church, the opera, *commedia dell'arte,* and romanticism. From the eighteenth century, when Carlo Goldoni and Carlo Gozzi wrote excellent, light-hearted comedies, to the end of the nineteenth century, when Gabriele d'Annunzio captured the popular theatre of Italy and Europe with his fiery, flamboyant style, Italy's viewpoint had been fundamentally romantic and optimistic. But Pirandello, probably the greatest Italian playwright since Plautus, was cloth of a different color. Like Strindberg he was the product of disillusionment. His loss of faith was not confined to conventional religion but included a loss of faith in realism, in science, and in humanity itself—at least in humanity as it existed in his day. In a search for some basis for existence and human behavior, he cut through conventional barriers of form and thought but found only a chaos of complexity that provoked bitter, grotesque laughter. In fact, some have regarded the fierce sanity with which he views life as closely akin to insanity.

His life had obvious bearing on what he wrote. Following the birth of their third child, his wife became hopelessly psychotic. Among other things she persisted in the delusion that he was unfaithful, even though he stayed at home continuously and turned over to her all his meager earnings as a schoolteacher. He refused to commit her to a mental institution, although she made life a torture to him and to their children. In view of such experience it becomes easy to understand the origin of Pirandello's basic preoccupation with the question of what is real and what is unreal. In play after play he attacks this theme with brilliant variations and originality.

In *Right You Are If You Think You Are*, we are introduced to a situation in which a wife living with her husband in a top-floor apartment is never permitted to meet her mother, although the two converse daily— the one from the street and the other from the garret window. Suspicious neighbors in search of the truth demand an explanation, and the husband provides a very plausible one. His wife, he tells them, is not the daughter of the woman in the street at all. Her daughter was his first wife, who died; this is his second wife. However, the mother has refused to accept the reality of her daughter's death, and since this delusion brings the old lady happiness, the husband perpetuates it by preventing her from meeting his second wife face to face. Such an explanation is entirely satisfactory until the neighbors are given an equally convincing account by the mother, who informs them that the wife is really her daughter but that the husband suffers from the delusion that she died and that he remarried. To humor him the mother submits to the strange practice of conversing with her daughter from the street. Finally the wife is asked to clear up the mystery, but she refuses to do so since the truth would destroy the happiness of either her "mother" or her husband. The one other character who throughout the play acts as a mouthpiece for Pirandello and could clear up the mystery to satisfy the idle curiosity of both neighbors and audience breaks into loud laughter as the play comes to an end.

This is a far cry from the neatly contrived happy and satisfying end-

FIGURE 6:4 Pirandello's *Six Characters in Search of an Author*. A University of Minnesota production; directed by Tyrone Guthrie.

ings of sentimental and well-made plays that make up the vast bulk of theatrical entertainment. It is the bitter outcry of an idealist who has found modern life unbelievably confused and inadequate. Instead of tears, however, Pirandello chooses laughter, especially at the neighbors and fools who are always so sure that they know, or will soon know, the answers.

While *Right You Are* most clearly reveals Pirandello's view of life, it is not necessarily his best or his most important work. *As You Desire Me*, *Henry IV*, *Naked*, *Six Characters in Search of an Author*, and *Tonight We Improvise* are among the most theatrically effective. In the last two he fascinates us by exploring the differences between actual reality and and stage reality. To most minds such a subject would be nothing more than a theme for an academic lecture, but through Pirandello's wit and sensitivity the intellectual is made dramatic, a grotesque mixture of intense tragedy and biting comedy. His plays may not be pleasant, nor are they ever likely to be popular, yet they seem bound to live, for no one has more vividly reflected the confusion and suffering of the twentieth century. He won the Nobel Prize for literature in 1934.

EXISTENTIALISM

In France Jean-Paul Sartre (b. 1905), Albert Camus (1913–1960), and others tried to lay a philosophic foundation for the alienated and disillusioned intellectuals of the mid-twentieth century. The devastation of World War II and especially the development of the atom bomb forced most intellectuals to recognize that something had to be done and be done quickly. Old beliefs, prejudices, and patterns had led the human race to the brink of self-destruction. People had to find new patterns and new values unfettered by the old. If there was no God, then life had meaning only because human beings had given it meaning. The danger that a few powerful people might assign life a meaning and then force this meaning on the masses was, and still is, very real and terrifying. Nor was the danger limited to the so-called totalitarian countries, for some of the most skillful brainwashing of all was to be found in commercial advertising and in the power of public relations. Sartre's search was for a rediscovery of self, a reassertion of each person's individual right to choose for himself or herself, to assign his or her own values, to vote "No" to either the tyrant or to the group — by dying if necessary. Existentialism, therefore, tries to reassure individuals that their own private experiences are unique and more important than the values others try to foist upon them.

Of Sartre's many plays the best known is *No Exit*, which advances the idea that each individual creates his own hell. In *No Exit* there is no River Styx, no fire and brimstone, only a comfortable drawing room, but in it is something more terrible than physical torture — three evil but recognizably real people, doomed to live in the same room forever and equally doomed to hate and torture one another, as they conclude that "hell is other people."

Existentialism can be seen in American playwriting, although more as an influence than as a central theme. *J.B.*, by Archibald MacLeish, for example, is concerned with a man's quest to find meaning in existence and human suffering. The overwhelming majesty of creation is not questioned, but the place of humankind in God's infinite scheme remains a riddle unanswered.

The basic plot follows the Biblical story of Job, whose faith in God is put to the test by a series of undeserved misfortunes. At the beginning of the story, J.B., like Job and Oedipus before him, stands before us young, healthy, prosperous, fundamentally good, and full of abundant faith. Then the disasters begin: A son dies in the war, a small daughter falls innocent victim to a sex fiend, two other children die in an accident, bombs wipe out his home and wealth, his health breaks, and at last even his wife deserts him. In his agony J.B., like Job, pleads for an answer: Why has it happened? How has he sinned? What is the meaning? Three comforters appear: a psychiatrist, a clergyman, and a Communist. Each offers his ready-made answers — patent medicines and panaceas — but no real answers to the overwhelming facts of injustice or to the mystery of existence. By this point (in the New York production) the great circus tent symbolizing the man-made protection of philosophy and religion has collapsed. J.B. is exposed to the merciless facts, the fearful void of the universe and the riddle of God's will. Is man's misfortune as meaningless to God as that of a crushed earthworm to the plowman?

Many have complained that MacLeish raises questions that he does not answer, and this is true. No one can deny, however, that he raises profound questions.

THE THEATRE OF THE ABSURD

Although a good production can reveal much that is comic in a play by
Pirandello or other antirealistic writers, the main thrust is clearly serious. This ceases to be true as we turn to the theatre of the absurd. Grim
as the human condition may be, it is also comic. Why should people take
themselves so seriously? Is their attempt to fathom and alter the course
of the universe any more effective or less funny than the attempt of a
puppy dog to dominate a freight train as it thunders by? Perhaps one of
the most remarkable qualities of the human animal is that when conditions become bad enough, some of them can still laugh. Aristophanes
managed to do this as Athenian problems grew unbearable, and the
absurdists have managed to laugh in the face of our own civilization and
at the same time to shock and insult it.

Our first pure example of the absurd appears to be *Ubu Roi*, written
by a young Frenchman, Alfred Jarry, and first produced in Paris in 1896.
The play defies description. It resembles a grotesque animated cartoon.
Ubu is fat, dirty, impulsive—terrifying, but in a funny way, as he
slaughters both friends and enemies, devastating Poland as if he were
an overgrown baby playing senselessly at war in a sandbox. The production of *Ubu Roi* outraged even the liberals and survived for only two performances, but its influence was considerable, not only on the theatre
but also on the other arts, where dadaists, surrealists, and pataphysicists
established Ubu as king of the irrational.

While Jarry's *Ubu Roi* influenced a few artists, it remained almost
unknown to the general public. Over half a century filled with wars and
turmoil was to pass before other Paris productions thrust an awareness
of the absurd into the general consciousness of theatre-goers. Not the
first, but probably the most important, was *Waiting for Godot*, by an
Irishman, Samuel Beckett (b. 1906). To those accustomed to well-made
plays with morals, plots, and logical meanings, *Godot* was incomprehensible. We see two tramps—two hopelessly lost human beings—waiting
for Godot. They wait and wait and wait. Nothing really happens. Tyran-
ny and oppression, a master and a slave with a rope around his neck,
make an appearance, pause while the master has lunch, exit, reappear in
Act 2, and again exit. To pass the time the two tramps improvise games

and indulge in comic routines, but only one thing stirs any real ray of hope. Now and then it is rumored that Godot is coming, but he never comes, and the play, like life, drifts on in a void of absurdity and waiting. Some of the smart ones in the audiences assumed that the riddle of the play could be solved by omitting the last two letters from the title,

FIGURE 6:5 Beckett's *Waiting for Godot.* Jeff Chandler and Larry Gates in a Guthrie Theatre production; directed by Eugene Lion; designed by Gregory Hill.

but Beckett denied that his meaning was anything so simple as this. Is it a play about waiting and hoping, or about the absurdity of waiting and hoping? Beckett, like Pirandello, laughs but gives us no answer.

Even more enigmatic is Beckett's *Endgame*. Two characters live in ash cans. Apparently the bomb has done its worst, and the most significant action is the crushing of a live flea that one of the characters discovers in his pants — not because he believes that the flea might breed other fleas but because he fears that fleas might once more start a chain of evolution culminating in another human race!

Two years before the Paris production of *Waiting for Godot* another outstanding absurdist, Eugene Ionesco (b. 1912), caught worldwide attention with a wacky title to a wackier play, *The Bald Soprano*. The comic stupidity of middle-class existence, the inanity of modern conversation, and people's inability to communicate were among the things communicated to at least some members of the audience. Another short play, *The Chairs*, deals with the emptiness and tragicomic meaninglessness of human life. A third play, *The Lesson*, presents an outrageously humorous but frightening view of education. In it we see the professor change from an old pedant with a gentle, bumbling disposition into a dogmatic tyrant who literally destroys his pupils. Ionesco's most successful full-length play was *Rhinoceros*, which carries Tennessee Williams's "The apes shall inherit the earth" one step further, as each character in turn changes into the most pugnacious, short-sighted, thick-skinned, and stubborn of all animals, the rhinoceros.

Two other Frenchmen must be mentioned — Jean Genet (b. 1910) and Antonin Artaud (1896–1948). Although not really absurdists, both were rebels who had a great influence. Genet, an ex-convict, gained a following with his far-out plays, including *The Balcony*, *The Maids*, and *The Blacks*. Artaud's critical work, *The Theatre and Its Double*, became almost the bible of the absurdists and avant-gardists.

Among America's contributions to the absurd we must include Kopit's *Oh Dad, Poor Dad, Mamma's Hung You in the Closet and I'm Feelin' So Sad* and several outstanding early plays by Edward Albee (b. 1928): *The Sandbox*, *The Zoo Story*, and *The American Dream*. These are short plays which brilliantly slash at such things as the stupidities of middle-class American life, our inane ideals, and the supposed dominance of females. Albee's most successful play to date, *Who's Afraid of Virginia Woolf?*, is naturalistic rather than absurd. A middle-aged college profes-

FIGURE 6:6 *A Chorus Line.* The Broadway production; conceived, choreographed, and directed by Michael Bennett.

sor, his wife, and their two guests spend a night playing games that strip each other psychologically naked. And the naked essence of each proves to be far from beautiful.

But unlike the theatre of former ages, much of the theatre since 1950 does not lend itself to simple intellectual analysis. Many playwrights maintain that their plays must be seen and experienced rather than read. Some of the best plays, including Megan Terry's *Viet Rock* and Jean-Claude Van Itallie's *America Hurrah!*, grew partially from acting improvisations. This was also true of the musical hit of the seventies, *A Chorus Line*, for although conceived by the director Michael Bennett and refined into its final form by professional writers James Kirkwood and Marvin Hamlish, it was essentially a group creation. The result was superb theatre made from the scraps that playwrights and directors had formerly thrown away: from the tension, comedy, heartbreak, and humanity that go into the auditions of those who only make up a chorus line. In many ways *A Chorus Line* is the essence of naturalism: no romantic costuming or makeup, no star performers, no contrived ending, and no poetic speeches, just a bleeding slice of life from the theatre itself.

Perhaps the greatest stumbling block confronting one who would "explain" modern playwriting lies in its very nature. In past ages playwrights usually worked under the basic assumption that although life itself was complex, contradictory, and chaotic, art was not. The old artists tried to cut away the chaos and confusion until meanings could emerge. In other words, they assumed that life had meaning and purpose even though these were often hidden and complex. Existential writers and absurdists tend to deny this. To them the ultimate meaning, or truth, of existence is that life is meaningless, formless, contradictory, and therefore absurd and something to be laughed at.

Whatever else we may say, the modern theatre does mirror a large portion of the intellectual and artistic world in which we live—a shattered world that has lost its old values and is still struggling to find new ones. Those who cry out for "positive" theatre may have to wait for a "positive" world—a world in which life, not death, can again stand foremost in people's minds.

We should admit, however, that in this day and age there are always complications and exceptions. Thus although most avant-garde plays of protest and disruption have tended to be negative, a few, like the rock musical *Hair*, have been essentially positive, high-spirited celebrations ·of life and living. *Hair* was youth's answer to the pillars of the American Establishment, whose blind, uncritical conformity had led the nation into its ugly involvement in Southeast Asia. The play celebrated with long, free-flowing hair, with youth (all kinds and colors) with group love-ins, with burnt draft cards (library cards), and with unabashed nudity. Charles Marowitz, writing in *Plays and Players*, called it a "jubilant assertion of American revolutionary genius." *Jesus Christ Superstar* and *Godspell* likewise upset the more conservative members of the Establishment by transforming the New Testament into almost childlike celebrations of joy and love.

The complex but widespread rebellion in theatre during the third quarter of our century has had at least one great virtue: It has shattered the dominance of realism. Not that realism is dead—far from it—but realism has lost its power to serve as the standard—to dominate and discourage other forms. Likewise none of the newer forms are powerful enough to dominate or discourage realism. Artaud and his followers, while succeeding in giving us something new, failed in their expressed desire to destroy the old, including Sophocles, Shakespeare, and Shaw. As a result, the theatre today probably enjoys freedom that is unparalleled, and although this has resulted in an absence of clearly defined standards, it has also resulted in a theatrical milieu that is richly stimulating.

FIGURE 6:7   The Broadway production of *Hair*, 1969.

FREEDOM AND COMPROMISE

The blending of the old and new in playwriting is perhaps best seen in England which, in art as in politics, has always had a tendency to "muddle through"—to grow and change via the vague process of evolution rather than the sharply defined process of revolution. But whatever the reasons may be, England since the middle of the present century has been enjoying one of its most productive periods of playwriting.

The first important break with the well-made comedies that had dominated British playwriting during the 1930s and 1940s was John Osborne's *Look Back in Anger,* which appeared in 1956. The effect on London was somewhat the same as the effect that Eugene O'Neill had had on New York during the 1920s—the shock of a playwright determined to take both life and the theatre seriously. The play quickly became a rallying point for the "angry young men" of Britain's postwar society, who felt that they were being cheated and crowded out by an unimaginative, unprogressive, middle-class Establishment—an Establishment dedicated to its own self-preservation and to the maintenence of the status quo. Osborne's next important play, *The Entertainer,* concerns the sordid decline of Archie Rice, a cheap music hall entertainer (superbly played by Sir Lawrence Olivier). Archie's bankruptcy—financial, moral, and spiritual—was quickly associated with the decline of the British nation itself. But although Osborne paved the way toward the new, his plays are not greatly unlike many of those by O'Neill, Williams, and other realists. The primary change is simply in their subject matter—the shift to a concern with the frustration, alienation, and anguish of the less privileged members of British society.

The tendency of modern playwrights to find drama in the lives of characters that former authors had used merely as background players or pawns is brilliantly illustrated by *Rosencrantz and Guildenstern Are Dead,* first produced at the Edinburgh festival in 1966. The work of Tom Stoppard, another of England's important young playwrights, it concerns the dilemma of two of literature's most famous nobodies in Shakespeare's great classic, *Hamlet.* Instead of seeing them from Shakespeare's point of view—two nobodies (the king cannot even keep their names straight)—we see them from Stoppard's and their own point of view. They become two innocent, bewildered, well-meaning students who are summoned to the court of Denmark to try to cheer up their former classmate, Hamlet. They are rewarded with scorn; they catch glimpses of Hamlet's incomprehensible behavior toward the king and queen and Ophelia. Finally they are shipped off to England and death for no discernible reason as far as they can see. All this is, of course, profoundly existential: two innocent but funny fellows caught up in a malevolent universe in which powerful forces use them and finally destroy them

FIGURE 6:8 Stoppard's *Rosencrantz and Guildenstern Are Dead* at the Cleveland Play House; directed by J. Ranelli; design consultant, Fred Voelpel.

without explanation or meaning. But this existentalism is not self-conscious. Stoppard maintains, and quite honestly so, that he never writes about existentialism, alienation, or any other theory; he simply writes about human beings under stress.

The blending of old and new can also be seen in most of the works of Peter Shaffer, *The Royal Hunt of the Sun* (1964) probes deeply into the psychology underlying a clash between two civilizations, Spanish and Incan. The human conflicts and motivations behind Pizarro's conquests rather than the bare bones of history are the basic ingredients of the drama. In *Equus* Shaffer again delves into psychology. This time his concern is a case study of a shocking and bizarre crime: the blinding of six horses by a boy of 17. Like Stoppard, most of Shaffer's plays resemble those of O'Neill more closely than they do those of Beckett or Sartre, and yet they also contain much that is new: alienation, frustration, confusion, and uncertainty. Shaffer also makes effective use of frankly theatrical elements: masks and music in *The Royal Hunt of the Sun*, and men portraying horses with gleaming metal heads in *Equus*.

Finally we must consider Harold Pinter (b. 1930), controversial and enigmatic but generally considered to be the most important of England's living playwrights. A Jew, his early years included loneliness, London air raids, and some ugly anti-Semitism. This may account for much of the brooding sense of danger that lurks just beneath the surface of most of his plays. Critics also found absurdist tendencies, especially in his early plays, but like Stoppard he denies any conscious adherence to theories. He has said that in writing his plays he has simply tried to

FIGURE 6:9 Pinter's *The Caretaker*. Mark Lemos, Eric Christmas, and Jeff Chandler in a Guthrie Theatre production; directed by Stephen Kanee; designed by Jack Barkla.

find a situation involving a few characters and has then thrown them together and "listened to what they said." If so, his approach to playwriting is almost identical to that of Chekhov, the only real difference being that Chekhov was listening to the intelligentsia of old Russia whereas Pinter listens to the harsher and more shattered, alienated, and uncertain inhabitants of a decaying London—characters who tend to be existential even if Pinter is not. Sometimes the decay takes us into the slums. In *The Caretaker*, for example, Davies, a dirty old tragicomic bundle of loneliness and aggression, is led into a junk-filled room where he is alternately befriended and terrified by two weird but intensely human brothers. The atmosphere is sordid and menacing, and yet a good production never fails to provoke gales of laughter.

Qualities of menace, danger, and uncertainty are still heavy when Pinter shifts his setting from city slums to a room in an upper-class apartment as he does in his *No Man's Land*, the hit of London in 1975–1976 and of New York in 1976–1977. In this play two decaying intellectuals (superbly played by Sir John Gielgud and Sir Ralph Richardson) engage in lacerating duels of words. Grim, dangerous, and sometimes poignant matters are involved, as in most of Pinter's plays, and yet the the result is often almost farcically funny.

But even though Pinter denies any direct influences from absurdists or existentialism, he freely admits his debt to writers like T. S. Eliot. Certainly one of the striking features of Pinter is his use of language—a mastery over the rhythm and fragmented jargon of present-day speech which Eliot first captured in his poetry. Pinter also admits his debt to the fact that like Shakespeare and most of the better playwrights, he is a practical all-around man of the theatre—actor and director as well as playwright.

Many other young playwrights in Britain deserve attention, and some of them might even excel those discussed here. Moreover, exciting plays are being written behind the Iron Curtain and elsewhere, but it is always dangerous to pass judgment on anything so alive and complicated as playwriting today. The important thing is its freedom and diversity. Perhaps never has playwriting—much of it very exciting and much of it unbelievably bad—been more alive.

CHAPTER 7

DRAMATIC THEORY AND CRITICISM

Having glanced at 2500 years of playwriting, what have we learned? What are the basic elements of drama? Are there any lasting standards? Can playwriting be taught?

Fifty years ago a scholar could have given a reasonably definite answer to such questions. Today there are no definite answers. Answers vary according to each individual's philosophy of life. The entertainer, the realist, and the absurdist each sees theatre from an almost entirely different point of view. The following ideas are essentially the views of realists and rationalists—views that generally dominated the thinking in college classrooms during the first half of the twentieth century. If they stimulate a desire to know more, or even a desire to disagree, they will have served their purpose.

CHARACTERISTICS OF THE GREAT PLAYWRIGHTS

Great playwrights have a tendency to be born at the right time. Allardyce Nicoll reminds us that a giant of playwriting is usually surrounded by a group of lesser giants. Sophocles, Shakespeare, Goethe, Ibsen—

none stood alone. Perhaps this is because a great playwright needs the stimulus of keen competition, or perhaps a great playwright and his or her colleagues all grow from the same source, as, for example, from the spirit of national exuberance that flooded Elizabethan England following the defeat of the Spanish Armada.

Great names usually emerge near the beginning of a period. In other words, the spadework has been done, the giant has had models as influences but not such perfect models that there is little hope of ever rising above them.

They have usually had early, as well as practical, experience in a living theatre. They have known their audiences and they have known their theatres. They have also tended to be individuals of mature judgment with insight into life and character. This, as Nicoll observes, has resulted in his or her being a "late starter and long endurer." A surprising number of the best playwrights did not begin writing until their late twenties or thirties.

FIGURE 7:1 Daumier's *Literary Discussion in the Second Balcony*.

One other characteristic of great playwrights might well be remembered by students who would shake the foundations of both theatre and philosophy with their first play: Great dramatists have usually begun by first writing many skillful, well-made, and entertaining plays. *The Comedy of Errors* preceded *King Lear*.

A FOUNDATION FOR CRITICISM

In *The Playwright as Thinker*, Eric Bentley does a brilliant job of convincing us that popularity and box-office appeal are inaccurate guides to the worth of a play. Unfortunately, he is not as successful in establishing an alternative basis of judgment. Bad as the judgment of audiences may be, scholars and critics down through the ages seem to present an even more dismal record. Critics do not agree on even basic fundamentals, though Aristotle, writing in the century following Sophocles, gives us a masterly analysis in his great critical essay, *The Poetics*. Liberally interpreted, this famous work does much to establish a foundation for criticism. Among other things, it defines drama as an imitation of individuals in action. It divides drama into six elements: plot, character, thought, diction, song, and spectacle. Finally, it establishes drama's purpose, or rather tragedy's purpose, as a purgation of the soul through the tragic emotions of pity and terror.

Volumes have been written about these principles, but for the present we must content ourselves with a few paragraphs. Aristotle's concept of drama as an imitation of individuals in action is of vital importance. Action, not the word, lies at the core of drama. Elmer Rice points out that *scene, act, play*, and *show*, as well as *actor, director, performer*, and *producer*, all place the emphasis on doing and seeing rather than on reading or listening: "Charlie Chaplin and Mickey Mouse conquered the world without words of tongue or pen."[1] Wise directors often urge beginning actors to concentrate on the action behind the words rather than on the words themselves—on the thing to be accomplished rather than on the words used in trying to accomplish it. For most people a play is not really a play until it is presented on the stage. The actors do not tell us what happens; they show us what happens.

[1] Elmer Rice, *The Living Theatre* (New York: Harper & Row, 1959), p. 138.

PLOT

Aristotle places plot foremost in his list of elements that compose drama, since plot provides the basic framework for the action. It is the story line, the scheme of action that enables the characters, ideas, and other ingredients to reveal themselves. The weakest type of plot, according to Aristotle, is the episodic plot, in which one event follows another with little or no causal effect or relationship. The strongest is the involved plot, such as the plot of *Oedipus the King*, in which each action tends to grow out of some preceding action, and the very struggle of the tragic hero to free himself becomes the force that destroys him.

Many attempts have been made to analyze and define plot structure, but drama, like life itself, refuses to be neatly pigeonholed—except in the minds of certain pedagogues. The theory of Ferdinand Brunetière, published in *La Loi du théâtre* (1894), if not taken too literally, may be as useful as any in the analysis and appreciation of many plays. His theory makes conflict the essential element in drama, and we must admit that conflict tends to be dramatic and exciting whether on the athletic field, in daily life, or on the stage. Directors, actors, and critics find that the majority of plays tend to yield greater meaning and dramatic value if viewed in terms of conflict. Melodrama, for example, is often little more than a conflict between villain and hero for the lovely young heroine. In *Macbeth* we see conflicts between men (Macbeth versus Macduff), between a man and the powers of evil (Macbeth versus the witches), between motives within a given character (Macbeth's agony of indecision beginning with "If it were done when 'tis done"), and there are many others. We can safely conclude, then, that conflict is a powerful ingredient in the structure of most plots, but we cannot rely on it blindly. Too many outstanding plays, like *Our Town, The Cherry Orchard* and *Waiting for Godot,* yield little of their true values through an analysis of their plots or conflicts.

CHARACTER

We should remember that action is only half of Aristotle's individuals in action. Individuals (or at least animals and objects with human characteristics) constitute the other half. The argument as to whether action or characterization is the more important is about as useful as the argument about the chicken and the egg; they are both parts of a whole and so interwoven and interrelated that neither has an independent existence. It is true that Kotzebue and other writers of melodrama tended to emphasize action and plot at the expense of character, whereas Chekhov and other naturalists tended to emphasize character at the expense of action, but such evaluations are probably more academic than essential.

One concept concerning character that the beginning student might do well to consider is the difference between dramatic and nondramatic characters — between the people we see in excellent plays and the run-of-the-mill average that we encounter in daily life. The naturalists may argue that a great playwright is great partly because he or she gives us completely lifelike characters. This was the aim of Zola and others except for one thing: Their lifelike characters were highly select individuals. In fact, naturalists sometimes turned to the gutters in search of lifelike human beings who were at the same time interesting enough to hold an audience for two hours. In general, then, what do we demand of an interesting or dramatic character? The answer is dangerous, for any human being could be effective on stage if introduced into exactly the right situation at exactly the right moment. In other words, we sometimes need a perfectly dull, normal person as a foil or contrast to the main characters. We sometimes need ugly people; we sometimes need stupid people; in fact, variety and contrast are basic ingredients in any richly characterized play. But in spite of all this, we can still state in general terms that the theatrical character is a heightened character — more colorful, more sensitive, more striking, perhaps more attractive, at least more something than the average individual. In fact, a commonplace remark about exceptionally colorful people that we encounter in real life is, "He (or she) ought to be on the stage!"

As we have seen, leading characters in tragedy are almost invariably men or women of exceptional intelligence and sensitivity. We recognize them as potentially great individuals who are therefore capable of giving us deeper insight into human existence as they struggle with the catastrophies that descend upon them. We might also remind ourselves of Ben Jonson's theory that a comic character is someone with too much of something. Characters in both comedy and tragedy, therefore, tend to be people who are exceptional in some way.

Perhaps the most universal quality of important characters in all forms of drama is sensitivity. We are interested in the individual who responds quickly, deeply, and impulsively to a given stimulus, who is keenly aware of the moment, who is alive to the situation. But even here there are exceptions, for Buster Keaton's comic art was founded on a total absence of sensitivity. Perhaps Keaton was the exception that proved the rule. Moreover, as an artist he showed superb sensitivity in recognizing the enormously humorous possibilities of the totally insensitive deadpan character he always portrayed.

THOUGHT

As we have seen, thought was the element of primary concern to the realists as well as a powerful factor in almost all great plays. Shaw maintained that he wrote plays because more people listened when he spoke from a stage than from a soapbox. Arthur Miller once said, "I don't care about saving the theatre, I'd just like to help save the human race!"

One aspect of thought in drama causes much confusion. The realists and most teachers have insisted that a good play must do more than entertain; it must have something to say. Yet, in America at least, we are warned against propaganda. Just what is the difference between having something to say and being a propagandist? Probably to most people the play that presents ideas with which we disagree is propaganda. Mordecai Gorelik points out that radical Soviet critics see nothing inartistic about agitational Communist plays that we would regard as pure propaganda, but they look upon plays like *Winterset* as bourgeois propaganda.[2] Though the problem remains complex and confusing, we can at least condemn certain types of propaganda, for example, the type that slavishly follows the party line, whether the line be Communist, capitalist, or monarchist. We can also condemn the type of propaganda that is crudely and unskillfully presented, whether the message is the virtue of honesty or the horror of capitalism. But when the idea (or the propaganda, if you prefer) is one's own and is presented with imagination, insight, and dramatic skill, it may well become great art. In fact, Gorelik presents the challenging thesis that the old art-for-art's-sake writer is only great when he presents new and challenging ideas, whereas the

[2]Mordecai Gorelik, *New Theatres for Old* (New York: Samuel French, 1947), pp. 361ff.

propaganda writer is only great insofar as the ideas are presented with great artistry.

DICTION, OR LANGUAGE

There is no substitute for command over the magic of words. If anyone doubts this truth let him consider the following passage from Lee Simonson's *The Stage Is Set*. Two of Hamlet's greatest soliloquies, "To be, or not to be" and "O, that this too too solid flesh would melt," are here rewritten as Simonson suggests they might be rendered by a naturalist playwright. Hamlet becomes plain Henry; he sits in a dirty back yard, where children have fashioned a melting snowman.

> HENRY Damn my stepfather; lecherous old bastard. If I could only kill him. But I'm a snivelling introvert. All I can do is complain. I can't do anything. . . . Mother—mother's nothing but a whore. No! I shouldn't have said that. Forgive me, mother. . . . But it drives me almost mad to think of it. God! if I could only kill myself—get away from it all. There's nothing to live for. *(He hunches more deeply into his coat collar).* I'm afraid! Afraid to do anything. Afraid of death. *(He shivers).* Spooks. What they told me when I was a kid. Just afraid of the dark—but it sticks. It gets me. *(Looking at the snow man).* I'm just so much mush—mush like you. *(He breaks into bitter laughter, takes off the battered derby from the snow man's head and salutes him elaborately).* If I could only thaw with you tomorrow—thaw, just dissolve, trickle into the earth—run off into the sewer, etc., etc.[3]

Perhaps the barren quality of naturalist language was simply a reaction against the overexalted eloquence of the nineteenth century. Perhaps it was part of the machine age. We have already noted how Maxwell Anderson, T. S. Eliot, García Lorca, and others tried to return to the poetic form. It should also be remembered that prose in the hands of writers like Strindberg, Chekhov, O'Casey, and Pinter has achieved great vividness, rhythm, and imaginative richness of expression. In any event, whether in prose or verse, word magic must be present. It is one of the great differences between life and art.

[3]Lee Simonson, *The Stage Is Set* (New York: Harcourt Brace Jovanovich, 1932), p. 435.

SONG AND SPECTACLE

Song and spectacle and the other technical elements of dramatic production will be discussed in Part Three. Obviously they are not as essential as the first four elements, and yet if skillfully used they often enhance the beauty and aesthetic values of the theatrical experience. Critics are still somewhat confused as to just what Aristotle had in mind by song. Some see him as primarily concerned with the cadence or lilt of the spoken lines, particularly in lyric passages. Others interpret song as meaning a formal musical background. We should remember that such an interpretation was responsible for grand opera. Perhaps the main thing that the beginner should realize is that embellishment, whether aural or visual, can either enhance dramatic values or clutter and destroy them. It all depends upon the taste and skill with which the embellishment is done.

One word of caution should be inserted before leaving even this brief summary of *The Poetics*. Any illusion that a study of Aristotle can make one either an infallible judge of plays or an outstanding playwright is shaken when we remember that the great Greek plays were written before, not after, his essay and that Shakespeare, Molière, Lope de Vega, and so many of the best dramatists were either ignorant of his work or politely ignored it. It is even true that during certain periods Aristotle's ideas, slightly misinterpreted and slavishly applied, served to hinder the development of drama rather than help it. The mystery behind the creation of great art tends to remain a mystery.

DRAMA AND THE AUDIENCE

As Elmer Rice points out, there are two phases to any work of art: (1) *self-expression* — an idea, a dream, or a concept that the artist feels he or she must get off his or her chest and (2) *communication* — the sharing of the art object with others.[4] But while the basic urges for expression and communication remain the same in all arts, the practical realization of

[4] Rice, op. cit., pp. 1–13.

these urges varies widely. The painter, for example, having finished a canvas, finds the process complete, ready to be communicated on its own merits to other individuals or groups of individuals now or in the future. The writer of plays, like the composer of symphonies, faces a vastly more complex problem. His or her work of art is not complete until performed by a complex organization of other artists (actors, directors, designers, etc.) known as a theatrical company; moreover, it is almost never performed for one or two individuals but for a large, specially assembled audience. These facts concerning the art of the theatre do not necessarily make drama better or worse than an individual art like painting, but they do complicate the process of judging it. Properly speaking, we can never say we saw *Hamlet;* instead, we saw Gielgud's production of *Hamlet* at such and such a theatre on such and such a date. The written script of *Hamlet* is recorded, of course, but, as pointed out in the opening chapter of this book, it is doubtful whether some readers actually get much more out of the script of Hamlet than they would out of the written score of Beethoven's *Ninth Symphony.* Consequently, those whose critical theories fail to include the reaction of an audience when evaluating drama are on dangerous ground. The proof of Shakespeare's greatness lies not only in the fact that he has been universally acclaimed by critics, but also by the fact that his plays have held audiences for over 350 years.

The theatre's need to attract and hold an audience functions as both a curse and a blessing. Audience reaction has undoubtedly discouraged many worthy new playwrights who happen to be a bit too advanced for their time. On the other hand, audience reaction also contains basic elements of common sense and an unflattering honesty that have weeded out much of the esoteric, the pretentious, and the egocentric. It therefore seems wise to consider a few of the practical questions that reasonably intelligent play-goers are likely to ask following an evening at the theatre.

WAS IT ENTERTAINING?

No matter whether a romanticist, realist, or absurdist, the playwright, like the speaker, must first catch and hold an audience; other values, if any, are dependent upon this. We can go even further and say that entertainment by itself has value, even though such value may be only momentary. Its aftereffects are neither harmful nor useful; it "struts and frets its hour upon the stage and then is heard no more." We in the audience return home neither better nor worse for the experience.

What, then, is wrong with being merely entertaining? Nothing is wrong with it, but other things are better. Moreover, in the twentieth century mere entertainment is cheap because it is so abundant. Commercialism and competition have forced radio, television, and to a lesser extent, motion picture productions to concentrate so much on momentary, interest-catching entertainment that we are surfeited by it. Pink ice cream and pop may be wonderful in small quantities, but not as a steady diet.

WAS IT AN EXPERIENCE?

To some people an experience implies an escape from life into the romantic world of vicarious experience, the world of daydreams and wish fulfillment, the world as it should be. In small doses this form of escape may not be dangerous, but if overdone the world of melodramas, romantic novels, and soap operas may seriously affect one's capacity to deal with real life. Few of us win the game in the last 30 seconds, slaughter the outlaws and escape unscathed, or end up in the moonlight with the person of our dreams in our arms. The mature, well-adjusted personality must develop a tougher, more realistic sense of values. The right kind of theatre can help one develop such a sense of values. Or, in the words of Harold Clurman, "Good theatre offers an escape—an escape into reality!"[5]

If human beings gain wisdom through living, they can also gain it through art, for art is in large measure organized experience that people share together. Those who know Shakespeare, Sophocles, Ibsen, Shaw, Strindberg, Chekhov, and O'Neill see life honestly in myriad patterns and see it both as it should and as it should not be. Accordingly, their ability to make wise decisions, to take disaster and disappointment in stride, to realize that they are neither alone nor the first to have been humbled and troubled by existence, should make them better, more stable, and more understanding human beings.

---

[5] Harold Clurman. (Speech given at American National Theatre and Academy, New York, February 1959).

WAS IT MORAL?

This question is difficult to deal with, since there is neither common agreement nor a logical definition of what we mean by moral; yet probably more plays are condemned on the grounds of being immoral than on any other.

To Artaud even the theatre of Sophocles, Shakespeare, and Shaw was based on an obsolete, dishonest system of values. To the "respectable" modern citizen the theatre of the absurd is shocking, indecent, sensational, and obscene. Each regards the other as hideously immoral. Any play running counter to established customs, laws, or especially the religious standards of a group is likely to be condemned; yet the great thinkers and religious leaders themselves have usually run counter to established norms. Of course they, like the playwrights, have often paid bitterly for their failure to conform. The problem is confusing. Ibsen's *Ghosts,* now a thoroughly respectable play, was once condemned as the essence of filth and indecency. Aristophanes' *Lysistrata* deals frankly with sex but does so for the basic purpose of debunking the greatest of all evils, war. *What Price Glory?* was one of the first plays to use brutal profanity, but it did so in order to debunk war. On the other hand, many seemingly pious melodramas imply that the villains had the right idea; their luck simply ran out in the last act. Popular success stories with their happy endings may wreck more lives than all the Restoration comedies put together, for they lead one to expect the impossible of life. To be moral the theatre must at least be honest. The great author may be concerned with good or evil, with the foolish or heroic. He or she may select, organize, rearrange, or condense his or her material, but the result should be fundamentally honest. From this standpoint *Cat on a Hot Tin Roof* may be more moral than *Pollyanna.*

One other observation seems valid. The great playwrights have usually been humanitarians and staunch believers in humanity. They have tended to see beyond racial, religious, and national barriers. They have been liberals and frequently iconoclasts. Because of this they have shared the fate of other liberals and have felt the lash of scorn and abuse, especially in their own day. Yet because of the very ideas for which they were persecuted by their contemporaries, they are often hailed as saints and prophets by succeeding generations.

WILL IT BE REMEMBERED?

It is true that the spectator seldom pauses immediately following a performance to say, "Will people remember this play?" Yet in the long run this is one of the most valid tests of good art. Critical evaluation of a play seems to follow an inevitable sequence: After a play's first flush of success comes a period of decline, for the next generation is sure to rebel against anything its parents valued. Not until the third, fourth, or fifth generations do we look back with objectivity and begin to select works of unusual value as the classics of a given style or age. Plays and playwrights that reemerge after this inevitable decline, that prove to have lasting worth, that can be produced again and again, are almost certain to have the stuff of which great dramatic literature is composed.

CLASSIFICATION OF DRAMA

Bowing to convention, let us look briefly at the standard classifications of drama: tragedy, comedy, farce, and melodrama. These have already been treated to some extent as they emerged historically, but we will now consider them together in order to draw comparisons and contrasts.

Let us begin by making it perfectly clear that any classification of plays is subject to the same imperfections and contradictions that we encounter when we try to classify or stereotype human beings. Only in ancient Greece was the line between tragedy and comedy clearly defined; and even there the greatest of tragedies, *Oedipus the King*, abounds in irony, which is a definite form of humor, while the most hilarious of comedies, *Lysistrata*, has a deeply serious purpose behind its laughter.

In essence, however, the terms *tragedy* and *comedy* distinguish two fundamentally different ways of looking at life. One can examine human life with a passionate hunger to understand—the tragic way; or one can assume an intellectual attitude and laugh at human follies—the comic way. Of course, one can also mix the two attitudes in numberless and varying proportions, alternating from one to the other, half-crying or half-laughing at the same time, and this is exactly what most of the best playwrights, especially since the time of Shakespeare, have tended to do. Every student knows that Shakespeare contrasted the horror of Duncan's murder with the comic entrance of Macbeth's drunken porter, but only those who most appreciate tragedy realize the tremendous contribution that thoroughly integrated humor makes in *Hamlet, Antony and Cleopatra,* and even *King Lear.*[6]

In the eighteenth century, as we have seen, styles of playwriting increased until we were able to distinguish farce, burlesque, ballad opera, sentimental comedy, high comedy, bourgeois tragedy, and neoclassic tragedy. Today the list has multiplied and subdivided until classification becomes more absurd than Polonius with his, "Tragedy, comedy, history, pastoral, pastoral-comical, historical-pastoral, tragical-historical, tragical-comical-historical-pastoral." In spite of this there may still be value in glancing at the four traditional forms: tragedy, melodrama, comedy, and farce.

TRAGEDY

Tragedy is commonly regarded as the greatest and most noble form of drama—an exaltation of the human spirit. In spite of the fact that it generally depicts characters involved in some terrible catastrophe, tragedy gives us a fundamentally optimistic and liberal view of life. The tragic playwright examines life intently and passionately during great crises in the lives of great personalities. From such an examination we gain wisdom and insight, moments of great beauty, and admiration for humanity even in its defeat. Citizens of a mature and healthy nation should be willing to engage in such soul searching without asking that the facts be colored by romantic hues, happy endings, or melodramatic techniques.

It should be emphasized that the tragic hero or heroine must be a person of some stature. In general there is little dramatic value in seeing a small mind or soul involved in tragic circumstances, someone who in time of crisis simply falls back on cliches and on trite patterns of behavior copied from bad novels or soap operas. The tragic hero or heroine must be capable of independent thought and action, capable of new insight, capable therefore of increasing our human understanding and

[6] See Calvin Quayle, "Humor in Tragedy" (Ph.D. diss., University of Minnesota, 1957).

compassion. This does not mean that the tragic hero of today must be a king or nobleman; such characters as Ibsen's Mrs. Alving, O'Casey's Juno, Williams's Blanche Du Bois, Miller's Willy Loman, and other "common" men and women have sufficient depth and universal significance to make them worthy, if not equal, successors to the giants of the Greek classics and Shakespeare.

MELODRAMA

Whereas the term *tragedy* is commonly associated with the noblest form of drama, melodrama is commonly associated with the most disreputable. Even in life, to accuse someone of being melodramatic is to stigmatize him or her with a vague aura of phony emotionalism and exaggeration. Obviously, such sweeping generalizations are not justified, for some of the dullest and most ridiculous plays ever written have been tragedies, while some of the greatest, including *Hamlet* and *Macbeth*, have contained strong elements of melodrama.

In a brilliant defense of the much maligned word *melodrama*, James Rosenberg points out that melodrama is certainly not true to life, nor does it pretend to be, but that it is true to the theatrical, the exciting, the stimulating, the highly selective, and the sometimes illuminating view of life.[7] On the whole, however, we must admit that the word *melodrama* tends to be associated with the sentimental nineteenth-century melodramas, that is, with plays that strive for the momentary rather than the lasting, the contrived rather than the organic, the exciting rather than the penetrating, and the happy ending rather than the logical or honest ending. In this extreme form melodrama probably deserves the fate that has befallen it, but it is seldom found in its extreme form. No one seems quite certain whether plays like *Ghosts, Camille, A Streetcar Named Desire, Juno and the Paycock*, and *Death of a Salesman* are tragedies or melodramas or just plain serious dramas. Moreover, it is highly unlikely that their authors were concerned about such classifications. For the most part, each well-written play is like each human being: a complex mixture of qualities which makes each person and each play unique.

---

[7] Robert Corrigan and James Rosenberg, *The Context and Craft of Drama* (New York: Intext, 1964), pp. 168–185.

COMEDY

In contrast to tragedy, the comic attitude, as we have already seen, chooses to laugh at the follies of humankind rather than cry out in anguish or weep over them. In general the comic situation, though it may be painful to those involved, is not painful to members of the audience. The conclusion of a comedy does not leave major characters dead or bereft of the desire to live. The foolish old man in love with a young girl, the pompous fop who struts his way into an embarrassing downfall, and the clever rogue who gets caught in his own trap are typical comic characters in typical comic situations.

Satire is generally regarded as the highest form of comedy. Aristophanes, Molière, and Shaw are among those who have made brilliant use of its power in ridiculing follies. Characterization, verbal wit, and cleverly contrived plots have, of course, contributed much to the merriment of the plays of such authors; but behind all the laughter and even the slapstick of such comedies, there has invariably been an idea, a protest, or a purpose that provokes thought and discussion. Laughter is a unique possession of the human animal and an indication of intelligence. In fact, there is something healthy and admirable about nations or individuals that can laugh at their follies rather than weep, quarrel, or fight over them.

FARCE

Of all the forms of drama, farce is probably the most confusing. The common tendency is to see in it the same relationship to comedy that melodrama bears to tragedy — in other words, a low, popular, comic form of entertainment in which fast action, contrived situations, physical mishaps, and even puns or obscenities lie at the root of its outrageous merriment. Though there is some validity in this common view of farce, closer examination of the genre reveals disturbing complications. Just as Shakespeare's tragedies contain strong elements of melodrama, most of the world's greatest comedies tend to rely heavily on farcical elements. Aristophanes and Molière were incorrigible in this regard. The famous screen scene in Sheridan's *School for Scandal*, the duel in Shakespeare's *Twelfth Night*, the mourning scene in Wilde's *The Importance of Being Earnest*, and the arena scene in Shaw's *Androcles and the Lion* are but a handful of the innumerable farcical situations used by great playwrights to promote their serious satire.

Farce and satire may be partners rather than enemies. Therefore, if we wish to place a value judgment on the various forms of comedy, our chief concern should not be with the comic device employed — pun, pratfall, or polished repartee — but with the purpose behind the device. Judged on this basis, a surprising number of so-called high comedies become trivial indeed, while many a low, rollicking farce strikes at the heart of some of society's most distressing evils. Charlie Chaplin's films, for all their horseplay and incredible flights of fancy, contained so much social criticism that America banished him!

In an excellent dissertation on the psychology of farce, Eric Bentley surprised most of his followers by defending farce, pointing out the therapeutic value of the outrageous acts committed in its name. He almost reaches the conclusion that farce might be used to replace psychiatrists, for it can go far toward relieving the inhibitions and frustrations of our modern world.[8]

In conclusion, if we think of farce as a type of comedy that sells its soul for a laugh, then farce may deserve its rank near the bottom of the heap. If, on the other hand, we think of farce as a comic situation in which physical activity, exaggerated characters, and outrageous antics are used to provoke ideas as well as laughter, then wise people will pause long before relegating farce to an inferior position. Too much of our great literature, too many of our great stage comedies, abound in such "low qualities," whereas too many of the dullest and most insipid plays are completely free from such entertaining antics. The pratfall done by the right character in the right place at the right time may not be so low after all.

THE CRITICAL REVIEW

In recent years there has been a growing concern about the role of the critic or play reviewer who evaluates a play, usually for the daily press, after opening night. Obviously, evaluation of new plays and perfor-

[8] Eric Bentley, ed., introduction to *Let's Get A Divorce and Other Plays* (New York: Hill & Wang, 1955).

mances is needed. Unfortunately, too much importance is often ascribed these reviews by both the potential audience and the artists themselves. All who participated in the long labor of production await the reviews with fear and anticipation; the entire company hungers to be praised for a job well done. Frequently, however, they receive — and often deserve — a scathing review which leaves them enraged, frustrated, martyred, and convinced that the critic is crazy.

There are many faults in this system which allows a few people to judge for the whole public. Too few of the newspaper critics really know the theatre well enough, and some yield to the pressure to turn out exciting journalism for the sake of editors and readers rather than balanced judgment for the sake of the players. The public itself is mainly to blame, since it enjoys sweeping praise or condemnation, which is clear and simple, rather than balanced judgment, which is often disturbing and confusing. The public is also a victim of the great leveling impulse of democracy: We like to see anyone better than ourselves "get theirs." To some extent they share with the critic a vision of the artist as an egotist who needs to be knocked down occasionally. Unfortunately, most of the really promising young actors, designers, directors, and playwrights are essentially shy, insecure, and easily frightened. Harsh criticism is especially rough on the young playwright who feels that he or she must hit a home run the first time at bat. Shakespeare, Ibsen, Molière — none would have survived in present-day America, for their early efforts would have been ridiculed, and sensitive artists often cannot, or will not, take it.

What can be done? We can hope for more critics with the rare combination of high standards, a knowledge of theatre, a deep understanding of human nature, and a dedicated desire to improve the theatre, but there is little that a student of theatre can do about this.

On the other hand, students of theatre can do something about adjusting their own attitudes. They can realize that theatre blows hot and cold; that the harsh words of the critic were probably more than balanced by the extravagant praise of friends and relatives; that although unjustly condemned in this play they probably received more praise than they deserved in the last one. In other words, they can develop a philosophy that enables them to maintain balance; they can take a long-range view, refusing to take any one criticism too seriously. Nothing helps more than numerous evaluations of a given performance or production. If all of the better students in a theatre department were required to write reviews, some illuminating truths could be discovered. Someone will invariably think it is the best production he or she ever saw, someone else will think it the worst, but if one reads all the reviews, significant patterns emerge.

Maybe college students should be less eager to have their work reviewed by professional critics. Critical evaluation by an outstanding staff after a production has closed and cooled is far safer and more educational.

In concluding this section on plays and playwrights, the reader should be warned that the preceding pages do not pretend to be more than an introduction to the world of dramatic literature. Hundreds of important plays and playwrights have not even been mentioned; nor is it to be expected that those who know drama best will agree with everything that has been said. Readers who are interested will find a wealth of material for further study — above all, the plays themselves. Books about plays may help in the process of acquiring an appreciation of the drama; but the play, as King Lear would say, is "the thing itself."

Whatever literary or critical standards of judgment we apply, the fact remains that the contribution of dramatic literature to the sum total of human culture is tremendous. As Helen Hayes once wrote:

> When I consider how many of the world's greatest minds — Sophocles, Aristophanes, Shakespeare, Goethe, Molière, Ibsen, Shaw — have clothed their ideas in the dramatic form; when I consider how the theatre has cut through the barriers of national, religious, and racial prejudice; when I consider the enjoyment, the enrichment, and the enlightenment it has brought into the lives of countless millions down through the ages — I become very proud of my profession.[9]

---

[9] Helen Hayes, from a statement contributed for a brochure campaigning for the construction of a theatre at the University of Minnesota, 1952.

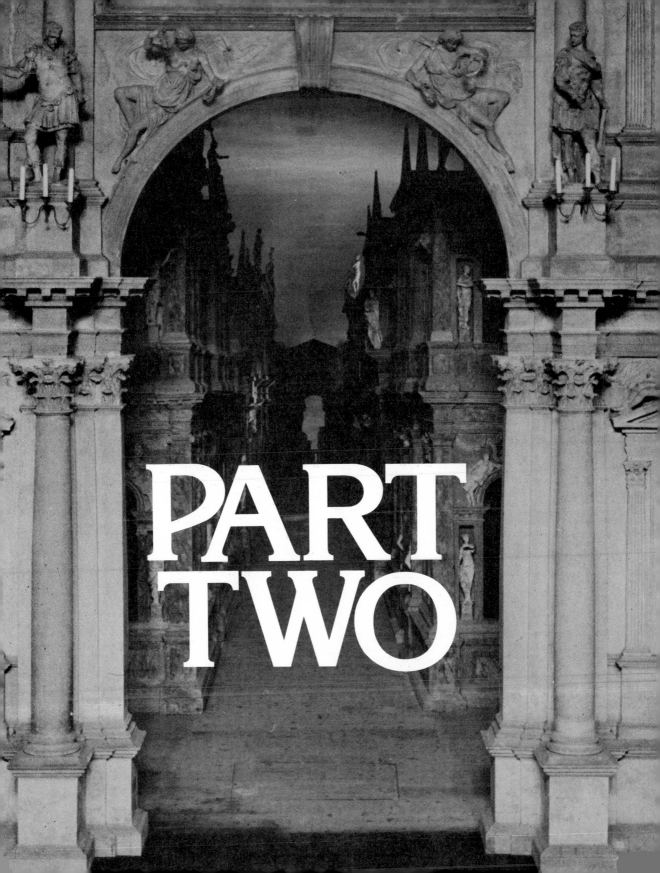

PART TWO

DIRECTING AND ACTING

CHAPTER 8

DIRECTING

Although a comparative newcomer to the theatre, the present-day director ranks second in importance only to the playwright in the process of presenting a living play on the stage. This is especially true, as we shall see, in the amateur theatre, where the director is often the only professional present. Even on Broadway names like David Belasco, Tyrone Guthrie, and Elia Kazan have acquired recognition once accorded only to stars or playwrights.

Historically the term *director* dates only to the latter half of the nineteenth century, even though certain managerial functions have always had to be assumed by someone. In Attic Greece that someone was often the playwright; in England, the most outstanding actor of the company. Along the way other combinations have functioned with varying degrees of success in supervising rehearsals and getting the play on the boards. But the idea of a director, or *régisseur*, is practically a twentieth-century development.

The need for such an artist arose from abuses of the old system. A few extreme examples will illustrate: In 1886 Edwin Booth and Lawrence

Barrett combined their energies to give the American theatre what was generally regarded as the greatest company ever assembled. Kitty Molony, starry-eyed young actress with the group, faithfully recorded the events of the season, including numerous instances that give us insight into rehearsal practices of the day. "Ten days," she tells us, "proved enough to get the company letter perfect in *Richelieu, Macbeth, Hamlet,* and *Othello.*"[1] A few more rehearsals and the entire repertoire, which also included *Richard III, Katherine and Petruchio, The Merchant of Venice, The Fool's Revenge, Brutus, Don Caesar de Bazan, A New Way to Pay Old Debts,* and *King Lear,* was ready to be performed! True, this was not the same as preparing each of these plays for an opening today. These were standard pieces. Actors already knew most of the lines, and stage business was largely traditional; even so, the lack of rehearsal seems to us appalling. During this rehearsal period Booth himself gave only cues; if a full speech was necessary, "Mr. Doud read it." Consequently Molony is able to relate how she stood enthralled in the wings on the opening night to see Booth as Richelieu *for the first time.* She describes the excitement and uncertainty of being propelled through the trap *for the first time* on the opening night of *Macbeth,* and the near-disaster when on the same night she almost ruined the show by having not the faintest idea of how to apply her makeup for her part as one of the bloody apparitions.

Such instances could be multiplied, but further examples are unnecessary. It suffices to point out that the following practices in play production were the rule rather than the exception during most of the nineteenth century:

1. The rehearsal period was short: only a few hours for a repertory piece, seldom more than a week for a new one.
2. Costume and makeup were largely left to the actors and consequently were motivated by a desire to attract attention. At best they exhibited a confusing multiplicity of styles.
3. Scenery was usually conventional and only slightly adapted to the needs of the play.
4. Small parts and crowd scenes were practically ignored or were trusted to any supernumeraries who happened to be available.

---

[1] Katherine Goodale, *Behind the Scenes with Edwin Booth* (Boston: Houghton Mifflin, 1931), pp. 11–29.

Obviously, the difficulty with such theatre was the absence of some artist with power over not only one actor, not only a group of actors, not only the scenery, sound, lights, costumes, properties, and makeup, but with responsibility for all these things—for seeing that all worked together to create an organic whole, the play itself. It was with the emergence of such an individual that the director, or *régisseur*, was born.

THE APPEARANCE OF THE DIRECTOR

Just who deserves the title of the first director has never been determined. There is, however, much to justify beginning with the Duke of Saxe-Meiningen, a royal amateur whose company first appeared in Berlin on May 1, 1874. The actual directing of the plays was done by his stage manager, Ludwig Kronek, but it was the duke who set the tone and standards for the company, and it was he who justly or unjustly received the credit. A strict disciplinarian, his rehearsal period was long and thorough. There were no stars; every part was considered important, and the crowd scenes, hitherto left to the mercy of supers, became the object of some of the company's most effective work. Scenery, lighting, costumes, makeup, and properties were carefully planned and blended into the total effect. Above all, worn-out traditional stage business was discarded, and new action was painstakingly adapted to express character and situation. During the last quarter of the nineteenth century, the duke's company toured extensively throughout Europe. Its influence was enormous, for it demonstrated the excellence that could be achieved when concentration was centered through a director upon the whole rather than the parts.

Reinforcing this practical demonstration of the director's importance were the writings of two men, Adolphe Appia and Gordon Craig. Appia (1862–1928), an artist and a scholar, owed many of his ideas to Richard Wagner. Wagner had been one of the first to cry out for a fusion of all the stage arts, and in many respects his ideas stand alongside his great musical dramas as landmarks in any history of directing. It was Appia rather than Wagner, however, who gave the clearest expression to the thesis that scenery, lights, acting, music, and the rest must be fused into an organic whole. Scenery, he insisted, should be three-dimensional in order to harmonize with three-dimensional actors. Under his imaginative touch, lighting became a powerful dramatic element reinforcing the dramatic effect of both the actor and the scenery and blending all visual elements together.

But Appia was essentially a scholar, modest and rather quiet, and his excellent works, such as *Die Musik und die Inscenierung,* were not widely read. (Most of Appia's major works were not available in English until the 1960s.) It remained for Edward Gordon Craig (1872–1966), son of Ellen Terry, to add the showmanship and exaggeration that was to catch the attention of theatres large and small throughout the world. Today there are those who still worship Craig as a genius and others who regard him as little more than an utterly impractical and overbearing windbag. Truth obviously lies between the extremes. To be sure, he exaggerated. To him the director was a superartist to whom even the playwright was subservient. He even went so far as to suggest that the living actor should be replaced by an *Über-marionette* capable of doing anything and everything that the imagination and genius of his director could conjure up. At the same time, it was probably Craig's boldness and exaggeration that attracted attention. Everyone soon knew of him and, through him, of a new theatre artist, the director.

During the years immediately before and shortly after the turn of the century several great directors emerged. In Paris, André Antoine at his Théâtre Libre brought to the theatre a new naturalism, simplicity, and conviction. In his opinion the stage director was to the drama what description was to the novel—the source of comment upon and illumination of the dialogue. Antoine planned the stage movement with painstaking care. His settings were naturalistic, sometimes to the extreme.

Max Reinhardt (1873–1943), in Germany and later in America, contributed productions that were imaginative, theatrically effective, and spectacular. He almost achieved Craig's dream, the director as superartist; one of his greatest productions, *The Miracle,* used a wordless script, while most of his other efforts resulted in productions that were more characteristic of Reinhardt than of the author. In America, David Belasco, mentioned earlier as a playwright, attained fame also as a director, bringing realism to a height never before thought possible. To achieve this he introduced a long and well-organized period of rehearsal, which included a thorough coordination of every element of the production, especially technical effects. His intensely personal work with actors was much more thorough and effective than most people suppose. Stanislavsky admired him, for they held much in common.

But it is perhaps in Russia that the various styles of directing may best be studied, not because Russian directing was better, but because in Russia the various theories of directing tended to be more radical, revolutionary, and sharply defined. Greatest of all Russian directors was Constantin Stanislavsky (1863–1938). Like the Duke of Saxe-Meiningen, who influenced him, Stanislavsky came to the theatre as an amateur, dissatisfied with the cheap and shallow ways of the commercial stage. Most of his principles of production resembled those of Saxe-Meiningen or went beyond them. Whereas the duke usually rehearsed a play for about five weeks, Stanislavsky stretched the period to as much as nine months—two years in the case of *Hamlet*. In Stanislavsky's company, the Moscow Art Theatre, the importance of bit parts became almost a religion. A fundamental axiom of the Art Theatre was "There are no small parts; there are only small actors"; accordingly, the greatest stars, even Stanislavsky himself, frequently appeared in bit parts. Devotion to the play rather than to the actor's personal success was crystallized by such standards as: "One must love art; and not one's self in art."[2] Numerous technical improvements were also made, chiefly in the area of greater authenticity and realism. Nor was Stanislavsky a slavish naturalist; some of his plays were exciting excursions into sheer theatricality.

But it was in the realm of acting that Stanislavsky's greatest contribution lay. In this he differed from Saxe-Meiningen, who had been something of a despot. While it has been said that Stanislavsky could imitate the duke's despotism when necessary, his basic method centered on stimulating actors to create for themselves. This probably accounts for much of the group loyalty and continuity that has characterized the Moscow Art Theatre. Actors with imagination and ideas had a chance to share in the creative process, and many of the greatest remained loyal to the company, giving it a character of permanence quite unusual in the world of the theatre.

In sharp contrast to the group effort and fundamentally naturalistic style of Stanislavsky stands the work of Vsevolod Meyerhold (1874–

---

[2] For these and other guiding principles see Constantin Stanislavski, *My Life in Art* (Boston: Little, Brown & Company, 1924), pp. 298–299.

1932). One of Stanislavsky's most brilliant pupils, he finally became so irritated by the quietness and naturalistic restraint of the Moscow Art Theatre that he broke away to set up a system of his own. He regarded the theatre not as a pale imitation of life but as something greater and more expressive than life. He probed for the essence of human behavior rather than the mere reproduction of conventional behavior as seen in daily life. He called for the banishment of pretense; everything was to be frankly theatrical. Actors often spoke directly to the audience; no attempt was made to mask spotlights or to disguise the elaborate scaffolding used to support ramps, springboards, and other paraphernalia on which his players (more acrobats than actors) were expected to perform.

Meyerhold's method of directing was as revolutionary as the style of his productions. He was the dictator—the superartist from whom all ideas sprang. At rehearsals his common statement was, "Observe me and do likewise."[3] He created all the parts; the performers merely imitated. His theatre was brilliant because he himself was brilliant. When he disappeared his theatre likewise disappeared.

Even in Russia, however, not all the best directors were identified with a definite style. One of the greatest, Eugene Vakhtangov (1883–1922), tended to take a compromise position, basing his work on the deep inner sincerity of acting characteristic of the Moscow Art players but heightening and sharpening this with some of the theatricality of Meyerhold. Vakhtangov's results were brilliant, and although he died in 1922 at the age of 39, his theatre still continues.

The compromise made by Vakhtangov seems characteristic of the best directors in England and America. As Cole and Chinoy have observed, most American directors are essentially pragmatic.[4] This was especially true of the really successful old pros of the British and American stage—men like Tyrone Guthrie, George Abbott, George S. Kaufman, and Moss Hart, who learned their profession the hard way, the natural way: by living, breathing, watching, and talking theatre; writing plays; acting in plays; and, finally, by directing plays. Even the really successful method directors, including Elia Kazan, Harold Clurman,

[3] See Norris Houghton, *Moscow Rehearsals* (New York: Harcourt Brace Jovanovich, 1936), chap. 4.
[4] Toby Cole and Helen Krich Chinoy, eds., *Directing the Play* (Indianapolis: Bobbs-Merrill, 1953), p. 65.

Robert Lewis, and Joshua Logan, were far more pragmatic and flexible than true believers in the method like to admit. None hesitated to break away from psychological naturalism whenever he felt that it would improve a production to do so; Kazan, for example, used many epic theatre techniques in directing both *J.B.* and *Sweet Bird of Youth*. Contradictions between theory and practice may be seen even in the methods of Stanislavsky himself, who, though world-famous for having encouraged actors to create for themselves, often demonstrated ideas, acted out bits of business, and even read lines for actors. In directing, it is results that count. Rules and systems are but a means to an end and are of value only to those with enough taste, judgment, and theatrical sensitivity to know when, how, and where to use them. The proof of the directing is in the performance.

Even such a brief view of a few directors from Saxe-Meiningen to the present day is enough to suggest that the director is of tremendous importance in shaping the destiny of the modern theatre. This is particularly true in the noncommercial productions of American high schools, colleges, and communities. In fact it is reasonably safe to say that the quality of a school production will depend very little upon the school's size, location, or general type, but almost entirely upon the skill and imagination of the director. It is conceivable that a sincere group of professional actors could get together and, without a regular director, produce an excellent play, but in the nonprofessional theatre the director is practically indispensable. He or she may stimulate the actors to create the play for themselves, after the method of Stanislavsky or may create it for them, after the manner of Meyerhold, but his or her skill (or lack of it) will soon determine the success or failure of the group.

Yet in spite of their obvious importance, directors do well to remind themselves that this importance is only indirect; their glory, if any, rests on their ability to make plays, not necessarily themselves, look great. This view has been seriously challenged, in recent years especially, by directors of absurdist or improvisational theatre. To them the director should be a creative artist, not an interpretive one. In accordance with the theories of Artaud, they go to a greater extreme than even Craig and Meyerhold in establishing the director as the supreme creative force in the theatre. Artaud, they remind us, was in outright rebellion against plays and playwrights. He urged the theatre to return to its primitive function: shocking, enthralling, and exciting the audience with sights and sounds. He had turned to the Oriental theatre, with its stress on production and spectacle, for a model. To Artaud the script was little more than an outline or a starting point. The director, with the help of the actors and technicians, was expected to be the real creative force. In America these ideas gained practical realization in schools of acting and in the achievements of improvisational groups, especially in the work of the Living Theatre under the leadership of Julian Beck and Judith Malina.

And yet for the most part, stage directors still prefer to think of themselves as artists who transform the printed page into life on the stage. This in no way implies that they are less imaginative or creative than the so-called creative artists. It simply means that their creativity and imagination are dedicated to the production of an author's script. To them, the play is the thing.

THE TRAINING OF THE DIRECTOR

Since the director is of such importance in creating a successful modern theatrical production, it would seem that our immediate concern should be to set up schools in which we could train as many directors as possible. The difficulty is that training a director is not as simple as training a mechanic or a typist. One is confronted immediately with the question of how and to what extent direction can be taught. Tyrone Guthrie pondered this problem and concluded, "The only way to learn how to direct a play is to get a play, to get a group of actors who are simple enough to let you direct them, and direct."[5]

Of course, it is unfair to quote such a brief comment from Guthrie's excellent book. He would have been the first to insist that this is not the whole answer or even a very good answer, and yet he hit upon an element of truth that educators—especially some American educators—should ponder. Overly simplified faith and optimism were characteristic of our nation's irrepressible youth. We had faith that we could make people good if only we passed enough laws, that protection from all the ills of life could be provided by purchasing enough insurance, that any-

---

[5] Tyrone Guthrie, *A Life in the Theatre* (New York: McGraw-Hill, 1959), p. 157.

neurotic to the p
and yet if the art
on the other hand
alone is not enou

PLANNING

Perhaps the first
much can I see o1
black marks that
mental or emotio
rial may literally
Taming of the Shi
howl with deligh
type. He or she m
from the printed
without a vivid c
fectively without

This ability t
mysterious inbor
in on the rich wo1
of dramatic litera
having been expc
able traumatic lov
sheltered, souls v
battle with wood
for ice cream, and
movie star. It is tl
lively imagination

Nor must th
Many of the best
first reading of a
produce the play,
environment, and
ing the play from
real people in a re
alizing opening 1

thing could be sold by enough high-powered advertising, that every team could be a winner if it only practiced enough, and that we could flood the nation with outstanding stage directors by simply offering enough college courses in stage direction. Unfortunately, the stage director, like the writer and the public speaker, is first and foremost a total human being: a complex of all that one has inherited plus all that one has acquired by living, especially during the crucial early years of childhood. No college course in stage direction can hope to match the importance of such personal traits as intelligence, tact, and leadership; nor can a college course instill the necessary physical and emotional capacity to endure hard work, to love dramatic literature, or to experience the indispensable desire to bring literature to life on the stage.

On the other hand, the only attitude more foolish than the one that assumes that conscious training could make a director out of anybody is the attitude that conscious training is of no value whatever. Even if we limit our discussion to college training, we can quickly compile a host of benefits. To begin with, let us glance at some potential contributions of college courses in general. Courses in art and music have obvious value; psychology digs at the very roots of human behavior; physics can provide a basic understanding of sound and light; and above all, the study of dramatic literature concerns the very core of a director's work.

Any college with an excellent theatre department offers other aids to the would-be director. First is the chance to see plays, some of which will probably be excellent and some very poor; but an occasional failure may accelerate rather than inhibit the learning process. Then there is the practical work in acting, stagecraft, lighting, designing, costuming, and playwriting, plus conversations, arguments, and excitement—theatrical atmosphere in general. In fact, the art of directing almost seems to be acquired by osmosis. Take the right kind of human beings, soak them for a few years in a healthy, stimulating theatrical environment, and they are likely to come out saturated with whatever it takes to be a director. This was obviously the chief way Moss Hart, George Abbott, and many others learned to direct.

But having admitted the importance of heredity and early environment, plus the value of education in general and of theatre experience in particular, there is still room for a specialized course in stage direction itself. Above all, such a course affords the chance Tyrone Guthrie calls for: to learn to direct by directing in a situation in which competition is

keen and c
ed for real
evaluation
the ideas a
clude that
in directin
memorizin
rich and sti
ty to learn l

Even with
plexity of th

the dire
excitabl
foreman
an analy
he arms
and voc

In othe
sensitivity c
ciency and c
not be mutu
as well as th
well as the a
artistic geni
nizational a
painting and
they choose,

6 The subject of c
dren's Theatre I
Creative Dramat
7 Guthrie, op. cit.

the play in every detail as it might appear on the stage in the perfect production. But regardless of method, the director's enthusiasm, dreams, and imagination must somehow be aroused.

Most teachers and texts on directing put great stress on analysis—analysis of such elements as theme, purpose, characterization, style, and period. Such analysis can be very useful if well done, not only because of the clear insight it affords for directors but also because it helps them communicate this insight to actors. The only trouble is that formal analysis can easily degenerate into academic drudgery. Accordingly, Harold Clurman, like most professional directors, tends to be skeptical about its value. On the other hand, the thoroughness with which a good professional director explores the possibilities of a script would put most college students to shame. Clurman, Kazan, and other method directors tend to search in depth for the basic motivating factors:—the wants, drives, and desires of the various characters. They dig for the factors that humanize a play and make it emotionally exciting, then search for ways to translate these drives into action. One has only to read the correspondence between Elia Kazan and Archibald MacLeish concerning the production of J.B.[8] or the penetrating analysis that went into Kazan's production of A Streetcar Named Desire[9] to appreciate the energy and imagination that went into his preliminary work as a director.

Such an analysis tends to take the form of sketchy notes; for example, the following is from a director's analysis of Sophocles' Electra:

Drives
Hunger for justice and revenge.

Murderers of her father, far from being punished, have gloated and prospered. Have banished her brother, have ruined her life.

Obsessed with determination to be strong and true—contempt for weakness and compromise.

Underneath, but distorted, is hunger for love: yearning for father, brother, life and love that might have been.

8 "The Staging of a Play," Esquire, May 1959, pp. 144–158.
9 Cole and Chinoy, op. cit., pp. 296–310.

neurotic to the po
and yet if the art t
on the other hand
alone is not enoug

PLANNING

Perhaps the first q
much can I see on t
black marks that ma
mental or emotiona
rial may literally be
Taming of the Shrew
howl with delight.
type. He or she must
from the printed pag
without a vivid conc
fectively without hav

This ability to e
mysterious inborn gi
in on the rich world o
of dramatic literature
having been exposed.
able traumatic love af
sheltered, souls who
battle with wooden g
for ice cream, and no g
movie star. It is the rea
lively imagination can

Nor must the valu
Many of the best direc
first reading of a scrip
produce the play, howe
environment, and actio
ing the play from any l
real people in a real wo
alizing opening night—

thing could be sold by enough high-powered advertising, that every team could be a winner if it only practiced enough, and that we could flood the nation with outstanding stage directors by simply offering enough college courses in stage direction. Unfortunately, the stage director, like the writer and the public speaker, is first and foremost a total human being: a complex of all that one has inherited plus all that one has acquired by living, especially during the crucial early years of childhood. No college course in stage direction can hope to match the importance of such personal traits as intelligence, tact, and leadership; nor can a college course instill the necessary physical and emotional capacity to endure hard work, to love dramatic literature, or to experience the indispensable desire to bring literature to life on the stage.

On the other hand, the only attitude more foolish than the one that assumes that conscious training could make a director out of anybody is the attitude that conscious training is of no value whatever. Even if we limit our discussion to college training, we can quickly compile a host of benefits. To begin with, let us glance at some potential contributions of college courses in general. Courses in art and music have obvious value; psychology digs at the very roots of human behavior; physics can provide a basic understanding of sound and light; and above all, the study of dramatic literature concerns the very core of a director's work.

Any college with an excellent theatre department offers other aids to the would-be director. First is the chance to see plays, some of which will probably be excellent and some very poor; but an occasional failure may accelerate rather than inhibit the learning process. Then there is the practical work in acting, stagecraft, lighting, designing, costuming, and playwriting, plus conversations, arguments, and excitement—theatrical atmosphere in general. In fact, the art of directing almost seems to be acquired by osmosis. Take the right kind of human beings, soak them for a few years in a healthy, stimulating theatrical environment, and they are likely to come out saturated with whatever it takes to be a director. This was obviously the chief way Moss Hart, George Abbott, and many others learned to direct.

But having admitted the importance of heredity and early environment, plus the value of education in general and of theatre experience in particular, there is still room for a specialized course in stage direction itself. Above all, such a course affords the chance Tyrone Guthrie calls for: to learn to direct by directing in a situation in which competition is

keen and d
ed for real
evaluation,
the ideas an
clude that d
in directing
memorizing
rich and stir
ty to learn by

Even with the
plexity of the t

the director
excitable, u
foreman of
an analytic
he arms him
and vocabul

In other wo
sensitivity of an
ciency and orgar
not be mutually
as well as the exe
well as the artist.
artistic genius oft
nizational ability
painting and writ
they choose, work

⁶ The subject of director t
dren's Theatre Director,'
Creative Dramatics in the
⁷ Guthrie, op. cit., pp. 152-

the play in every detail as it might appear on the stage in the perfect production. But regardless of method, the director's enthusiasm, dreams, and imagination must somehow be aroused.

Most teachers and texts on directing put great stress on analysis—analysis of such elements as theme, purpose, characterization, style, and period. Such analysis can be very useful if well done, not only because of the clear insight it affords for directors but also because it helps them communicate this insight to actors. The only trouble is that formal analysis can easily degenerate into academic drudgery. Accordingly, Harold Clurman, like most professional directors, tends to be skeptical about its value. On the other hand, the thoroughness with which a good professional director explores the possibilities of a script would put most college students to shame. Clurman, Kazan, and other method directors tend to search in depth for the basic motivating factors:—the wants, drives, and desires of the various characters. They dig for the factors that humanize a play and make it emotionally exciting, then search for ways to translate these drives into action. One has only to read the correspondence between Elia Kazan and Archibald MacLeish concerning the production of *J.B.*⁸ or the penetrating analysis that went into Kazan's production of *A Streetcar Named Desire*⁹ to appreciate the energy and imagination that went into his preliminary work as a director.

Such an analysis tends to take the form of sketchy notes; for example, the following is from a director's analysis of Sophocles' *Electra:*

Drives

Hunger for justice and revenge.

Murderers of her father, far from being punished, have gloated and prospered. Have banished her brother, have ruined her life.

Obsessed with determination to be strong and true—contempt for weakness and compromise.

Underneath, but distorted, is hunger for love: yearning for father, brother, life and love that might have been.

⁸ "The Staging of a Play," *Esquire,* May 1959, pp. 144–158.
⁹ Cole and Chinoy, op. cit., pp. 296–310.

thing could be sold by enough high-powered advertising, that every team could be a winner if it only practiced enough, and that we could flood the nation with outstanding stage directors by simply offering enough college courses in stage direction. Unfortunately, the stage director, like the writer and the public speaker, is first and foremost a total human being: a complex of all that one has inherited plus all that one has acquired by living, especially during the crucial early years of childhood. No college course in stage direction can hope to match the importance of such personal traits as intelligence, tact, and leadership; nor can a college course instill the necessary physical and emotional capacity to endure hard work, to love dramatic literature, or to experience the indispensable desire to bring literature to life on the stage.

On the other hand, the only attitude more foolish than the one that assumes that conscious training could make a director out of anybody is the attitude that conscious training is of no value whatever. Even if we limit our discussion to college training, we can quickly compile a host of benefits. To begin with, let us glance at some potential contributions of college courses in general. Courses in art and music have obvious value; psychology digs at the very roots of human behavior; physics can provide a basic understanding of sound and light; and above all, the study of dramatic literature concerns the very core of a director's work.

Any college with an excellent theatre department offers other aids to the would-be director. First is the chance to see plays, some of which will probably be excellent and some very poor; but an occasional failure may accelerate rather than inhibit the learning process. Then there is the practical work in acting, stagecraft, lighting, designing, costuming, and playwriting, plus conversations, arguments, and excitement—theatrical atmosphere in general. In fact, the art of directing almost seems to be acquired by osmosis. Take the right kind of human beings, soak them for a few years in a healthy, stimulating theatrical environment, and they are likely to come out saturated with whatever it takes to be a director. This was obviously the chief way Moss Hart, George Abbott, and many others learned to direct.

But having admitted the importance of heredity and early environment, plus the value of education in general and of theatre experience in particular, there is still room for a specialized course in stage direction itself. Above all, such a course affords the chance Tyrone Guthrie calls for: to learn to direct by directing in a situation in which competition is

keen and difficulties abundant, but in which real plays are being direct-ed for real audiences. A course in directing also offers a chance for self-evaluation, comparison, and criticism. Finally, it offers a chance to study the ideas and methods of great directors. It therefore seems safe to con-clude that directing can be taught—perhaps, more accurately, that skill in directing can be improved. This is not accomplished, however, by memorizing a few rules or formulas but primarily through exposure to a rich and stimulating theatrical environment that includes the opportuni-ty to learn by doing.[6]

DIRECTING: THEORY AND PRACTICE

Even with the best of training, the good director, because of the com-plexity of the task, is hard to find. According to Guthrie,

> the director, then, is partly an artist presiding over a group of other artists, excitable, unruly, childlike and intermittently "inspired." He is also the foreman of a factory, the abbot of a monastery, and the superintendent of an analytic laboratory. It will do no harm if, in addition to other weapons, he arms himself with the patience of a good nurse, together with the voice and vocabulary of an old-time sergeant-major.[7]

In other words, the job of directing calls for the imagination and sensitivity of an artist, the skill and patience of a teacher, and the effi-ciency and organization of an executive. These qualities, of course, need not be mutually exclusive. Skill in organization should help the teacher as well as the executive, and imagination should assist the executive as well as the artist. Unfortunately, in real life this is seldom the case. The artistic genius often lacks both the patience of the teacher and the orga-nizational ability of the executive. In some other arts—for example, in painting and writing—this presents no serious problem. Painters can, if they choose, work 24 hours one day and none the next, be irritable and

---

[6] The subject of director training is treated at greater length by the author in "Training for the Chil-dren's Theatre Director," in Geraldine B. Siks and Hazel Dunnington, eds., *Children's Theatre and Creative Dramatics in the United States* (Seattle: University of Washington Press, 1961).
[7] Guthrie, op. cit., pp. 152–153.

neurotic to the point where few people can bear to associate with them, and yet if the art they produce is great, they deserve to be great. Theatre, on the other hand, is a group art that demands teamwork. Artistic ability alone is not enough; ability as a teacher and executive is fundamental.

PLANNING THE PRODUCTION: THE DIRECTOR AS ARTIST

Perhaps the first question the would-be director should ask is, "How much can I see on the printed page?" One person can examine the little black marks that make up a page from *King Lear* without receiving either mental or emotional stimulation, while another reading the same material may literally be moved to tears. Or one may read a page from *The Taming of the Shrew* and think, "How utterly dull," while another may howl with delight. Obviously the good director is related to the latter type. He or she must be capable of extracting the play's dramatic essence from the printed page. A director can no more hope to direct effectively without a vivid concept of the play than a speaker can hope to speak effectively without having something to say.

This ability to extract the full value from the printed page is not a mysterious inborn gift, for it changes with experience; therefore, to tune in on the rich world of experience that others have recorded on the pages of dramatic literature, one must have lived. This has little to do with having been exposed. Some can go through wars, famine, and innumerable traumatic love affairs and yet experience less than other, apparently sheltered, souls who have known no greater warfare than a childhood battle with wooden guns, no greater hunger than a childhood craving for ice cream, and no greater love than a secret passion for some faraway movie star. It is the reaction to experience that counts. Sensitivity and a lively imagination can work wonders with very little experience.

Nor must the value of plain hard work and willpower be ignored. Many of the best directors probably receive little more from a hurried first reading of a script than the average reader. Once they decide to produce the play, however, they read and reread, visualizing characters, environment, and action. Some stimulate their imaginations by removing the play from any limitations of the stage, visualizing characters as real people in a real world. Others employ an opposite technique, visualizing opening night—crowds, orchestra, lights, curtain, and, finally,

---

Description
When we first see h[...]

Thin, hollow-eyes, g[...]
Almost pathological [...]
Own brother does n[...]

Yet she was born a [...]
    the most fortun[...]

Her mother (Clytem[...]
A brilliant and beau[...]
Iphigenia her "pet."[...]
Busy in social whirl.[...]
Inclined to hurt and [...]

Electra, even as chil[...]

Her father (Agamem[...]
Away from home [...]
    Handsome, kin[...]
She was his favorite [...]
Emotional crisis wh[...]

What happened?
Clytemnestra besid[...]
Electra quite unmo[...]

Shortly afterwards, [...]
Electra accidentally [...]
Violent reaction, bu[...]
Cold politeness. [...]
Electra begins to "n[...]
One hope during te[...]

The great day! [...]
Victorious return. C[...]
Hero's welcome for [...]
And then—before s[...]
    speak to her—[...]
    with bronze-he[...]

Weeks that followe[...]
Electra saves Orest[...]

the play in
production.
dreams, and
    Most te
analysis of s
period. Such
the clear ins
communicat
sis can easil
Clurman, lik
value. On th
sional direct
lege student
tend to seal
drives, and c
humanize a
to translate t
dence betw
production
production
imagination
    Such an
the followin

Drives
Hunger f

Murdere
        pere
Obsessec
    ness
Underne
    life a

8 "The Staging of
9 Cole and Chinoy

Her satisfaction in thus thwarting Clytemnestra and Aegisthus is short.
    Now she is constantly watched.
Years of grey dullness — years of endless waiting.

Chrysothemis and citizens of Argos make the best of it, adjust to the new
    rulers.
The crime goes unpunished — almost forgotten.

Electra more and more desperate.
Old love for her father now transferred to Orestes.
Daydreams of his return, nightmares of his death.

At this point the play begins.
Two "strangers" arrive from Corinth.
News of Orestes!
The urn with his ashes! Then the recognition scene! (No wonder one of the
    greatest in all literature.)

Lest the tragedy become one-sided and melodramatic, we should glance at a portion of the case for Clytemnestra:

Drives

Wants to live, to enjoy.
Wants to justify her love for Aegisthus, to justify the murder of Agamemnon.
Wants safety — freedom from fear — mainly fear of her own children.

Description

Healthy and wonderful appetite for life — like Rosalind Russell in *Auntie Mame.* Very handsome, intelligent; infinite variety like Cleopatra.
Disarmingly frank about love and sex.
Always good taste and style.

The above excerpts are obviously not intended for scholars or readers, but for actresses and directors. They are 95 percent imagination and 5 percent research, and yet such "case studies" can do much to humanize characters — to start the process of making the characters live for the director, who in turn tries to make them live for the actors and actresses and eventually, through them, for the audience. But such probing into characterization is only one of the many forms of analysis that may fire the director's imagination and enthusiasm. Sometimes the theme of the

Description
When we first see her:

Thin, hollow-eyes, gaunt — like war victim.
Almost pathological, almost animal.
Own brother does not even recognize her at first!

Yet she was born a Princess — beautiful, intelligent, destined to be one of
   the most fortunate.

Her mother (Clytemnestra):
A brilliant and beautiful woman but cold toward Electra.
Iphigenia her "pet."
Busy in social whirl.
Inclined to hurt and ridicule.

Electra, even as child, resented mother's vanity and sexy flirtations.

Her father (Agamemnon):
Away from home much of the time. Great hero in her eyes. The King!
   Handsome, kind, very fond of her.
She was his favorite: gifts, games, spring morning walks together.
Emotional crisis when he left for war with Troy.

What happened?
Clytemnestra beside herself with rage and grief over sacrifice of Iphigenia.
Electra quite unmoved — had been jealous.

Shortly afterwards, trauma!
Electra accidentally happens on Clytemnestra and Aegisthus in act of love.
Violent reaction, but suppressed.
Cold politeness.
Electra begins to "mother" sisters and brothers.
One hope during ten long years — "Someday my father will come home!"

The great day!
Victorious return. City wild with rejoicing.
Hero's welcome for Agamemnon.
And then — before she could give his treasured gifts — before he could even
   speak to her — before she could even touch him — he was cut down
   with bronze-headed axe!

Weeks that followed horrible.
Electra saves Orestes from death. He escapes into exile.

director is, of course, an unachieved ideal. Some directors succeed because they are artistic geniuses of such brilliance that in spite of eccentricities and disorganization, they still manage to produce exciting results. Others, with mediocre imaginations as artists, succeed through excellent management, including the loyalty, morale, and enthusiasm they stimulate in those about them. Still others succeed because of their gift in teaching, especially in teaching beginners to act.

No two directors are exactly alike. Techniques and systems that work for one may be useless in the hands of another. Stage directing, like other arts, displays a chronic antagonism toward standardization, and although beginners can learn much from others, there are still many secrets that they must discover for themselves. Textbooks, theories, or formulas can never replace intelligence, imagination, and an honest desire to transform a written script into vivid and meaningful life on the stage.

of the most amazing things I have ever experienced in the theatre; for not only the lines I had previously noted, but almost every line in the scene, took on new life and meaning.

But in most cases directors are not so fortunate as to find a single suggestion that ignites a whole scene. They must usually work slowly in much greater detail, preferably with only two or three actors at a time, coaxing meaning and life into each line and each action. Finally, in dealing with hopelessly untalented actors, directors reach an inevitable decision: they can let the actors remain as bad as they are and thereby ruin the scene, or they can resort to the technique of imitation. In early stages this need not require slavish imitation. If the line reads, "Leave the room, sir," the director may read it, "Get out of here." Only in the last stages of desperation should a director resort to performing a scene line by line in the hope that the actor can at least learn something by imitation. Unfortunate as this may be, there are times when it is better than nothing.

One other item should be noted before leaving the matter of demonstration and imitation, and that is that they are not necessarily directly related. It is possible for a director to read a line or perform a bit of business simply as an efficient means of communicating a new idea or concept to an actor, with no thought in the mind of either the director or the actor that an imitation is intended. It is as if the director had said, "Look, what about this possibility?" and the actor had responded with, "Excellent, let me try it." By the next rehearsal, both have probably forgotten where the idea came from and have probably assumed that it was always there. The kind of demonstration to avoid is the type that causes an actor to say at the next rehearsal, "Let me see, how did you want the line read?" Or perhaps even worse, "Oh, if I could only do it like you did!"

Run-throughs   It is possible to rehearse a play with such meticulous care that the separate pieces appear to be excellent, yet the total effect is a failure. In fact, this is one of the most common of the maladies that plague amateur dramatics. Every word is pronounced with vigor and every phrase hammered home with stress, but the things that matter— the story, the humanity, the drama—have all been lost. To gain perspective, to see the play as a whole, the director should occasionally move back in the auditorium and let the play run without interruption. Most textbooks recommend this procedure during polishing or coordinating director is, of course, an unachieved ideal. Some directors succeed because they are artistic geniuses of such brilliance that in spite of eccentricities and disorganization, they still manage to produce exciting results. Others, with mediocre imaginations as artists, succeed through excellent management, including the loyalty, morale, and enthusiasm they stimulate in those about them. Still others succeed because of their gift in teaching, especially in teaching beginners to act.

No two directors are exactly alike. Techniques and systems that work for one may be useless in the hands of another. Stage directing, like other arts, displays a chronic antagonism toward standardization, and although beginners can learn much from others, there are still many secrets that they must discover for themselves. Textbooks, theories, or formulas can never replace intelligence, imagination, and an honest desire to transform a written script into vivid and meaningful life on the stage.

CHAPTER 9

ACTING

Of the arts and crafts that compose theatre, acting is probably the most glamorous and fascinating, as well as the most controversial and confusing. From Thespis to Albert Finney, the fickle public has exalted beyond all proportion those few who somehow caught its fancy, while ignoring, if not abusing, others of almost equal ability. Nor is the fickleness of fame the only confusing factor about acting: Its theories are complex and contradictory; advocates of special techniques violently oppose one another; and the crowning irony of all is that those with no formal training whatever sometimes excel others who have spent most of a lifetime in study and practice.

Some of the perplexity is due to the momentary quality of the art. Until the movies came to provide a record of what was said and done, the actor's art was preserved only in the memories of those who experienced it. Then, too, the final appeal of acting is subjective. Acting is great only if it produces a great effect upon a given audience. But the audience is not a fixed phenomenon. Its tastes and habits vary like the fashions in dress. Our great-grandparents applauded actors who played to their audiences, maintaining a warm, friendly relationship. With the advent of realism such acting was branded as "elocutionary," and the naturalistic approach became the vogue. Today we in turn have grown impatient with naturalistic actors who, in their excessive fear of playing front or projecting their voices, present the audience with the inexpressive profile and mumbled speech of daily life. Instead we cry that art should be greater, more vivid, more expressive than life. In fact, some nonillusionistic styles of acting, such as those employed in epic theatre and especially in happenings, carry frank theatricality and actor-audience contact to an extent that would have startled even our great-grandparents.

But in spite of the complexity and intangibility of the art, isn't it possible to discern a few lasting standards and values? In spite of their many differences, haven't most of the greatest actors had much in common? Let us begin with a quick sampling of history, by looking briefly at a few of the stage immortals.

THE HISTORY OF ACTING

THE ACTORS OF THE CLASSICAL AND MEDIEVAL PERIODS

Thespis was not the only actor in Greece whose name has survived; there are many, including Aeschylus and Sophocles, who, like Thespis, performed in their own plays. Wearing built-up shoes (cothurni) and a mask with a high headpiece (onkos), and performing in huge outdoor theatres, these actors must have found great volume, rich intonation, and a certain degree of stylized movement necessary.

On the other hand, the common concept of classic acting as highly conventionalized and artificial may be misleading. Remember that Thespis was the first actor, Aeschylus was the first to use two actors on stage at the same time, and Sophocles the first to use three. As a new art acting had had little opportunity to crystallize into any stereotyped code of behavior. While this does not mean that Greek acting was natural, it does suggest that it was comparatively fresh and original. Cole and Chinoy cite examples that bear out the impression that classic acting was by no means devoid of impulse, inspiration, and emotion.[1] Aesop, a

---

[1] Toby Cole and Helen Krich Chinoy, eds., *Actors on Acting* (New York: Crown, 1970), pp. 14–15.

Greek-born actor, performing in Rome, became so emotional while playing Atreus that he accidentally killed one of the servants; the great Polus in playing Electra made the tragic heroine's grief convincing to himself and to his audience by carrying the ashes of his own son in the urn supposed to contain the ashes of Orestes.

Whereas Greek actors usually enjoyed relatively high social standing, those of Rome were almost without exception foreigners and slaves. One actor finally gained such prominence, however, that he was awarded his freedom. This was Quintus Roscius (c. 126 B.C. – 62 B.C.), who was

Figure 9:2 Comic actors. From a vase painting.

primarily a comedian rather than a tragedian. His success won him fame and the friendship of the great Cicero. To this day to call an actor a second Roscius is to pay him one of the highest of compliments.

From the death of Roscius there is a span of 1600 years to the *commedia dell'arte* players. Here was acting in one of its most intriguing phases, for in these troupes the players were supreme. They used no scripts, no memorized lines, no elaborate scenic effects. Following nothing more

FIGURE 9:3 Commedia del'arte: horseplay, imagination, and vitality.

than a rough scenario, these audacious performers faced their audiences prepared for anything. Singing, dancing, quick wit, and alert imaginations combined to spin together some of the finest spontaneous theatre the world has ever known. According to one account,

> they were as chock-full of malice as of wit. . . . They were not willing, like silly school-boys, to recite only what they had learnt from a master. . . . They had only to receive a scenario, which someone had scribbled on his knee, to meet their stage manager in the morning to arrange the outlines of the plot . . . the rest they could invent themselves. . . . They had a store of proverbs, sallies, charades, riddles, recitations, cock-and-bull stories, and songs jumbled together in their heads. . . . They seized opportunity by the forelock and turned the least accident into profit. They drew inspiration from the time, the place, the color of the sky, or topic of the day, and established a current between their audience and themselves out of which the mad farce arose, the joint product of them all. . . . Harlequin, armed with blacksmith's tools, draws four of Pantaloon's soundest teeth. He waits on Don Juan at table and wipes the plates on the seat of his breeches. . . . There is only one plate of macaroni between them and they eat it in floods of tears. . . . Their extravagant fancy broke loose before an audience and burst into fire and soared to the sky, a marvel of balance. Explosions of wild laughter followed, and wild confusion, and a medley of caricatures, dreams, buffooneries, scurrility, poetry, and love.[2]

Although this is obviously an imaginative rather than an objective record of what a *commedia* performance was like, it does suggest its exciting possibilities. Actors capable of such brilliant improvisation must have been hard to find, even though most of them specialized in the playing of only one character. Among the players who mastered this art of improvisation was the beautiful, talented, well-educated Isabella Andreini (1562–1604), who won fame and admiration wherever she appeared. Foreshadowing the glamor that so often has attached itself to great actors and actresses were the tributes extended at the time of her early death. The greatest of these came from her husband, the famous actor and manager Francisco Andreini, who in his sorrow left the stage, never to appear again.

[2] Philippe Monnier, ''The Venetian Theatre and the Italian Comedy of the Eighteenth Century,'' *Mask*, January 1911, pp. 104–105.

FIGURE 9:4   Strolling actresses dressing in a barn; a 1738 etching by William Hogarth.

THE ACTORS OF ENGLAND

Our knowledge of acting during the Elizabethan period is limited. Shakespeare's company, the Lord Chamberlain's Men, with Richard Burbage as the leading man, appears to have championed a more lifelike style than its rivals. Certainly Hamlet's advice to the players indicates that Shakespeare was striving for a more convincing effect than that achieved by those who "saw the air with [their] hands," "tear a passion to tatters," "out-Herod Herod," and "split the ears of the groundlings."[3]

During the Restoration, women first appeared on the English stage. Mrs. Bracegirdle, Mrs. Barry, and the fabulous Nell Gwyn were among those who emerged as favorites. They, along with such stars as Thomas Betterton, began to assume such importance that by the middle of the eighteenth century, the players tended to overshadow the play, a tendency likewise seen in France, Italy, Germany, and America.

[3] William Shakespeare, *Hamlet,* act 3, sc. 2.

In England the most famous of the eighteenth-century actors was David Garrick (1717–1779). He entered the theatre not as a stage-struck student of acting, but as an amiable, intelligent, witty businessman. His approach was fresh, original, and natural. "If this young fellow is right," cried Quinn, leading actor of the old school, "then we have all been wrong." Garrick had none of the arty, temperamental, or neurotic qualities that the general public seems so determined to associate with acting. He was a close friend of Samuel Johnson, Oliver Goldsmith, and other leading figures of his day. He was an excellent executive and one of the best managers the Drury Lane Theatre ever had. Unlike some stars, who were inclined to "hog the show," Garrick surrounded himself with an

FIGURE 9:5 David Garrick caught between comedy and tragedy; a painting by Sir Joshua Reynolds.

outstanding company and was responsible for giving a number of actors and actresses, including Sarah Siddons, a boost toward success. As to his acting, he seems to have been extremely versatile. His contemporaries regarded him as equally effective in both comedy and tragedy, although today there is a tendency to favor the reports of his comedy. His style, while regarded as very natural in his day, was "not above the stops, starts, and drawn-out death scenes that drew applause."[4] He also played most of his roles in lavish contemporary costume, but in spite of what may seem minor shortcomings, he brought freshness, health, and common sense to the theatre of his time.

Those who insist on believing that actors should be eccentric and temperamental take delight in pointing to Edmund Kean (1787–1833), who followed Garrick by half a century. Kean was the typical artistic genius, and his genius had the usual roots in a life of suffering and misery. His debut at Drury Lane as Shylock reads like a romantic extravaganza. Almost overnight he had London at his feet and within a few years had amassed a fortune. Tales of his tragic power are numerous. During a performance as Sir Giles Overreach in Massinger's *A New Way to Pay Old Debts*, his final scene is reported to have achieved such a pitch of intensity that "One of the actresses on stage, Mrs. Glover, overcome with fright at the horror depicted on his countenance, fainted; [Lord] Byron at the same time was seized in his box by a convulsive fit; whilst women went into hysterics and the whole house burst into a wild clamour of applause."[5] Coleridge remarked: "To see Kean was to read Shakespeare by flashes of lightning."[6] Though obviously intended as a compliment to the brilliance with which Kean illuminated certain Shakespearean passages, this remark contains connotations that are apt in quite another sense, for Kean was erratic and undependable. He gave bad performances as well as inspired ones, made enemies in both England and America, and undoubtedly hastened his own death by alcohol and dissipation. But at his best there is no denying that he was a genius—romantic, inspirational, and unpredictable.

England's leading actor toward the close of the nineteenth century again presents a character contrast to the eccentric genius of Edmund

---

[4] Cole and Chinoy, op. cit., p. 95.
[5] J. F. Molloy, *The Life and Adventures of Edmund Kean* (London: Ward and Downey, 1888) p. 248.
[6] Cole and Chinoy, op. cit., p. 327.

Kean, for Sir Henry Irving (1838–1905) was above all things respectable and conscientious. Like Garrick, he excelled both as an actor and as a manager. Born in poverty and obscurity, not unusually gifted in either voice or body, he achieved success through infinite care in perfecting details. No one has ever done more to elevate the stage in the opinion of those outside the theatre. He insisted that the actor, as a member of a learned profession, was entitled to the same esteem and respect as the doctor or the lawyer. His own conduct was exemplary. He presented what were considered masterpieces of literature with the strictest reference to historical accuracy. In recognition of his contributions, he was knighted in 1895, the first actor to be thus honored.

THE ACTORS OF FRANCE AND ITALY

Like England, France produced more than its share of great stars. To begin with, there was Molière himself, who rates, along with Garrick and Roscius, as one of the great comedians of all time and who in his plays conducted a witty crusade against the affectation and bombast of players in rival companies. Then there was Michel Baron (1653–1729), one of Molière's young actors, who carried the natural style into tragedy and did so with tremendous success. Intoxicated by his fame, he is reported to have maintained that the world had known only two truly great actors, Roscius and Baron. In 1691, at the age of 38, he retired from the stage, convinced that there were no more worlds to conquer.

Perhaps the most famous of the early eighteenth-century French actresses was the beautiful Adrienne Lecouvreur (1692–1730). Her acting followed the natural style of Baron, and her tragic death (she was poisoned at the height of her fame) has inspired both poets and playwrights. According to Voltaire, she "almost invented the art of speaking to the heart, and of showing feeling and truth where formerly had been shown little but artificiality and declamation."[7]

From nineteenth-century France came Sarah Bernhardt (1844–1923) and Benoît Constant Coquelin (1841–1909). Bernhardt, "the divine Sarah," was undoubtedly one of the world's great personality actresses. Temperamental and sensational on stage and off, she was always color-

[7] Ibid., p. 148.

ful and easy to publicize. During her early years she vacillated between the stage and the Church. Her entire life was spiced with temperamental outbursts and love affairs. In her later years she often slept in a casket. Yet on the stage, with the help of a magnificent voice, she maintained her reputation as the world's greatest actress for nearly half a century.

In contrast to the eccentric genius of Bernhardt, Coquelin was famed for his logic and mental control. He established what Stanislavsky called the representational school of acting, which advocated creative imagination, study, and emotion during rehearsals but insisted upon complete objectivity during performance. In other words, he believed that the performance should be fundamentally intellectual imitation of what had been worked out during rehearsal. This unemotional approach was challenged by Sir Henry Irving, and a great controversy ensued, which we will consider later.

Sarah Bernhardt's greatest rival was the Italian actress Eleonora Duse (1859–1924). The contrast between the two was as marked as that between Garrick and Kean. Duse's private life was restless and tragic, but on stage she exhibited a sincerity and quiet greatness that will always be admired. Bernhardt always played Bernhardt, but Duse submerged her own personality in the role. Her objective was to live the part; her style was simplicity and sincerity. Duse made one film, which has been preserved, and while she was ill at the time, over 60, and hampered by a hopeless script, her acting has not aged. Present-day audiences who have seen the film have been struck by the truth and dignity of her performance. In contrast, Bernhardt's films of the same period seem overacted and sometimes ridiculous. This leads to the conclusion that Shaw, as usual, was right, for he chose Duse as the greater of the two, maintaining that Bernhardt projected only her own charm but that Duse projected the charm of whatever character she portrayed.

The sincere approach of Duse was combined with the inspirational power of the romanticists in another Italian actor, Tommaso Salvini (1829–1916). Everyone who saw him seems to agree that in roles like Othello he was unequaled. A deep, almost religious sincerity seemed to characterize his playing. Like Duse, his aim was to live the part. Tradition has it that long before the performance began he assumed the spiritual, as well as the physical, character of Othello and remained completely in character until the performance concluded. He began his portrayal of the Moor with such simplicity and quietness that audiences were at first unimpressed, but as the poisoned suggestions of Iago began to take effect, he gradually changed into one of the most powerfully tragic figures ever seen. It was from watching Salvini that Stanislavsky received many of the impressions that were to lay the foundation of the Moscow Art Theatre and the Stanislavsky system of acting.

THE ACTORS OF AMERICA

In nineteenth-century America, at least three actors managed to gain international fame. The first, Edwin Forrest (1806–1872), was a man of enormous physical vigor with a powerful voice. His acting was characterized by rough realism and tragic dignity. Strong-willed, violent-tempered, and egocentric, he made enemies in both England and America. His sensational feud with the English tragedian William Charles Macready culminated in the disastrous Astor Place riot. The trouble that led to this outbreak had begun several years earlier when Forrest, playing in London, was hissed during a performance of *Macbeth*. Accepting the rumor that Macready was responsible for the insult, Forrest attended his rival's performance of *Hamlet* and deliberately hissed Macready. The audience was shocked, and the fiery old English actor was so choked with rage that he was momentarily unable to continue the performance. Ill will continued to mount until during Macready's visit to America in 1849, the hot-tempered partisans of each clashed in a bloody riot inside and outside the Astor Place Opera House in New York, and many persons were killed. It is perhaps fitting that such a rugged individual as Edwin Forrest should have been the first American actor to attract international attention. Certainly he had many of the qualities commonly associated with the frontier.

In most respects Edwin Booth (1833–1893), America's second and perhaps greatest actor, was a marked contrast to Forrest, for his style of playing is usually referred to as quiet, intelligent, and profound. The son of the English-born tragedian Junius Brutus Booth, Edwin grew up in a theatrical environment. Although his father did not want him to act, the fates ruled otherwise. By the time he was 31, Booth was generally recognized as outstanding, particularly in *Hamlet*, which ran for a record of 100 nights. At this climax of success came the shock of his brother's assassination of Abraham Lincoln. Temporarily Edwin retired from the stage, but he eventually returned to give some of the greatest perfor-mances the American theatre has ever seen. Hamlet was still his most distinguished role. His melancholy temperament and essential loneli-ness gave to the famous character a depth and understanding that may well have been unequaled. His acting, however, was moody and un-even; one might see a great performance or a mediocre one. But in spite of these limitations, the fact remains that few, if any, have equaled Ed-win Booth at his best.

The third outstanding American actor of the nineteenth century was Joseph Jefferson (1829–1905). Those who doubt the actor's importance in the creation of great theatre should pause to consider the case of *Rip Van Winkle*. In the hands of anyone else, the play has always been me-diocre, but with Jefferson as Rip it acquired qualities of greatness. Both as an actor and as a man, Jefferson excelled in human warmth, kindli-ness, and understanding. His autobiography contains some excellent hints on acting, as well as much common sense about both the theatre and life in general.

As for the twentieth century, it seems safer to avoid the hazards of arbitrary selection that would be entailed in the selection of four or five from among the many outstanding actors and actresses of our day. Moreover, it is doubtful that further discussion would greatly advance our basic purpose in this chapter, which is to try to discover something about the fundamentals of the art of acting itself. Several relatively com-plete analyses of the background and training of successful actors have as yet failed to throw much light on the subject.[8] Carefully conducted psychological studies of actor personalities, aptitudes, and interests have fared little better.[9] Actors and acting simply refuse to be neatly cod-ified. As we have already seen, there seems to be no common pattern. Some, like Kean, are temperamental and neurotic; others, like Garrick, dependable and level-headed. Some, like Bernhardt, project their own personalities; others, like Duse, the personalities of their characters.

---

[8] For a summary of these, see Elsie Turner, "A Study of the Background and Training of Fifty Promi-nent American Actors," (M.A. thesis, University of Minnesota, 1954). Another excellent source is Cole and Chinoy, op. cit. The authors draw no dogmatic conclusions; they allow the actors to speak for themselves. The reader is free to study, to reflect, to test in terms of his or her own experience, and finally to draw his or her own conclusions.

[9] Francis E. Drake, "A Study of Personality Traits of Students Interested in Acting" (Ph. D. disserta-tion, University of Minnesota, 1949).

Some, like Coquelin, try to perform with mental objectivity; others, like Irving, to feel the emotions they portray. More detailed study would reveal that many great actors came from theatrical families, though many others did not; that some succeeded through unquenchable determination, though a few maintained that they did not even want to act. We would find, however, that most did have some early experience with the stage, that most lived interesting lives, that most did not slavishly imitate the systems or techniques of others, and that most knew how to work and work hard. Yet even these rather obvious statements are subject to qualification.

SCHOOLS OF ACTING

Leaving the actors themselves, let us turn to teachers, textbooks, and schools of acting in an effort to learn something about the art. Prior to the twentieth century the approach to acting was essentially external. Teachers and texts tended to stress stage techniques, movement, voice, diction, and pronunciation. If we view acting as a response to an imaginary stimulus, the nineteenth-century (and earlier) schools of acting were concerned almost exclusively with the response, and usually with an attempt to codify and standardize the response. In the hands of uninspired and unimaginative teachers, this eventually led to the stilted posturing and declamation of the elocutionary system. Textbooks literally pictured standard poses for each emotion and each attitude; elaborate charts dictated the correct positions for hands, head, feet, and torso. The better actors and teachers struggled against this elocutionary trend, especially since it was so completely at odds with the new theatrical trend toward realism or naturalism. Finally they found their new messiah in Stanislavsky, who evolved a new approach to the problem that has come to be known as the Stanislavsky method, or simply as the method.

Essentially, Stanislavsky tried to establish a system or technique for setting one's creative and imaginative faculties to work. His system is based on the assumption that if actors are truly sensitive to the stimulus of the imaginary situation, their reactions will largely take care of themselves. Stanislavsky recognized that in order for the response to be effective, body and voice should be relaxed and healthy, free and sensitive to shades of thought and feeling, but the core of the response was

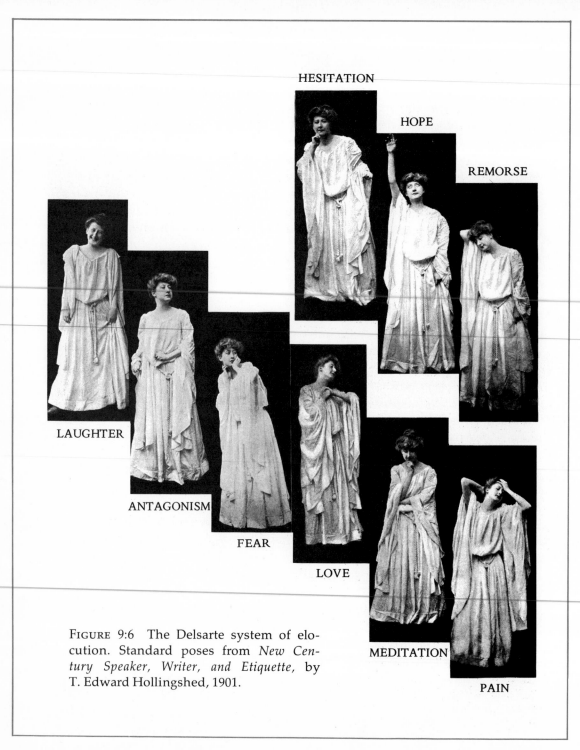

LAUGHTER

ANTAGONISM

FEAR

HESITATION

HOPE

REMORSE

LOVE

MEDITATION

PAIN

FIGURE 9:6 The Delsarte system of elocution. Standard poses from *New Century Speaker, Writer, and Etiquette*, by T. Edward Hollingshed, 1901.

left to individual actors, not thrust upon them mechanically by rules, charts, instructors, or the example of other actors. The essential question for each actor was, "What would I do if I were this character and confronted with his or her situation?" As a result, such things as imagination, concentration, memory of emotion, dramatic action, objectives, and relaxation became typical units of study for students of the Stanislavsky method.

Stanislavsky's influence was especially strong in America, partly because his method was espoused by members of the Group Theatre (which included such talented artists as Lee Strasberg, Harold Clurman, and Elia Kazan), partly because it was ideally suited for the realistic and naturalistic plays of the period, and partly because it harmonized with the liberal ideals of educational theatres in American colleges and universities.[10] But this widespread enthusiasm for the method may have been its greatest weakness. No one has yet devised a way to protect a great man or woman from his or her well-meaning but inadequate disciples or to protect a good idea from uninspired and overly rigid imitation. A method cult soon developed, whereby the actor's inner life was pampered and exalted with little regard to the needs of the play.

Moreover, as Maxine Klein points out, the method, as interpreted by most of its American disciples, has tended to have a "slowness, a heaviness, a lack of vigor," largely because it has usually focused on the small moments of human experience rather than "the spectacular, the extraordinary, and the magnificent."[11] Then too, method actors and actresses have tended to be notoriously difficult to direct and, worst of all, have tended to forget the audience, even caring little whether they could be seen or heard. Motion picture and television cameras could pick up their subtle expressions and mumblings, but on the stage they were uninteresting and even a bit insulting to audiences, who felt cheated and left out.[12]

These limitations became painfully apparent as resident professional theatres began to be established across the country, and as directors turned to England or Canada in an effort to find actors who could be

---

[10] Stanislavsky's Moscow Art Theatre visited New York in 1923. His first and most influential book, *An Actor Prepares*, was published in English in 1936.

[11] Maxine Klein, *Time, Space and Design for Actors* (Boston: Houghton Mifflin, 1975).

[12] Those who wish to gain a fairly complete, sensible, and witty view of the method would do well to read Robert Lewis, *Method—or Madness?* (New York: Samuel French, 1958).

seen and heard. As a result, many acting teachers in America during the third quarter of the twentieth century turned from the method to a stress on vocal and physical development that resembled some of the more serious work of the elocutionists. Game playing, inspired largely by the work of Viola Spolin, also became popular. Moreover, not only has the content of acting courses been in a state of turmoil, but there has been bitter controversy concerning the very type of school in which acting should be taught. Stripped to its essence there were two basic approaches: (1) the professional schools, patterned after the European model, believed that training for a career in acting should start somewhere during the high school years and be concentrated into about three years of intensive work on the art of acting and (2) the American approach, which was far more indefinite, extending over a much longer period—children's theatre in elementary schools, dramatics in high schools, an undergraduate major in college, specialization in acting in a graduate school, followed by an internship in a professional company.

There are, of course, infinite variations of the above patterns, but so far there has been no conclusive evidence as to the relative effectiveness of any of them. This has often prompted cynics to repeat the adage, "Actors are born, not made."

CAN ACTING BE TAUGHT?

As already mentioned, a newcomer may sometimes outshine others who have spent most of a lifetime struggling with the art. In such instances someone always comes forth with a solution: "The newcomer was born with talent, the others without." This is very convincing until someone asks, "But what is talent?" One who wishes to keep acting veiled in mystery can reply, "A special gift with which some are endowed." One who wants to understand, however, must search for a more rational explanation. The question then becomes, "Are actors born inherently different from other human beings?" If actors are inherently different, no one has as yet isolated the difference. Tests, reasonably numerous in recent years, have failed to disclose any particular traits or aptitudes of unusual significance.[13] In general, the term *talent* is probably used as if it

---

[13] Drake, op. cit.

were synonymous with general effectiveness. As such, the term is not objectionable. But if used to imply some mysterious or special gift, it may become little more than a protective escape for the incompetent teacher, who, unable to get results, dismisses the student as "untalented." Talent is probably nothing more mysterious than the total pattern of abilities and aptitudes involving voice, body, personality, past experience and a knack for abandoning oneself to the world of make-believe. In other words, the actor or actress, like the director, is first of all a total human being, a complex bundle of habits, memories, and attitudes, not just a few specialized techniques learned in a dramatic school.

At the opposite extreme from the contention that actors are born and that it is all a matter of talent lies the view that the beginner in acting should consider himself or herself as humble and as helpless as the beginner in other arts, such as instrumental music. This view, while useful in motivating a lazy student, is essentially false, for as already admitted, a beginner can and often does act and act rather well. Imagine a beginner in violin or piano offering a public concert after practicing a few hours per day for three or four weeks! The difference is not hard to understand. The beginning musician can be assumed to have scarcely touched a violin or piano, whereas the beginning actor has been using his instruments (body, imagination, and voice) for better or for worse since the day he or she was born. Acting, then, is not so much an entirely new skill as it is a matter of adapting what one already has to a new situation. This has disadvantages as well as advantages. It throws a premium upon the intangible thing called *attitude*. It requires a delicate adjustment: The actor or actress must concentrate most of his or her attention upon the play — the imaginary situation — at a time when the real social stimulus, success or failure before an audience, is enormous. It may be more difficult for actors to gain perfect control of their instruments than for musicians to gain perfect control of theirs, but in the beginning actors are far ahead.

To return to the question of whether acting can be taught, it seems obvious that acting is neither wholly a matter of unborn talent nor wholly a matter of learning all from the beginning. It can be taught, provided that we think of teaching in the largest sense of that term, as the guiding and controlling of environment. Narrowed to the space of a few hours in a classroom, it is hard to say. Wonders are sometimes achieved during a single class or a single rehearsal, but again it is no reflection on the teacher or the student if habits and attitudes acquired over a lifetime are not easily changed. The teaching of acting is a challenging, frustrating, but fascinating task.

TO FEEL OR NOT TO FEEL

Today we tend to classify actors and actresses into two groups: method actors and technique actors. Such classification is seldom very accurate. There are endless compromises and variations and almost as many theories as there are actors. All this relates to an earlier controversy, which also tried to divide actors and actresses into two schools: (1) those who attempted to feel the emotions they portrayed—to live the part—and (2) those who tried to perform unemotionally, relying on rules and technical skill.

This question was originally posed in 1770 by the French philosopher and critic Denis Diderot, who startled many of his contemporaries by insisting that the actor should remain completely insensible to the emotion he portrays. The controversy reached a climax in 1888 when the English critic William Archer published a book on the subject entitled *Masks or Faces?* In spite of his thorough attempt to solve the problem, he ended in a rather inconclusive compromise, and the controversy still continues.

Logic tells us that in the final analysis it does not matter whether actors feel or not, as long as they present a pattern of voice and action that will make the audience feel. Those who doubt this should consider the shadows on a movie screen. Although the actors who created these shadows may have felt, the shadows themselves certainly do not feel, and yet these shadows move millions to tears, laughter, excitement, and all the vicarious sensations of romantic love. But proponents of feeling, although forced to admit that an actor does not have to feel in order to cause an audience to feel, still insist that a basic question remains: Are actors more likely to assume correct outward patterns—patterns that will convince and move their audiences—when feeling or not feeling?

They insist that actors, especially young ones, who feel and believe in what their characters in the play say and do are much more likely to be convincing. Otherwise, young actors tend to communicate not the drives and desires of their characters but their personal drives and desires as actors: their personal eagerness to succeed, their struggle to remember the next line, their elation when the comic line gets a laugh, their strained anxiety when it does not. Professionals may be able to think irrelevant thoughts and cover them up with technical skill, but raw beginners seem likely to make an audience understand, feel, and believe whatever they themselves understand, feel, and believe.

When Stanislavsky's theories were first proclaimed, proponents of feeling were elated, for he stated that good actors should experience the emotions they portray not just once or twice during rehearsals but to some extent during every performance. On the other hand, many were perplexed by Stainslavsky's scorn of actors who tried to portray emotions in general. Finally it became clear that the great problem all along had largely been one of semantics: words like *emotion* and *feeling* simply have widely different connotations to different people. For example, anyone who has worked any length of time in the theatre is familiar with the young actor or actress who tries too hard, struggles to force an emotion, and gets excited about acting for the sake of acting. Helen Hayes, Katharine Cornell, and other opponents of feeling cited such behavior as examples of what happens when an actor or actress tries to feel the part. Stanislavsky, on the contrary, cited almost identical behavior as an example of *not* feeling the part. As he saw it, most young actors who become emotional and excited on stage were really being excited by their own emotions as actors; emotions which probably had nothing to do with the emotions that the character in the play would experience. Thus *emotion* has worn at least two contrasting faces. Those opposed to emotion have seen it as the source of amateurish straining and uncontrolled ranting. Those in favor of emotion have seen almost the exact opposite, a relaxed state of deeply felt understanding—a belief in the imaginary situation—a creative state not unlike that of the author when he or she wrote the play.

A second factor has also caused difficulty: the complex and seemingly contradictory nature of the emotions. It is highly probable that many of those who have argued most vehemently against feeling are the very ones who were gifted with a great capacity for feeling. They may have argued against feeling because, being full of feeling, they felt the need for control. We all tend to assume that others need what we need.

This may explain why an intellectual like Sir Henry Irving argued for feeling, while the emotionally charged Coquelin argued against it. Even more significant is the fact that actors and actresses who have consciously tried not to feel may have unconsciously employed one of the most subtle techniques for inducing genuine feeling, for a conscious desire not to give way to emotion is a common ingredient of emotions in real life. Parents grieving over the death of a child do not try to feel sorrow. They struggle not to feel sorrow, to control themselves, but as they talk to old friends tears are likely to come in spite of all efforts to the contrary. In actual practice, then, the best proponents on both sides of the controversy have attained remarkably similar results through remarkably similar methods.

The great argument, then, seems largely to have been a semantic one, complicated by the fact that the whole subject of the emotions is extremely complex and largely beyond direct conscious control. The controversy may have created some lively discussions, but it also had its negative results. The impression was created that acting must either be emotional (creative) or mechanical (technical), whereas the truth is that great acting has always been both creative and technical. With this in mind, let us look more carefully at some of the basic principles and techniques involved in each.

THE CREATIVE APPROACH

Perhaps the most significant element about the Stanislavsky method is that it really tries to be creative. There are many who argue against this, maintaining that acting is only an interpretative art, not a creative one. One value of the interpretative view is that it tends to keep the actor or actress humble and subservient to the playwright and the director. But the word *interpretative* also carries a less fortunate connotation, an implication that the actor or actress is a sort of second-rate artist whose job requires little insight or imagination. This simply is not true. While there is obviously a difference in the degree of creativity required by the average playwright and the average actor or actress, the difference is not so sharply defined as one would at first suppose. For example, a story that Shakespeare read in Holinshed's *Chronicles of England, Scotland and*

Ireland appealed to him; he intermingled it with his own experience, expressed it through his own artistic medium, poetic tragedy, and named it *Macbeth*. Verdi in turn read *Macbeth*, digested it in terms of his own experience, then expressed it through his artistic medium, the opera. If both Shakespeare and Verdi are creative artists, then why not the great actor who performs the role of *Macbeth?* He, too, reads the story, digests it in terms of his own experience, and expresses it through his own artistic medium, acting. Thus, one can argue that each is interpretative, since each gives us his or her interpretation of some phase of life, art, or experience. But whether we use the term *creative* or *interpretative*, the fact remains that all true artists have much in common. A good actor, like a good playwright, brings much imagination, skill, sensitivity, and depth of insight to his or her art.

Within the field of acting itself, however, the term *creative* has a somewhat special significance. It implies that the actors themselves are fundamentally responsible for creating the patterns of expression that will best express their roles. This is a contrast to earlier systems such as Delsarte's, in which actors were expected to perform according to a set of rules laid down by the master. It is likewise a contrast to the system employed by some directors who make their actors and actresses little more than puppets. The director under the Stanislavsky system is important, but only as a teacher who assists, guides, and stimulates. The actors may use help from any source possible, but it is still their responsibility to play the role, not necessarily according to the textbook, not necessarily according to what the director says, not in imitation of the way Edwin Booth or Helen Hayes played it, but in the best possible way that they themselves can play it. This requires thinking, imagination, and creative effort.

Many of the principles of the creative approach have been mentioned already, but because of the importance of the method in modern acting, whether one likes it or not, it seems wise to develop the subject more fully. We shall therefore take a closer look at some of its basic techniques. Keep in mind, though, that divisions of any kind in the Stanislavsky system are highly arbitrary. Actually, all the steps tend to be interwoven and interrelated. For example, the best way to relieve muscular strain is to concentrate on one's objective, while in order to concentrate on one's objective it is necessary to get rid of muscular strain. What Stanislavsky was striving for was a creative attitude. The various creative

When this happens, it becomes easy to play the scene in the play with sincerity and conviction, for the actor or actress now understands it emotionally as well as intellectually. He or she can believe it because a similar thing actually happened to him or her.

In a sense, memory of emotion is nothing but a conscious application of the old principle that we know things only in terms of our own experience. Usually, sensitive artists find that such identification in terms of personal experience functions quite subconsciously and automatically. We read a scene from a play and find it to be deeply moving or exciting without having to probe consciously for the personal experiences that have enabled us to tune in so effectively on its tragedy and excitement. Memory of emotion, when used as a conscious technique, becomes most valuable when, for some reason, a scene that should be moving leaves us cold. In such cases, deliberate probing in the storehouse of our own experiences may provide the answer. Of course, the personal experience that the actor recalls is rarely identical with the one he must portray. According to Boleslavsky, a memory of how one once annihilated a particularly obnoxious mosquito can provide the imaginative actor with a sufficient emotional basis for the convincing portrayal of bloody murder on the stage.[14]

JUSTIFICATION AND BELIEF

To act well, most actors and actresses find it important to believe in the artistic logic and integrity of what they are doing. If the play is poorly written or the action required by the director is false, they find it difficult to be convincing. On the other hand, the great actor or actress is often a wizard at thinking up reasons that will justify even awkward action or bad lines. Charlie Chaplin had an amazing faculty for projecting a naive belief into situations that most actors could only have forced into pure ham. Whether a comedian, a tragedian, or an actor in a fantasy, actors must seem to believe in the artistic truth of everything they say and do if the audience is to believe in their performance.

[14] Richard Boleslavsky, *Acting, The First Six Lessons* (New York: Theatre Arts Books, 1933), p. 44.

PROJECTION

What is said and done on stage must be seen and heard by the audience. Even in the most intimate scenes, sweet nothings must be murmured in a voice that projects to the balcony! The simple requirements of audibility and visibility form the basis of numerous stage conventions and techniques: turn front, kneel on the downstage knee, deliver important lines forward, and dozens of others. Obeyed slavishly and without judgment, such rules can make the actor or actress look ridiculous. Taken simply as a means of achieving the general ends of being seen and heard, they contain the wisdom of long experience, and the earnest beginner will welcome the help they can give.

THE ACTOR'S BODY

Related to the problems of audibility and visibility are the instruments of expression themselves, the voice and the body. The value of a free, responsive voice and a rhythmic, expressive body cannot be overemphasized. How to develop such a voice and such a body is another matter.

Actually, voice and body are closely interrelated, or, more accurately, the voice is simply one of the highly specialized functions of the body. Consequently, teachers usually begin the training of either by first considering the body, for it is less complex and more tangible than the voice. Improvement in one is likely to effect improvement in the other, for the root cause of difficulty in both, as far as the beginner is concerned, usually lies in unnecessary muscular strain, which in turn is probably due to such psychological factors as anxiety, fear, stage fright, and insecurity. One approach toward improvement, then, lies in doing something to relieve these unnecessary tensions. Achieving a better psychological adjustment may help; some hints for this will be discussed later when we consider stage fright. Physical exercise may also be beneficial. At least, a physiological-mechanical approach in dealing with the major muscle systems of the body is not as dangerous as it may be in the case of voice.

But whether the approach is mechanical, psychological, a combination of the two, or something else entirely, it should, if successful, relieve unnecessary tension. Note, however, the word *unnecessary*, for the body must not only be relaxed, it must be expressive. The athletic champion is also free from unnecessary tension, but don't forget that the real reason he or she is a champion is that he or she runs faster, jumps higher, or hits harder than anyone else on the field. The same is true of the great actor or actress. It is focus, control, and coordination of energy that count, not an absence of energy. Some help toward gaining a free, expressive body may be found by returning imaginatively to the uninhibited, expressive days of childhood. Freedom in use of the body may also be gained from athletics and dancing, but whatever the technique, the objective to strive for is a body that without strain or affectation expresses feelings and ideas, not just with the face muscles, not just with the voice, not just with the hands, but with the coordinated power of the entire body. Good acting, while never strained, has vitality.

THE ACTOR'S VOICE

The training of the human voice has suffered from quackery, superstition, and exploitation. On the other hand, marvelous results have frequently been achieved. The same teacher may, with the same methods, succeed with one student and ruin the voice of another. All in all, the problem is so complicated that we will consider here only a few general principles.

1. The whole process of speech is an overlaid function; that is, each part of the vocal mechanism used in expressing ideas also serves some more primitive function in connection with such acts as eating or breathing. Speech is achieved only by burdening this mechanism with an enormously complicated and ever-varying pattern of tensions and relaxations. The complexity involved in speaking a simple sentence is overwhelming. A clumsy, ignorant teacher may therefore do infinite harm in throwing this complicated system out of adjustment.

2. Largely because of the stress of modern living, there is a tendency for voices to be strained, breathy, high-pitched, and poorly placed. Physiologically this is due to unnecessary tension in muscles that should be relaxed; psychologically it is due to the fears, anxieties, and insecurity responsible for the tensions. Most good voice teachers are

masters at gaining relaxation and confidence. The bad ones may do little more than make the student acutely conscious of his or her voice. This consciousness frequently leads to still more tension, which in turn leads to an even worse voice.

3. Amazing improvements are frequently made in voices simply by working for confidence and better psychological adjustment. Many a young voice that rings with assurance and energy in the friendly environment of the playground becomes embarrassingly weak and ineffective in the strained, unfamiliar environment of the stage or platform. Even the inexperienced teacher can attempt to transfer the confidence and assurance of the one to the other. Anything that relieves fear and strain will almost invariably help the voice — at least, it can do no harm.

4. A general desire to speak with greater audibility and clarity than in ordinary life can also be motivated without danger. Most people use a better-than-ordinary voice when speaking on the telephone, probably because they instinctively feel the need for more clarity and care. Students often make remarkable vocal development during the production of a single play simply because they sense the necessity for better-than-normal voice production.

The Iris Warren approach, which clearly recognized the psychological as well as the physiological aspects of voice and was introduced to America largely through the efforts of Kristin Linklater, has often achieved freedom and power without strain or artificiality.[17]

Except for a few common-sense techniques such as these, it is probably best to leave voice training to experts. Speech defects, especially serious ones like stuttering, should be referred to qualified speech therapists. Well-meaning tampering is dangerous.

STAGE FRIGHT

As already indicated, one of the actor's or actress's most difficult jobs is to keep his or her faculties concentrated primarily on the elusive and intangible process of giving convincing theatrical life to a character. This job is hampered by numerous distractions, the worst of all being self-consciousness, which usually attacks in the form of stage fright. In

[17] See Kristin Linklater, *Freeing the Natural Voice* (New York: Drama Book Specialists, 1976).

the final analysis, this is a personal problem and one that both speakers and actors must conquer for themselves. Perhaps the following hints will help.

1. It is reassuring to know that stage fright is natural and, in mild forms, even desirable. After all, an appearance before a large audience *is* a social crisis, and nothing can convince the intelligent person otherwise. Nor is the nervousness always an indication that one is self-centered. It may result from fear of letting down the cast, the director, or the school rather than fear for one's own reputation. To some degree, then, nervousness is a sign of intelligence and sensitivity, and both of these qualities are desirable, if not indispensable.

2. It is comforting to know that the chemical and bodily changes that occur during an attack of stage fright are the same as those necessary for the heightened activity of outstanding acting. Athletes, actors, and speakers commonly find that their fear leaves them as soon as they really get into the game, the play, or the speech. Adrenalin poured into the blood under the stress of fear becomes an asset as soon as the individual begins meeting the challenge of the job.

3. Plenty of well-motivated action often helps to relieve stage fright, since it absorbs excess nervous energy and also serves as a distraction technique. One can be reasonably certain that an actor or actress whose first entrance calls for him or her to turn on the lights, notice the room, cross to the fireplace, begin making the fire, hear the telephone, and cross to answer it, still dangling a stick of wood in one hand, will not have difficulty with his or her opening lines.

4. Putting the actor's mind to work may also relieve the tension of stage fright. He or she should focus interest on something within the play and try to make the character's ideas and arguments serve the same function as his or her own ideas and arguments would in a real-life situation. The psychological significance of this is much greater than most people suppose. It rests on the reasonably well-established theory that when the higher brain centers are active, the emotions, which tend to be localized in the lower brain centers, fall under control. It follows that nothing can be more helpful than a belief in something about the play: its message, its importance, a character's wishes and desires — anything that gives the mind something reasonably tangible to grasp, to work on, to believe in — something outside of, and more important than, the self.

An idea that arouses some emotional conviction is best, partly because it makes concentration easy and partly because such emotional interest will supplant the emotion of fear, which is the essence of stage fright.

5. An increasingly popular approach to acting has been developed by Viola Spolin and others. It consists largely of uninhibited and imaginative game playing. While the approach appears to be valuable in many ways, it is especially effective in freeing students from self-consciousness or stage fright.

6. One of the best and most practical methods of opposing stage fright is for the young actor or actress to develop gradually. One who begins by working backstage, then progresses to mob scenes, then to bit parts, then to minor roles, next to supporting roles, and at long last to leads is unlikely ever to experience the crippling terrors of acute stage fright.

CONDENSATION AND FOCUS

Perhaps the most important techniques in theatre grow from the fact that art has form and purpose. Life tends to ramble on endlessly with a complexity largely beyond human comprehension. Its meaningful moments are usually hopelessly cluttered with the ordinary, the uninteresting, and the distracting. Everything in a play, on the other hand, should have significance and interest. Most of the play's problems of condensation and elimination have already been solved by the playwright before the actor or actress enters the picture, and yet much remains to be done. Distracting, meaningless movements, though perfectly natural in life, can ruin a show. Ideas half-formed and fragmentary, as they may be in life, are seldom effective on stage. Mumbled and repeated words, not noticeable in most conversations, can be disastrous to the actor. In mob scenes, unity of effect must sometimes be achieved through the director's insistence that everyone share in the hero's victory, even though from the standpoint of logic some characters would be hostile or indifferent. On stage there is a tendency to freeze when the other person speaks. Stage reactions, especially surprise, tend to be broader than is characteristic of most sophisticated adults. In other words, much of the movement and business that a good stage director requires of an actor or actress is primarily for the purpose of composition, picturization, or rhythm and is not necessarily the most natural thing that the character would do.

Glancing back at the two approaches to acting, the creative approach seems to be fundamental. Generally speaking, the actor or actress can never be too imaginative, too understanding, or too sensitive to the stimulus of the imaginary situation. Stanislavsky deserves credit for having evolved a system for developing this indispensable part of the actor's equipment that many had previously considered as fixed and innate. On the other hand, it must never be forgotten that art is not purely a matter of responding to imaginary stimuli. It must be an *effective* response. Such basic things as visibility, audibility, and the demands of composition are indispensable to the actor or actress who would serve his or her function in the total process of conveying the play to the audience.

THE ART OF CHARACTERIZATION

Versatility in characterization, once considered to be one of the actor's most important resources, almost became a lost art during the first half of the twentieth century. Traditionally, from Thespis, who played all the roles in a play, to Stanislavsky, who took great pride in his ability to play numerous roles during a single season, versatility in characterization had been of vital importance. An actor or actress with a limited range was simply not considered to be an accomplished artist. Even the great Edwin Booth usually included one or two comedies in his repertory just to prove that he could play something besides Hamlet and Richelieu. The trend away from such versatility toward typecasting, whereby actors specialize in playing themselves, or at least a single type of charac-

FIGURE 9:7 Far from playing it straight and conservative, Stanislavsky was a master of theatricality and characterization. These are only a small sample of his creations. *(a)* Ivan in *Tsar Fyodor. (b)* Famussov in *Trouble from Reason. (c)* Larverger in *Love Potion. (d)* Gayev in *The Cherry Orchard. (e)* General Krutitski in *Enough Stupidity for Every Wise Man. (f)* Rippafratta in *The Mistress of the Inn.*

(a)

(b)

(c)

(d)

(e)

(f)

ter, began toward the end of the nineteenth century when New York producers started to form *combination companies.* These were companies that specialized in the production of one play only: special scenery, special props, special costumes, and special players. Critics and audiences seemed to find these combination companies an improvement, but the actors suffered. The boredom of playing the same role during a long run was stifling to the actor's development as an artist; moreover, versatility was no longer of importance. Motion pictures furthered the trend toward typecasting, and, finally, the arrival of method acting, as interpreted by the rank and file of its American disciples, frowned upon anything not obviously germane to the actor himself as "phony." (These lesser disciples of the method seemed to be unaware that Stanislavsky himself was a master of characterization and that America's best method directors, especially Clurman and Kazan, laid great stress on characterization in their productions.)

As far as directors, playwrights, and audiences were concerned, typecasting was not a problem, especially in New York or Hollywood, where the pools of talent were almost unlimited: all types, ages, kinds, and colors. But outside of New York and Hollywood the tendency to imitate the pros and frown upon characterization has been deadly. This has been especially true in schools, where casting is limited to young people, most of them healthy and monotonously normal.

There were always exceptions, of course. Lon Chaney gained fame from his sensational characterizations in such movies as *The Phantom of the Opera* and *The Hunchback of Notre Dame.* Handsome young Hal Holbrook astounded America by transforming himself into Mark Twain, yet on the whole, the exciting art of characterization tended to disappear. Acting teachers and directors no longer seemed to think it important. Lacking skillful professional models, amateur characterizations (when unavoidable) tended to become broad and unconvincing: crude putty noses, stereotyped dialects, and the inevitable lame leg plus a quavering voice for old age. To avoid such cliches many directors insisted that their young actors just "play it straight," which for the most part resulted in dull productions, for the life of most plays is deeply embedded in the genuine but colorful individuality of the characters.

With the return of professional repertory companies, plus new freedom from the more stifling aspects of realism, the art of characterization is beginning to revive. Teachers and directors are once more beginning to realize its vital importance.

(a)

(b)

(c)

(d)

FIGURE 9:8 Four characterizations by Paul Ballantyne. With the establishment of resident repertory theatres, such versatility and skill in characterization is again becoming important. (*a*) Crabtree in *The School for Scandal*. (*b*) Pischick in *The Cherry Orchard*. (*c*) Candy in *Of Mice and Men*. (*d*) Nanancourt in *An Italian Straw Hat*.

(a)

(c)

(b)

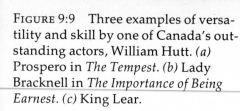

FIGURE 9:9   Three examples of versatility and skill by one of Canada's outstanding actors, William Hutt. *(a)* Prospero in *The Tempest*. *(b)* Lady Bracknell in *The Importance of Being Earnest*. *(c)* King Lear.

The major approach to genuine and exciting characterization seems to come from something inside actors themselves. In fact, the ability to mimic striking personalities, not only humans but also animals and objects, may be one of the inherent characteristics of good actors. Acting teachers who simply encourage students to develop their latent possibilities for versatility in characterization usually find the results surprising and stimulating. Michael Chekhov, in his book *To the Actor*, makes a convincing case for what he calls the "psychological gesture." Much of Stanislavsky's *Building a Character* is devoted to the subject, wisely pointing out that characterization can be approached not only from the inside but also from the outside through the choice of the right mannerisms, the right hand props, and especially through a skillful use of costuming and makeup.

MAKEUP

To most actors and actresses there is magic excitement in the smell of stage makeup. This is due not to its perfume but rather to its association with the exciting glow of the hour or two immediately preceding performance. In fact, one of the values of makeup may lie in giving the actor or actress something useful and definite to do during the nerve-racking preperformance period. This is not true of all of them. Some prefer peace and solitude, but the majority, if left alone with nothing to do, begin to worry, tense up, and anticipate various horrors of failure. The chatter, activity, and bravado of dressing rooms tend to buoy up such spirits. This makeup period also requires the actor to arrive at the theatre well before curtain time, thus providing a slight margin of safety in case of emergencies. It also gives dinners a chance to settle.

But the psychological value of makeup is deeper than the activity and atmosphere it provides prior to the opening curtain. Many actors and actresses, particularly when playing character parts, find that makeup stimulates them toward a more confident and effective performance. In some cases they almost hide behind masks and dare to say and do things that would embarrass them if said and done in naked faces.

But though the application of makeup has certain psychological values for the actor or actress, its more obvious functions lie in the fact

(a)

(b)

FIGURE 9:10 The magic of makeup. Two character makeups by Bill Barber, University of Utah. (a) Kelly Kennedy, before and after, as the Duchess of York. (b) Dave Radosivich, before and after, as Don Quixote.

that from an audience standpoint it counteracts stage lighting, delineates character, and in a large auditorium helps to project the features of the character to the audience. Of the three, delineation of character is by far the most important. Age, nationality, and personality are among the vital factors that makeup can help to convey. Note the word *help*. No makeup artist on earth can paint a convincingly harrowed and tragic expression over a bright, happy, unimaginative face. Just as makeup helps the actor, so the actor must help the makeup, and actors who are famous for characterization have flexible faces and sensitive souls. It is ordinarily a skillful combination of makeup, costume, and expression that achieves the desired effect.

Not all makeups require marked changes in appearance, however. Those commonly known as straight makeups aim at little if any fundamental change. In other words, the actor or actress has been essentially typecast as far as appearance is concerned, and it is only necessary to accentuate what he or she already has. Usually this results in an attempt to accent one's most attractive features according to the tastes of the time, but the tastes of the time vary. During the first quarter of the twentieth century, the makeup of stage heroes tended heavily toward the romantic, even the pretty side. Eyebrows and eyelashes were generally lined, cheeks heavily rouged, and the lips accentuated. During the second quarter of this century such a makeup would have been used by a male actor only if he were playing the role of some effeminate fop. The hero of that period tried to imitate the ruddy, sunburned complexion of the he-man. During the third quarter of this century the spirit of rebellion swept all standards aside. Tomorrow — who can say?

But whatever the prevailing style, students of straight makeup have an excellent chance for a frank evaluation of their own features. Hints on makeup as well as on hair styling and how to wear clothes have frequently turned rather plain people into very attractive ones, on stage and off.

The process of applying a straight makeup begins with the application of a base. Greasepaint in tubes is standard, although most actors prefer pancake for straight makeups. The objective in either case is to achieve an even, healthy complexion, and this usually requires a color more pink or ruddy than normal to counteract the prevailing amber of artificial lights. Next come subtle highlighting and shadowing to correct possible bad features, followed by the application of rouge and eye shadow. After this the makeup is carefully and thoroughly powdered with translucent powder that will set, but not alter, the basic effect. Lipstick is then applied, and finally eyelashes and eyebrows are lined with varying shades of brown, or on occasion blue, green, or black. For women mascara and artificial eyelashes may be useful. Needless to say, the style and grooming of the hair, the press and fit of the costume, and the ease and carriage of the actor or actress do much to complete the effect.

After the show the makeup is first dissolved with cleansing cream and then removed with cleansing tissue or a makeup cloth; finally, the face is washed with soap and water, and the job is complete. Good makeup should not be harmful to normal skin.

Character makeups are more interesting than straight makeups since they produce marked changes in appearance. In addition to the techniques already mentioned, the character actor, both male and female, employ a number of others, in many cases actually altering the shape of the face by the use of nose putty or other plastic materials. If nose putty is used it is first worked with the fingers until soft and pliable, then applied to the dry skin. Beginners often find that the putty insists on sticking to the fingers rather than to the nose, cheekbones, or chin as intended. Experienced actors avoid such a messy catastrophe by occasionally dipping their fingers into the greasepaint that is eventually to be used as a base. They continue to work and mold the putty until the edges blend into the skin and the desired shape has been achieved. They then smooth the base color across the rest of the face, and the foundation for the makeup, complete with new putty features, is prepared.

The second, and perhaps most difficult, technique that the character actor or actress employs consists of the application of highlights, lines, and shadows. How do they decide where to put these? That is where skill, art, and practice come in. If a formula or a few definite lines would suffice, then anyone could put on an excellent makeup, but this is not the case. It is more difficult to apply a good character makeup than it is to sketch the faces on paper, for the sketch artist can begin with a clean, blank piece of paper, whereas the actor must rework features and characteristics already there. Shadows and highlights can go anywhere on paper according to the dictates of expression, but in makeup they must generally coincide with the natural tendencies of the actor's own face. In fact, many actors proceed by assuming the attitude and facial expression of the character they intend to portray. Then, noting where the wrinkles and shadows tend to fall, they lowlight these with brown or maroon. Noting where the highlights appear, they accent these with white or a tint of the base. These shadows and highlights are then skillfully blended until the shadows and lines appear to be wrinkles or sunken areas,

FIGURE 9:11 Makeup and characterization. Three studies of Helen Hayes as Queen Victoria.

FIGURE 9:12 Some skullful and imaginative creations by Irene Corey for the Everyman Players. *(a)* Saint Paul. *(b)* Ken Holamon as the tortoise. *(c)* Jimmy Journey as the hare. *(d)* Job.

(a)

(b)

(c)

(d)

not lines of paint, while the highlights are blended until they appear to be ridges or bulges of flesh, not daubs of white.

In old-age makeups it is almost always necessary to paint out the natural lines of the eyes and mouth, replacing them with lines that give the illusion of wrinkled flesh. One who knows the art of makeup also pays careful attention to highlights and shadows on the arms and neck. An old-age mask painted on the front of the face of an otherwise carefree youth gives an unintentionally ludicrous effect.

Having applied nose putty, foundation, highlights, and shadows, there is little more that a woman can do except to powder the makeup, fix her hair, adjust her costume, and get into character, although for certain old-age types artificial eyebrows may work wonders, and of course accessories like spectacles have their value.

Men have the advantage, for not only eyebrows but beards and mustaches of every imaginable design can be added. These, when time or other limitations make it inadvisable for an actor to grow his own, are ordinarily made from crepe hair, which comes in braided form. This is usually unraveled, dampened, and stretched to remove most of the curl. Strands of this are then shaped, combed, and clipped. They are glued to the face with spirit gum. If well done the job is convincing at close range as well as from the auditorium. Generally a color of the crepe hair is selected that essentially matches the hair of the actor, although the effect will be more convincing if two or three related colors are carefully blended. The most common change in hair coloring is to go gray. For dignified old age, white mascara or liquid hair whitener is ordinarily used, though for certain dried-out outdoor types cornstarch may be superior. Metallic powders sprayed with lacquers are sometimes employed, not only to gray the hair but also to transform actors into blondes, redheads, or brunettes. There are occasions when wigs for both men and women are indispensable.

Many special techniques have not even been mentioned here, including the use of collodion, latex, wax, and other materials for molding the features. Fortunately, anyone really interested in the art of makeup can learn a great deal by simply studying Richard Corson's remarkable book on the subject.[18]

Many theatres rely on the services of a professional makeup artist in order to achieve the necessary degree of skill in this element of the production, but it is really the actor's problem. He may receive aid, and he should welcome the advice of the makeup specialist, but, after all, he should know his own face and character better than anyone else does. His pride in developing a complete characterization should stimulate him to purchase his own makeup and develop professional skill in its application, for an effective makeup can be one of the most practical steps toward the achievement of an exciting characterization.

[18] Richard Corson, *Stage Makeup*, 5th ed. (Englewood Cliffs, N. J.: Prentice-Hall, 1975).

PART
THREE

ARCHITECTS, DESIGNERS, & TECHNICIANS

CHAPTER 10

THEATRE ARCHITECTURE

While the play and the players are the central elements of the theatrical experience, there are other items whose contributions cannot be ignored. One is the playhouse in which the play is performed. Undoubtedly the grandeur of Attic tragedy was reinforced by the beauty and simple dignity of the Theatre of Dionysus under the open sky. The dynamic flow of action in Shakespearean tragedy was certainly assisted by the excellent acoustics and functional efficiency of the Globe and other Elizabethan playhouses. The realism of Ibsen and Chekhov was supported by the pictureframe stages of the late nineteenth century. Consequently, some knowledge of theatre architecture, some sense of its evolution, and some conception of which of its elements are universal and essential become necessities to anyone who would more fully understand and appreciate the art of the theatre.

283

FIGURE 10:1   The new British National Theatre. The unprecedented boom in theatre construction during the third quarter of the twentieth century reached its climax in March 1976, when Britain, in spite of a severe economic recession, opened a new $32 million theatre complex on the Thames. Under its roof are three theatres, seven bars, two cafeterias, a restaurant, and 135 air-conditioned dressing rooms, plus shops, offices, lobbies, and other facilities.

THE CLASSICAL THEATRE

THE ANCIENT GREEK THEATRE

There is no reliable information as to the kind of theatre in which Thespis may have performed while winning the first Greek tragic contest in 534 B.C. Horace mentions something about a cart, and from this fragment of evidence some have conjectured that Thespis probably stood on a cart in the midst of his chorus and acted for an audience that gathered about him (Figure 10:2). Others maintain that he stood on a table, and though neither idea can be backed by convincing evidence, the fact remains that Thespis would have been wise to stand on something, for this would have set him apart from and above his chorus, where he could have been better seen and heard by his audience. And the business of providing the actor with a better chance to be seen and heard by the audience is the fundamental function of all stages.

Most theatre architects, however, have also been concerned about functions in addition to audibility and visibility. For example, the most important architectural element of the early Greek theatre was a religious one, an altar to Dionysus. This in turn was surrounded by a large circle, the orchestra, within which most of the actors performed. Greek audiences, like all audiences, were also concerned with comfort, which soon led to some sort of seating arrangement. A hint as to what this first seating arrangement may have been comes from a historical fragment. About 499 B.C. the Athenians suffered a minor disaster when some wooden stands collapsed during a theatrical performance. This has led some scholars to conclude that early Greek performances might have been given on level ground, probably within the city, where some form of scaffolding for seating would have been necessary. But in any event,

FIGURE 10:2   Perhaps Thespis stood on a cart.

FIGURE 10:3 Aeschylus may have written his earliest plays for a theatre something like this.

whether because of this disaster or because of other factors, such as the theatre's growing importance as a community function, we know that within a few years the standard form of the Greek theatre, with its auditorium resting on the solid ground of a hillside, had evolved.

The Theatre of Dionysus at Athens, where the plays of Aeschylus, Sophocles, Euripides, and Aristophanes were first performed, is the most famous of the classic theatres, though many others were scattered

FIGURE 10:4 Perhaps Euripides wrote for a theatre something like this.

(a)

(b)

FIGURE 10:5   Ruins of
three ancient Greek
theatres before or
during restoration.
(a) The Theatre
at Epidauros.
(b) The Theatre of
Dionysus at Athens.
(c) The Theatre at
Delphi.

(c)

across ancient Hellas. The development of the Theatre of Dionysus seems to have been about as follows. Sloping down behind the Acropolis was a hillside that formed a natural amphitheatre for the audience. At the base of this hillside the Greeks laid out the two indispensable elements of their theatre: an altar to Dionysus and an orchestra circle about 90 feet in diameter (Figure 10:3). Although there is no reliable evidence, logic leads us to believe that wooden seats were next added on the hillside. Whether there was any scene building *(skene)* in the background during the early years seems doubtful. The main evidence indicating the lack of such a building is derived from the plays themselves, for the earliest extant plays of Aeschylus are set out of doors, while his later plays, together with the plays of Sophocles and Euripides, are usually (but not always) set before a building or palace. It is therefore logical to suppose that a scene building was added in the neighborhood of 470 B.C., or shortly after Aeschylus wrote *The Persians,* the last of his plays that could easily have been played without a building as a background.

But whatever its evolution, we have a good idea of the basic architectural features of the typical Greek theatre, for the ruins of many that were built of stone during the Hellenic and Greco-Roman periods that followed the great Attic period still remain. The best preserved of these is the one at Epidaurus, built, or at least begun, during the fourth century B.C. As Figure 10:5 indicates, there is little guesswork as to the features of either the auditorium or the orchestra. These have been well preserved. The *skene* has disappeared, however, as it has from all theatres of the Attic and Hellenic periods, and archeologists have quarreled bitterly over what the form of this important feature may have been. In general they agree that the *skene* had at least three doors and that in later Greek and Roman times the uses of these doors became traditional, the center door, for example, always leading into the palace of the protagonist. There is also general agreement as to the names of some of the parts. The entryway on either side (between the *skene* and auditorium) was called the *parodos,* and it was through one of these that the chorus made its entrances and exits. At some period in the *skene's* evolution, wings *(paraskenia)* and a forestage *(proskenion)* were added. The top of the forestage *(logeion)* probably served as a stage on which the actors performed, though this conjecture has been the subject of heated controversy.

As to the numerous stage machines and effects employed by the

(a)

(c)

FIGURE 10:6 Highly conjectural sketches of three Greek stage devices.
(a) The *eccyclema*.
(b) The *periaktos*.
(c) The *mechane*.

(b)

Greeks, there is little reliable evidence. The three major devices appear to have been the *eccyclema*, the *periaktos*, and the *mechane*. The *eccyclema* was a low platform mounted on wheels or castors in such a manner that it could be rolled out through the central doorway to reveal scenes that had supposedly taken place within the *skene*. Thus Clytemnestra kills Agamemnon inside the palace, yet a few moments later she appears before the chorus to justify the deed while seemingly standing over the body of the fallen king. Such a scene was probably made possible by placing the body of Agamemnon on the *eccyclema*, then rolling the whole bloody spectacle out on the forestage and into view of the audience (Figure 10:6a).

The second device was the *periaktos*. Its exact form and usage is shrouded in much guesswork and uncertainty, but it appears to have been a prism-shaped unit with different scenes or decorations painted on its three faces. By placing several of these *periaktoi* between the pillars along the front of the *skene*, something approaching a change of scenery may have been achieved by simply revolving each one-third of a turn, thereby revealing a new face to the audience.

The third device commonly used, the *mechane*, was apparently some sort of crane or derrick used primarily to raise and lower the gods. The effect must have been rather crude and obvious. In fact, Aristophanes may have been poking fun at the *mechane* as well as at Socrates when, in *The Clouds*, he used such a device to suspend the great philosopher in a basket.

So much for the typical Greek theatre, which in its time served the cause of Dionysus so nobly. As the years went by, changes occurred. We have already seen that after the death of Aristophanes the chorus declined in importance and that the old religious significance of the theatre died away. With these changes a full orchestra circle was no longer of importance. Consequently, in the Hellenic period the *skene* began to encroach upon the edge of the orchestra, while after the Roman conquest theatres usually reduced the orchestra to a semicircle and dispensed with the altar altogether. Auditoriums also tended to grow smaller; at last even these could no longer be filled, and the great open-air structures were abandoned to the elements.

THE ANCIENT ROMAN THEATRE

In general, there are marked similarities between the typical Roman theatre and the Greek theatre from which it descended. It should not be imagined, however, that all the plays in either Greece or Rome were performed in typical theatres. None of the great Roman playwrights wrote for such theatres. Seneca, it will be remembered, wrote closet dramas to be read or declaimed in polite circles, while both Plautus and Terence

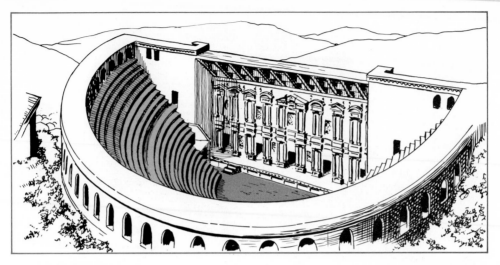

FIGURE 10:7   Sketch of a typical Roman theatre.

wrote for a temporary wooden type of theatre about which next to nothing is known except that it had a long, narrow stage representing a street with several houses.

As early as 154 B.C. a Roman theatre is reported to have been built of stone, but the Roman Senate, strict and puritanical during the early years of the Empire, condemned the structure and had it torn down. A hundred years later (55–52 B.C.) the great Pompey constructed the first permanent theatre—permanent because Pompey cleverly placed a shrine to Venus at the back of the auditorium, thus implying that the curved rows of seats were not the seats of a theatre but steps leading to a sacred shrine. This theatre became the model for others that were eventually constructed throughout most of the Empire.

The form of the Roman theatre inevitably invites a series of comparisons and contrasts with the Greek:

1. Unlike the Greek auditorium, which rested upon a hill, the Roman auditorium was usually a freestanding structure built up on level ground.
2. The scene building and auditorium of the Roman theatre were joined to form a single architectural unit.
3. The scene building of the Roman theatre was enlarged and lavishly decorated.
4. The auditorium was reduced to an exact semicircle, whereas in the Greek theatre it had extended beyond the semicircle.

FIGURE 10:8   Ruins of the Roman theatre at Orange.

5. The orchestra was reduced in size and also reduced to a semicircle.
6. The seating capacity, despite Rome's natural tendency to substitute quantity for quality, was usually (but not always) smaller than it had been in Greece. This was obviously because of the low social and artistic status of the theatre in Rome, in contrast to its vital importance in Greece.
7. The Roman theatre had a long, narrow stage with a roof above it.

Other practices of the Roman theatre, such as the stretching of colored awnings across the auditorium, the use of a front curtain (suspended from above and lowered as the play began), and even such sumptuous items as carpets and "air conditioning" (cold perfumed water that ran down the aisles) have been described by none-too-reliable sources (primarily Vitruvius and Pollux). But while there may be some doubt about decorations and other minor items, our basic information about Roman theatres is excellent, for the ruins of many still stand. Romans, like Americans, could build wonderful playhouses; their weakness lay in what they said and did in them.

THE MEDIEVAL THEATRE

Of the many stage types that appeared during the medieval period, only three major forms will be considered here: (1) the temporary platform stage of the strolling players, (2) the simultaneous stages used in producing the mystery and miracle plays, and (3) the wagon stages used in producing the English and German mystery cycles.

As to the stages of the strolling players, there were infinite variations, but the essential feature was a raised platform with a curtain as a background, behind which actors could retire from the sight of the audience (Figure 10:9). The spectators usually stood in front or on three sides of this platform, though there were exceptions. For example, when this type of theatre eventually made its way into the courtyards of the London inns, its stage was set up at one end of the yard in a manner that allowed most of the guests to watch the performance from the surrounding windows or balconies, a practice that eventually influenced the form of the Elizabethan public playhouse. It is interesting to note that the *commedia dell'arte* players clung to their simple platform stage even

FIGURE 10:9 Medieval platform stage.

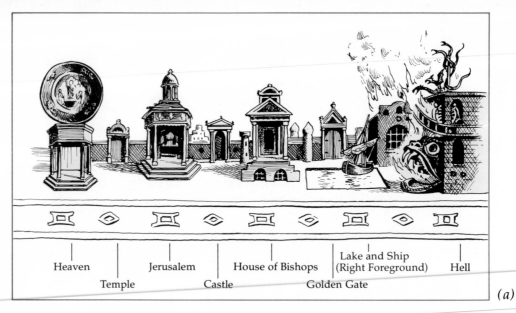

| Heaven | | Jerusalem | | House of Bishops | | Lake and Ship (Right Foreground) | | Hell |
| Temple | | Castle | | Golden Gate |

(a)

FIGURE 10:10   The simultaneous stage. The medieval practice of placing all scenes on stage before the performance began can still provide an excellent solution to the shifting problems of many plays. *(a)* The Valenciennes mystery play, 1547. *(b)* The stage with all the settings for *Old Four Eyes* an outdoor drama at the Burning Hills Ampitheatre, Mendora, North Dakota; designed and directed by Frederick G. Walsh.

(b)

FIGURE 10:11
Medieval
pageant
wagon.

when their skill won them invitations to appear in courts throughout Europe.

Simultaneous stages were first developed within the churches. The basic idea consisted of shifting the audience rather than the scenery. A sequence of booths or stations was constructed, each depicting a given scene; audiences then moved from one to another as crowds in a zoo move from the elephants to the lions to the monkeys.

As the theatre moved outdoors the simultaneous setting was retained, but the number of stations was modified so that instead of surrounding the audience they were confined to an arc, with heaven occupying the station to the actor's right and hell the one to his extreme left. Little or no provision seems to have been made for the comfort of the audience, although some spectators may have managed to find seats on the steps and balconies of the adjoining buildings.

This medieval idea of placing all scenes on stage at the same time appears again in the early Renaissance theatres of France (Figure 10:10). It is still seen and has been especially effective in staging American outdoor dramas such as *The Lost Colony* (see Figure 10:28c). Many modern proscenium theatres, including the beautiful Dallas Theater Center, designed by Frank Lloyd Wright, have small side stages flanking the main stage, thus providing at least three simultaneous locations for the players.

The famous wagon stages used in England and Germany provide an interesting variation of the simultaneous stage. Each stage or station for a given production was completely prepared before the performance began, but instead of setting it up simultaneously in the same location with all the others, each was mounted on wheels and moved from one audience to another throughout the city. These wagon stages were of two-story construction; the lower story was used as a dressing room and the upper as the area for the action (Figure 10:11). Each trade guild was usually assigned the responsibility for one wagon. Thus the garment makers might do the Adam and Eve episode and the carpenters the story of Noah. On the appointed day people gathered in city squares, and one after another the wagons appeared. Each performed its play and then moved on to the waiting crowd in the next square.

THEATRES FROM THE RENAISSANCE TO THE TWENTIETH CENTURY

Italy's rebirth of interest in things classical quite naturally stimulated a rebirth of interest in the architecture of classic theatres and, as we shall see, resulted in the construction of the Olympic Theatre *(Teatro Olympico)*, a beautiful and important playhouse that still stands. But Italy did more than restore the old: It contributed two very important books on the subject, the famous *Architettura* (1551), by Sebastiano Serlio, and *Practica di fabricar Scene e Machine ne' Teatri* (1638), by Nicola Sabbatini. Above all, however, Italy gave the world a new type of theatre, one that ignored both the forestage-facade tradition of the classic stage and the simultaneous stations of the medieval. It developed the Farnese Theatre, a proscenium theatre with a front curtain plus painted scenery that gave a pictorial illusion of place.

THE CLASSIC TRADITION: THE OPEN STAGE

The Olympic Theatre   The Olympic Theatre, built in the classic tradition, was the result of a deliberate effort on the part of a Renaissance group, the Olympian Academy, to construct a highly authentic replica of a classic theatre. The designer was the famous architect Palladio. He

FIGURE 10:12   Two views of the Olympic Theatre, built in Vicenza, Italy, in 1584. It was designed as a conscious attempt to duplicate the classic style.

died after the work was begun, and the building was completed by his son in 1584.

While essentially a classic theatre, there are several highly interesting differences between the Olympic Theatre and those of Greece and Rome. In the first place, Palladio's theatre moved indoors; in the second place, the central doorway of the stage was greatly enlarged and thus became a sort of embryonic proscenium arch, for behind this arch, as well as behind the side doorways, permanent perspective vistas were soon to be added (Figure 10:12). Thus even the Olympian Academy was not able entirely to resist the craving for the new pictorial perspective which was already thoroughly established in painting and, as we shall see later, had begun to find its way onto the stage.

But while the Olympic Theatre shows a pictorial influence, its basic form is clearly classical: a raised platform stage backed by a more or less permanent architectural facade. It is thus related structurally not only to Greek and Roman theatres but to all open-stage theatres, especially to the open-stage Renaissance theatres in Holland, England, and Spain. Note, however, that though related, it is not the ancestor of the theatres in these countries, for it was not built until 45 years after the theatre at Ghent (1539) (Figure 10:13) and eight years after James Burbage opened

FIGURE 10:13   A Dutch theatre at Ghent, 1539.

FIGURE 10:14   Performance in an English inn yard, about 1550.

his first Elizabethan theatre (1576). Yet directly or indirectly all had a common heritage in the classic theatres of Greece and Rome, and all show the same basic features: a platform stage backed by an ornamental facade containing three or more openings. In the case of the theatres of Holland, England, and Spain, however, the influence of the classic stage appears to have been indirect and probably unconscious. George Kernodle advances the theory that certain elements of the classic stage had been transmitted into art and through art (painting, sculpture, and the *tableau vivant*) to the stage.[1] The *tableau vivant* (a static scene posed by living characters) was especially important and may well have exerted a major though indirect influence on the type of Renaissance theatre that developed first in Holland and later in England and Spain. The Olympic Theatre's claim to distinction, therefore, lies in the directness of its relationship to the classic stage, for it was built with the expressed purpose of reproducing the classic form.

The Elizabethan Playhouse   Information regarding the exact nature of the English Elizabethan playhouse is extremely meager, for the theatres of Shakespeare's day were built of wood and have long since dis-

[1] George R. Kernodle, *From Art to Theatre* (Chicago: University of Chicago Press, 1944), chap. 1.

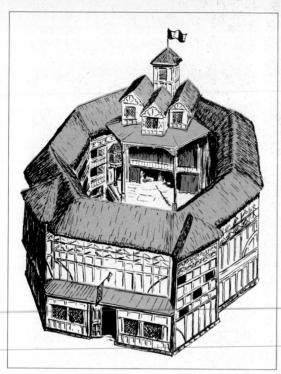 

appeared. Bits of evidence—a few old prints, a few descriptions, part of a building contract, and internal evidence from the plays themselves—provide most of the information on which our ideas rest.

The auditorium of the Elizabethan playhouse seems to have been entirely native and original. As already suggested, it apparently grew from the English inn yard where strolling interlude players had once performed while guests watched from their windows and commoners watched from the ground (Figure 10:14). In any event, the Elizabethan public playhouse likewise remained outdoors and still placed its groundlings in the courtyard, while patrons who could afford to do so watched from the galleries or boxes that surrounded the acting area (Figure 10:15).

In the typical Elizabethan playhouse the forestage, or apron, was very prominent. Usually it was wedge-shaped and extended well into the open pit or yard. Above it there may have been a porchlike structure, the shadow, supported by two pillars. Behind and on either side were proscenium doors with proscenium balconies above them, while in the rear center were two larger openings, the inner-below and the inner-above. The inner-below and perhaps the inner-above were equipped with traverse curtains that could be opened or closed, thus dividing the propertied inner stage from the unpropertied forestage (Figure 10:16).

FIGURE 10:15 *(facing page)* Two views of the John C. Adams reconstruction of the Globe Theatre.

(a)

FIGURE 10:16 Theoretical form and use of the Elizabethan stage, *(a)* unlocalized and *(b)* localized.

(b)

This Elizabethan stage was one of the most functional and efficient ever devised. As an example of the way in which it operated, consider the first act of *The Merchant of Venice:*

Scene 1. A street in Venice. (Curtain is closed; actors play on forestage.

Scene 2. Belmont, a room in Portia's house. (Curtain opens, revealing inner stage set with scenery and properties to suggest Portia's house. Portia and Nerissa discovered inside, but as dialogue begins they move onto forestage where they can be better seen and heard.)

Scene 3. Venice, a public place. (Same as Scene 1.)

Scene 4. Belmont, a room in Portia's house. (Same as Scene 2.)

Scene 5. Venice, a street. (Same as Scene 1.)

Scene 6. Venice, a room in Shylock's house. (Scenery and properties are changed behind the curtain during Scene 5; curtain opens, revealing Shylock's house.)

And so the plays went, not always with such formal alternation between forestage and inner stage, but always in a manner that would enable the players to keep the action moving. Sometimes the balcony windows above the proscenium doors were used *(Romeo and Juliet);* sometimes the inner-above was used (the monument scene in *Antony and Cleopatra).* In any event, we cannot avoid being impressed by the efficiency of this stage, which made possible the uninterrupted flow of action so necessary to the playing of Shakespeare.

Other features of the typical Elizabethan playhouse included machinery for flying effects, traps for ghosts, and a flag that was raised when the show was in progress. There were also devices for sound effects, including a cannon. In fact, Shakespeare's playhouse, the Globe, one of the most famous of all playhouses, burned to the ground when some of the smoldering wadding from its cannon ignited the thatched roof.

These public playhouses were many and popular, but they were not the only theatres to be found in England at that time. Plays were done in halls at the universities and in private indoor theatres, which were apparently patterned after the outdoor theatres except for the addition of a roof and the consequent necessity for artificial lighting. By far the most famous of these was the Blackfriars Theatre, where the boy players of St.

Paul's sometimes made themselves thorns in the flesh of Shakespeare and his companions. Finally there were the court masques, in which the new Italian picture-perspective theatre was the dominant form. Some of the theatrical spectacles prepared by the great designer and architect Inigo Jones (1573–1652) for presentation at court during the reign of James I reached extravagant heights of lavishness in both costuming and scenic splendor. We shall consider these further when we discuss scenic design.

The Spanish Corral   During the years when the Italians were building the Olympic and Farnese Theatres and the English were doing a booming business in their "wooden O's," the Spanish were crowding into their *corrales* to see the plays of Lope de Vega and Calderón. The Spanish auditorium had much in common with the Elizabethan playhouse. The Spanish native form had been a courtyard, or a *corral,* just as the English native form had been the inn yard, and the results were similar—a series of galleries surrounding the level ground of the *corral,* where the commoners stood. The stage itself was also the same type: an open stage platform without proscenium doors or windows but still employing a curtained inner stage. Scenery, if any, must have been meager, and yet in such a theatre the plays of Spain's Golden Age were first performed. We shall meet the open stage form again as we come to the present day.

THE PROSCENIUM TRADITION

As mentioned earlier, the unique contribution of Renaissance Italy to theatre architecture was the Farnese Theatre at Parma, which was completed in 1618 or 1619. As Kernodle points out, the roots of this playhouse are to be found in the visual arts, particularly in the newly developed pictorial perspectives of Renaissance painting.[2] Perspective painting, which had become highly developed in Italian art during the fifteenth century, made its way into the theatre in the early sixteenth century. These early perspective settings, for example those by Serlio (see Figure 11:2), were designed for a stage platform but although they may have been placed behind a frame, they were not placed behind a

[2] Ibid., chap. 6.

(b)

FIGURE 10:17 The proscenium theatre. From the construction of the Farnese Theatre until the middle of the twentieth century, the proscenium tended to dominate theatre construction in Europe and America. (a) The Farnese Theatre, constructed at Parma, Italy, in 1618 or 1619. (b) The ANTA Playhouse in New York as remodeled in 1954.

permanent proscenium arch. Kernodle also makes it clear that the proscenium of the Farnese Theatre did not appear as a sudden invention, nor was it simply a further enlargement of the central doorway of the Olympic Theatre.[3] Instead the proscenium developed gradually as the sixteenth century progressed. In other words, the Farnese Theatre is the first proscenium theatre only in the sense that it marks the culmination and combination of trends already developed. To repeat, it moved the stage behind a formal proscenium, equipped this stage with pictorial scenery that could be shifted, and further separated the audience area from the playing area by means of a front curtain, thus giving the world a new picture proscenium type of theatre, a type that was soon to be generally accepted throughout most of the Western world.

It was not long until both France and Italy began to incline toward the proscenium form. In France the native basis for the theatre had been the tennis court, which consisted of one or more galleries surrounding a playing area. To convert this into a theatre a platform stage was erected at one end, much as it had been in the English inn yard and the Spanish *corral*. Unlike the English and Spanish, however, the French displayed an early preference for the proscenium arch. This may have been because the great period of French playwriting came after, not before, the Farnese Theatre.

As the centuries progressed there was a tendency for both opera houses and theatres to become larger, especially to increase the stage floor area and flying space (the space above the stage area), thus making provision for elaborate and spectacular effects. The Hall of Machines (*Salle des Machines*), constructed in Paris in 1662, though it eventually proved to be a white elephant, illustrates the extent to which some of these tendencies went. On the great opening night the king and 100 members of his court were placed on one of the huge platforms and hoisted into the air. Approximately 1000 stagehands were required for the operation of the complicated effects. The stage was so enormous (its depth was 132 feet) that, when the Palais Royal burned to the ground in 1763 and the company moved into the then abandoned Hall of Machines for temporary quarters, instead of using the entire building they found the stage alone of sufficient size to serve as both stage and auditorium.[4]

---

[3] Ibid., chap. 7.
[4] C. Lowell Lees, "The French Influence upon Garrick's Staging Methods" (M.A. thesis, Northwestern University, 1932), pp. 57 – 58.

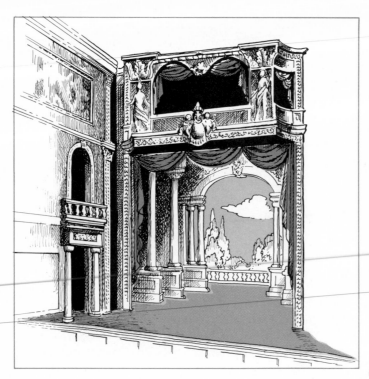

FIGURE 10:18 The Dorset Garden Thea- tre, an English Restoration playhouse, shows a com- promise be- tween the Elizabethan theatre and the proscenium theatre.

THE COMPROMISE: ENGLAND AND AMERICA AFTER 1660

Consciously or unconsciously, the theatres of Restoration England combined the two basic forms of the Renaissance stage. From the French and
the Italians, or perhaps from Inigo Jones, came the idea of the proscenium opening with its scenic perspectives. Perhaps from the same
sources came the ideas of moving indoors and of adding seats for the
groundlings and new elegance to the decorations. On the other hand,
Restoration theatres retained much that had been Elizabethan: the forestage, or apron, on which most of the action took place, the proscenium
doors and in some cases the proscenium balconies, and even the old
inner-below, which was simply enlarged and called a proscenium opening. Compare the sketches of a typical Elizabethan stage (Figure 10:15)
with the Dorset Garden Theatre (Figure 10:18) which was opened in
1671, and you will see that the break between the Elizabethan and Restoration theatres is not nearly as great as most people suppose. In fact if we
could compare Dorset Garden with the old indoor Blackfriars Theatre of
Shakespeare's day, we might find no essential distinction whatever.

During the eighteenth and nineteenth centuries the theatres of England, like those on the Continent, increased in size. Gas lighting was eventually introduced, and finally electricity, but the essential English form, the apron with its proscenium doors, was stubbornly retained even into the twentieth century.

What is commonly regarded as the first American theatre was built in Williamsburg, Virginia, in 1716. However, the most famous of the early theatres was the John Street Theatre in New York (1767). It was built by David Douglas, who has been called "the builder of theatres," for he constructed them almost wherever his famous company (the American Company, originally organized by Lewis Hallam) played. Both William Dunlap, in his *History of the American Theatre*, and Royall Tyler, through the mouth of Jonathan, his famous Yankee character in *The Contrast*, have left us descriptions of the John Street playhouse. It was set far back from the street, was painted red, and had a pit, a gallery, and a stage "of good dimensions." In 1798 the much finer Park Theatre opened its doors, also in New York. It burned in 1820, but a new theatre,

FIGURE 10:19 The Second Park Theatre, New York City, 1834.

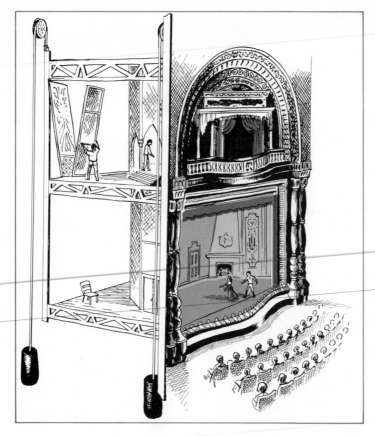

FIGURE 10:20
The elevator
stage of Steele
MacKaye's Mad-
ison Square
Theatre, 1879.

the Second Park Theatre, was soon completed where the old one had been. A famous painting of the interior (Figure 10:19) indicates that there was little difference between the basic form and quality of this theatre and theatres of the same period in London. The apron, flanked by proscenium doors and windows, is prominent, as are the rows of boxes that encircle the auditorium.

Not all plays in America were performed in regular theatres, however. In all countries and in all ages, stages have been improvised with complete disregard for basic architectural trends. For example, the first plays seen in the territory of Minnesota were performed by soldiers stationed at old Fort Snelling. These soldier shows, which began as early as the winter of 1821–1822, used barracks or mess halls—whatever was available. When the first professionals came up the river to St. Paul in the summer of 1851, they improvised a theatre in a hall located above a store. The companies that followed used similar makeshift facilities; one even played in the courthouse. It was not until 1857 that a building was constructed especially for theatrical purposes. This was the People's Theatre, which cost a sum total of $750. Rough and crude as the frontier itself, it burned to the ground a few years later. Not until 1867 did St. Paul get an adequate theatre, and even this was located on a second floor, with only one exit in case of fire or panic.

A complete history of nineteenth-century theatre architecture in other American cities would doubtless show thousands of innovations and variations. None, however, appears to have been new or fundamentally different, except the Madison Square Theatre (1879), which was built by Steele MacKaye and contained an elevator stage capable of shifting entire scenes by simply raising or lowering them (Figure 10:20). While the idea was not particularly successful in America, it did have an influence in Germany and marks the beginning of mechanical shifting devices. Of these the most effective to date have been (1) the revolving stage, which traces its origin from Japan through Germany and from there to the rest of the world, and (2) the wagon stage, which traces its origin all the way to the *eccyclema* of ancient Greece.

THE TWENTIETH CENTURY

The first half of the twentieth century, which produced spectacular technical achievements in most areas of human endeavor, had little effect on the legitimate theatre. The technical genius of the age found striking expression in motion pictures, radio, and television, but theatre architecture remained static. As we shall see, innovations in scenery and lighting were made during the second quarter of the century, but theatre architecture still lagged behind. To understand what happened, we must first turn to Broadway.

THE BROADWAY PLAYHOUSE

Until the end of the Second World War most American theatres, including college and high school auditoriums, tended to be patterned after standard Broadway playhouses. Since these were constructed for the purpose of crowding as many paying customers as possible into a 75-by-

100-foot rectangle of fabulously expensive Manhattan real estate, it is easy to understand why space for lobby, foyer, stage, and dressing rooms was so extremely limited. We can likewise understand the absence of shop and storage facilities, for in New York it is much less expensive to construct scenery elsewhere and truck it into the theatre. There is no need for storage space, since the house is rented to one show at a time, always in the hope that the new production will run forever! When the show closes, everything is disposed of, and the stage is completely cleared for the next tenant.

Even so, these Broadway playhouses are surprisingly well designed, considering their period and the purpose for which they were built. Most of the auditoriums are small, averaging about 1200 seats. Each has a main floor, a balcony, and often a gallery. This arrangement, plus the fact that most of them are quite wide, brings everyone reasonably close to the actors. Acoustically these small houses are excellent, and thus the primary functions, audibility and visibility, are well satisfied. The stages of these Broadway theatres, though cramped for space, are usually adequate, since only one play at a time is in production.

FIGURE 10:21 Henry Miller's Theatre. A typical Broadway playhouse of the early twentieth century.

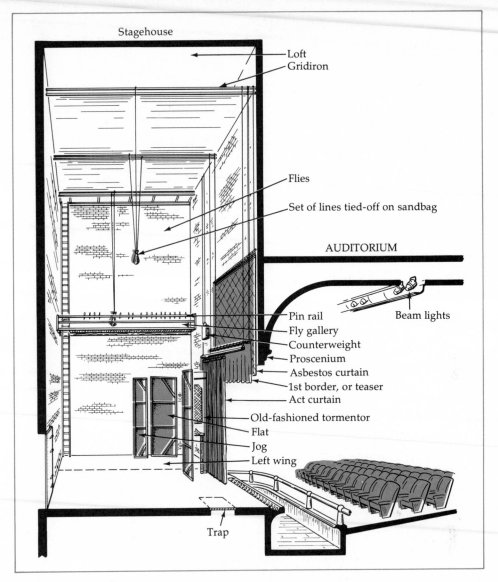

Stagehouse

Loft
Gridiron

Flies

Set of lines tied-off on sandbag

AUDITORIUM

Beam lights

Pin rail
Fly gallery
Counterweight
Proscenium
Asbestos curtain
1st border, or teaser
Act curtain
Old-fashioned tormentor
Flat
Jog
Left wing

Trap

FIGURE 10:22   Cross-section of a proscenium theatre (greatly simplified).

To those unfamiliar with the backstage area, a quick view of its major features should be helpful (Figure 10:22). Architecturally, a proscenium theatre consists of two major units, an auditorium and a stagehouse. The wall of the stagehouse, which divides it from the auditorium, is known as the proscenium. This contains the proscenium opening, through which the play is seen. Immediately behind this opening is a steel or asbestos curtain, which rides up and down in metal grooves and is used to divide the stagehouse from the auditorium in case of fire. Any portion of the stage floor that projects into the auditorium beyond this curtain is known as the apron, a feature practically nonexistent in most of the old Broadway houses. Stage space directly behind the proscenium opening includes the acting area, which of course varies according to the size and shape of the setting that encloses it. This area usually contains several traps (sections of floor that can be removed), which provide for such scenic necessities as Ophelia's grave. Space to the right side of the acting area (the actor's right as he faces the audience) is known as the right wing, that to the left as the left wing.

Above the acting area is flying space, or the flies. At the top of this is the grid, or gridiron, an iron framework that carries the sheave blocks (pulleys) and the lines (ropes or cables) used in flying (raising and lowering) scenery. The space between the gridiron and the roof of the stagehouse is known as the loft, and it is here that stagehands rig and adjust lines and sheaves in setting up for a new show.

On one side (sometimes both sides) of the stage is the fly gallery, a long, narrow gallery high above the floor where flymen handle the lines used in flying the scenery. As will be seen when we discuss shifting, lines are tied off around belaying pins which are inserted through holes in the pin rail, a large pipe or wooden beam that also serves as the top guard rail of the fly gallery.

Sizes and dimensions of stagehouses show a wide variation even among commercial theatres. In 1938 Burris-Meyer and Cole, after studying 38 representative American stages, supplied the following data as to average dimensions:[5]

Proscenium height	Proscenium width	Stage depth	Stage width	Gridiron height	Apron depth
28'1"	37'7"	31'1/2"	70'	61'	2'2"

All things considered, Broadway playhouses, though far from ideal, served the theatre well. The architectural crime lay in the manner in which architects outside of New York tended to imitate the bad features and eliminate the good features of the Broadway playhouse. Schools

[5] Harold Burris-Meyer and Edward C. Cole, *Scenery for the Theatre* (Boston: Little, Brown, 1938), p. 11.

during the first half of the century were the worst offenders. Auditoriums were expanded into barnlike caverns seating as many as 5000; stages were often compressed to little more than a speaker's platform; lobbies and dressing rooms were reduced and even eliminated; and shops and storage facilities were generally omitted, just as they had been in Broadway playhouses, but not for the same valid reasons.

Still, although the tendency to imitate the worst features of Broadway architecture dominated construction, there were exceptions. One was the Cleveland Playhouse (1916), where two proscenium theatres were combined under a single roof, allowing them to be served by shops, box office, and storage facilities common to both. Another was the State University of Iowa Theatre (1936) at Iowa City, which included several advanced features: (1) an intimate (500-seat) auditorium, (2) continental seating (rows far enough apart so that aisles were unnecessary), (3) stadium seating (an auditorium with a steep vertical slope), (4) a large revolving stage resting on an independent foundation, and (5) steel tracks that enabled large wagons to slide easily and accurately into position.

There were other important campus theatres, especially the Penthouse at the University of Washington, which will be discussed later, but such theatres tended to be exceptions until the end of the Second World War when a building boom, unprecedented in the history of the theatre, swept across America. The result has been staggering: Almost every college and university in America now displays a multimillion-dollar theatre or art center on its campus.

New playhouses have also blossomed for community theatres and for resident professional theatres. A few high schools have even been wise enough to include theatres (real theatres — not cafeteria theatres or basketball theatres) in their new plants. Ironically, almost the only area of America to lag far behind has been New York City itself, but even it finally joined the parade of construction with the ANTA Theatre in Washington Square and the Vivian Beaumont Theatre in Lincoln Center. All in all, America's passion for playhouse construction is a bit overwhelming and has been aptly described by Harold Clurman as the American theatre's "edifice complex."

More important than the sheer number of new playhouses are the facts that these playhouses are scattered all across the country and that exciting and widely varied new forms have been developed. Architects finally began to realize that educational and community theatres had needs and served functions different from those of the commercial Broadway playhouses. They are built on less expensive land and can better afford to expand horizontally. They are concerned with the production of seasons of plays and therefore need a building that is a self-contained producing plant. This means ample space for shops, storage, and rehearsal, plus offices for a permanent staff. In addition, it usually means classroom and teaching facilities. Finally, since the theatre is often intended to function as a cultural center for the school, the community, or both, there is need for rather spacious lobbies, comfortable lounges, and perhaps provision for such things as art exhibits.

But these striking advances in theatre construction have not been entirely free from error. The pendulum has frequently swung to an opposite extreme. Thus the auditorium, which during the first half of the century tended to be a monster that eliminated shop space, storage space, and dwarfed the peephole stage, has now been diminished in some theatres to a pitiful handful of seats facing the ugly dark proscenium of a cavernous stage. The prevailing style of decoration, once overloaded with gingerbread, plush, and elegance, has become as stark and depressing as a prison. The theatre, once a profit-making business, has become an art that can live only through generous handouts and deficit financing. The entrepreneur, once the dominant force in theatre construction, has been replaced by the designer-technician. Only when a personality as powerful as Sir Tyrone Guthrie enters the picture is there likely to be a theatre that achieves something approaching a balance between audience needs and backstage needs.

Huge stages with mechanical shifting devices, which would have been a godsend during the 1920s and 1930s when realism was in flower, are already obsolete. The cry today is for a theatre of involvement. Yet theatre planners have mistakenly assumed that involvement requires only a small auditorium. It requires instead an intimate relationship between audience and performer—a crowd of excited spectators surrounding or partially surrounding actors and actresses who can be seen and heard. A stage that is huge and out of proportion is quite as destructive to intimacy as an auditorium that is huge and out of proportion. There is a needed balance between audience and player that is not easy to achieve. In an attempt to achieve such a balance, forms other than the proscenium theatre have entered, or reentered, the picture.

ARENA THEATRES

Although the apron stage, as we shall see, has constantly offered mild opposition to the proscenium, the real revolt began in 1940 when the University of Washington opened its Penthouse Theatre. This was a playhouse constructed exclusively for arena staging. There was neither a raised platform for the actors nor the slightest vestige of a proscenium. As can be seen in Figure 10:23, the audience completely surrounded the performers. There are, of course, earlier examples of the idea. Enthusiasts for arena staging often maintain that primitive peoples probably placed the performer at the center of such a circle. They also point to circuses, bull rings, and arenas of all types to support their claims as to the basic naturalness of such an arrangement.

In the early 1920s Adolphe Appia recommended that a theatre be a large flexible space, while Robert E. Jones and Kenneth Macgowan wrote with imagination and enthusiasm about the possibility of producing

FIGURE 10:23   The Penthouse Theatre. The first playhouse constructed exclusively as an arena theatre, at the University of Washington, 1940.

FIGURE 10:24 A primitive arena indicates the naturalness of the form.

Shakespeare in one of the small circus arenas of Paris.[6] In 1924 Gilmor Brown opened his Pasadena Playbox, an intimate theatre in his own living room, where plays might be staged in whatever area of the room seemed most desirable (Figure 10:25). It was also in 1924 that Jacques Copeau established a playhouse without conventional stage or proscenium in a warehouse on the outskirts of Paris. In Russia a few years later Nikolai Okhlopkov developed an arena theatre as a means of achieving greater intimacy and realism.

But whoever deserves credit for its origin, the arena stage has assumed a position of genuine importance. Since the opening of the Penthouse Theatre at the University of Washington in 1940, arena stages have sprung up all over the country. One of the earliest and most successful was the Margo Jones Theatre-in-the-Round in Dallas, Texas, which from 1945 until the director's untimely death in 1955 was one of the most exciting theatres in America. Today almost every college in America has an arena theatre of some sort. Among them we find the beautiful Ring Theatre at Miami University and the Stadium Theatre built underneath a section of the football stadium at Ohio State. Several

[6] Kenneth Macgowan and Robert E. Jones, *Continental Stagecraft* (New York: Harcourt Brace Jovanovich, 1922), pp. 198–212.

of America's most successful resident professional theatres are arenas. The Alley Theatre in Houston, founded in 1947, has enjoyed an impressive record of success both in its old arena and in its new one. The Arena Stage in Washington, D.C., has also enjoyed an enviable reputation of success since its founding in 1950.

It seems too early to predict the future of arena staging with certainty but in all probability it is neither the theatre of tomorrow, as some of its enthusiasts predicted, nor the passing fad that its enemies supposed. It is rather a useful form of theatre with advantages and disadvantages like everything else. Among its limitations are the following:

1. The back of an actor or actress—from both an auditory and a visual standpoint—is less expressive than the front.
2. Scenery, which the arena eliminates, can often add to the player's ability to move and perform effectively.
3. The illusion of space and freedom (such things as the feeling of an open sky) is lacking.
4. The necessity of playing to all sides of the house tends to give a pattern of rotation to the action which can be disturbing.
5. Effective lighting is difficult to achieve.

On the affirmative side are the matters of cost and convenience. If every producing group had had a theatre like the one at the State Uni-

FIGURE 10:25   Gilmore Brown's Playbox at Pasadena was simply a large room which allowed flexible, informal staging.

Kerr summarizes the movement toward the open stage as follows:

The pressure toward a new shape, then, came insistently from all sides: from writers demanding the freedom to tell a new kind of story; from directors reaching desperately for fresh contact with their audiences; from audiences that must be wooed by the promise of an experience unlike that offered by rival and more accessible forms; from real-estate men who are realistic about what it takes to keep a playhouse solvent. All of our urges, whether generously creative or crassly economic, seem headed in a single direction.[8]

The direction referred to, of course, is toward the open stage or some variation thereof—toward an arrangement that permits an audience to see, hear, and share in a production without undue strain and without the aid of a public address system or opera glasses. It is a theatre, however, that still tries to provide a modified scenic background, a flexible environment for the action, and the powerful atmospheric advantages of modern lighting.

As the stage has broken through the proscenium and rejoined the audience, it has assumed innumerable forms and variations. While it seems wise to classify all of these as open staging, we can distinguish two major subdivisions, the apron stage and the thrust stage.

The apron stage extends into the audience in front of a proscenium stage, which is still used for much of the action. In modern practice this apron is usually mounted on a lift (elevator), enabling it to double as an orchestra pit for musical productions. Action is sometimes behind the proscenium and sometimes in front of it. The auditorium is usually quite wide and fan-shaped, representing a compromise between the regular proscenium and the thrust stage.

The thrust stage, as in the Festival Theatre at Stratford, Ontario, entirely eliminates the use of the proscenium stage, all the action taking place on the apron. Here the stage extends far enough into the auditorium so that the audience looking across the acting area sees spectators on the opposite side. Scenery, if there is any, is also thrust toward the audience rather than recessed behind a proscenium. Some of the greatest productions of our century have been staged in such theatres, and the form is becoming increasingly attractive to both professionals and amateurs.

[8] Walter Kerr, "The Theater Breaks Out of Belasco's Box," *Horizon*, July 1959.

FIGURE 10:30   The thrust stage. A form of theatre where the action never moves behind a proscenium. *(above)* The Stratford Festival Theatre, Ontario. *(below)* The Guthrie Theatre, Minneapolis.

lighting, and selects the sound and properties. Even on the most humble amateur level, however, one person cannot do it all. Help will be needed, and the wise leader will soon encourage and develop those who can help in the design as well as in the labor.

From an artistic standpoint it still seems to work best when a single artist designs lights, scenery, props, and costumes, but designers capable of doing so are becoming harder and harder to find. If more than one designer is involved, then the play's director will need to make sure that there is a close, and cordial, working relationship among them.

Although unity and harmony among all technical elements is obviously desirable, the following discussion, for the sake of clarity, will consider each element separately.

SCENIC DESIGN

Until the Renaissance, theatre architecture and the art of scenic design were essentially inseparable. In other words, there was a strong tendency for the visual background of the play to be a permanent part of the theatre itself: the architectural facade behind the player in the Greek, Roman, and Elizabethan theatres, the platforms or stations in the medieval. True, there was some consciousness of scenery: Aristotle credits Sophocles with its introduction; Vitruvius speaks of the *periaktoi* and other devices; and craftsmen of the medieval mystery plays must have lavished great imaginative skill on their stations, especially the hell mouth. But it was not until the picture-perspective settings of the Renaissance that the art of scenic design really assumed a place of its own.

It has already been mentioned that this idea of preparing a pictorial illusion of place was a natural outgrowth of the fifteenth-century interest in linear perspective, which had quite literally opened new horizons for Renaissance painters. In fact, some of these Renaissance painters, including the great Raphael himself, were among the first to design scenery. Thus there was a strong tendency to transfer to the stage the techniques of painting and perspective that had already been developed on canvas.

In general, the earliest pictorial backgrounds for the stage, like early backgrounds in painting, show an almost scientific and mechanical

FIGURE 11:1 A prize-winning design for Sophocles' *Antigone* by Sid Perkes, Utah State University.

preoccupation with perspective, almost as if the designer's primary objective had been to create the visual illusion of the longest possible street. This can be seen to some extent in the famous designs by Serlio which resemble architectural drawings (Figure 11:2). They have been called classic in contrast to the more romantic style that followed, for they tend to be intellectually and mechanically accurate rather than aesthetically or emotionally inspiring. There is an architectural hardness about these early settings, which in practice was heightened by the fact that they were not simply painted on a flat surface but were, whenever possible, built up in relief, using three-dimensional moldings and other solid features.

(a)

FIGURE 11:2   Serlio's famous designs for stage settings. Note the emphasis on mechanical perspective. *(a)* A tragic scene. *(b)* A comic scene.

The Italian monopoly on pictorial settings was of short duration. Early in the seventeenth century the English developed a passion of their own for scenic spectacle in their lavish court masques. As already mentioned, the man who was responsible for most of this scenic embellishment was Inigo Jones. He traveled a great deal, saw much, and learned much. To England he brought Italian scenic perspectives, the proscenium arch, and the contemporary continental systems of building scenery. But Jones was more than a borrower; he was an artist and innovator in his own right. His designs show a much freer and more florid style than those by Serlio. Most of his work has an imaginative and elab-

(b)

orate touch that is entirely individual. Perhaps his greatest innovation was the development of a system of changing scenes by sliding flats in grooves (Figure 11:3b), a system that remained standard in most English and American theatres for almost three centuries.

Any leadership that Inigo Jones or the English Court may have assumed in the matter of scenic design was cut short when the Puritans closed all English theatres in 1642. Theatrical attention returned to the Continent, especially to Italy, whose scenic artists achieved some spectacular results. In Venice, Giacomo Torelli is reported to have so overwhelmed his fellow citizens with some of his scenic effects that, believ-

FIGURE 11:3 *(above)* A theatrical design by Inigo Jones. The crack down the center indicates that this scene was to be painted on shutters. *(below)* Jones's method for shifting scenes consisted of a series of flats which fit into grooves at top and bottom so that they could slide on or off stage. In Scene I all sets of flats are in place on stage; the shift to Scene II, is accomplished simply by sliding the first flat of each set off stage.

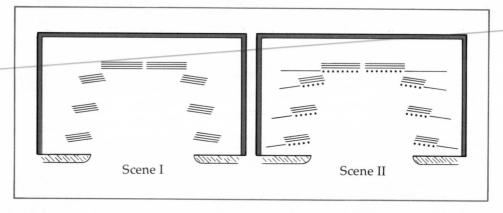

ing him to be in league with the devil, they tried to kill him. He fled to Paris, where his beautiful scenes and elaborate effects might be less dangerously appreciated. Although Torelli left Italy, many other designers did not; in fact the country fairly blossomed with scenic and operatic wonders. A study of the lavish baroque designs contributed by these Italian scenic artists during the late seventeenth, eighteenth, and nineteenth centuries is enough for a book in itself. The beginner should probably concentrate on remembering one name, Bibiena, a family name that stretched through four generations. From Giovanni Bibiena, the founder, to Alessandro and Carlo, the great-grandsons, the Bibienas created some of the most remarkable visual effects the theatrical and operatic world has ever seen. And while some later generations may have regarded such scenery as old-fashioned and outmoded, we must at

FIGURE 11:4 A design by Giuseppe Bibiena, 1719. His work represents the height of baroque elegance in scene painting.

Figure 11:5 Design for *A Christmas Tale* by Philip Loutherberg, David Garrick's famous scene designer.

Figure 11:6 Painted scenery (wings and backdrops) as in this woodland spectacle, 1778, dominated theatrical design from Inigo Jones to Tom Robertson.

least pay tribute to the skill, the patience, and the craftsmanship shown by the Bibienas and others like them. In their way these baroque settings achieved marvels of proportion, beauty, and scenic splendor.

Although painted scenery held the stage for three centuries, not all of it followed the lavish style of the Bibienas. Just as there was a close relationship between the designer and the painter during the Renaissance, so a similar relationship has been traced between designers and painters since the Renaissance.[1] The scene designer's tendency to follow paths already charted by the artist is not surprising, for it is logical that a comparatively individual art like painting should tend to be more experimental and exploratory than a group art like theatre. In any event, the romantic style of landscape painting, developed by such seventeenth-century artists as Salvator Rosa and Claude Lorrain, became popular in England by the beginning of the eighteenth century but did not reach the stage until toward the middle of the century. As far as the English theatre is concerned, the influence of these romantic landscape painters can be seen at its best in the work of Philip Loutherbourg (1740–1812). His settings, painted mostly for David Garrick at Drury Lane, had qualities of their own. He was especially effective in scenes featuring mist and wild mountain crags. Among the less gifted scene designers the tendency to imitate painters resulted in skillfully executed settings that were little more than out-and-out copies, while on the lowest level the copies were not even skillful. By the end of the nineteenth century most scenery was manufactured on a business basis by workers who used stencils, patterns, formulas, and the barest minimum of creativity.

THE REVOLT AGAINST PAINTED SCENERY

This tendency for painted scenery to be manufactured instead of created, to imitate good art or bad art with little taste or discrimination, may well have been an important factor in causing the scenic revolt that developed toward the end of the nineteenth century—a revolt against

[1] James R. Thompson, "Influences of Modern Painting on the New Stagecraft" (M.A. thesis, University of Minnesota, 1951).

the picture-painted scenery that had held the stage for almost 300 years. There were also other factors behind this revolt. Perhaps the theatre was once again merely following in the footsteps of the painter, who, as early as 1830, had moved toward realism and then, by the time of Ibsen, away from realism toward modernism. Perhaps the camera, with its ability to hold a mirror up to nature, was responsible for the general dissatisfaction with painted scenery. Or perhaps the new flat glare from gas or electric footlights and borderlights tended to highlight the false perspectives, painted shadows, waving pillars, and incongruous proportions that resulted when a player moving too far upstage loomed higher than the painted mountains. Whatever the reasons, the beginning of the twentieth century saw a widespread revolt against painted scenery.

Yet while critics agreed in their antagonism toward painted scenery, they were not in agreement as to an alternative. From the first there were two major schools of thought: the realists, who sought to remedy unconvincing painted scenery by making it "real", and the anti-realists, who sought to remedy the same unconvincing scenery by making it frankly theatrical, an art in and of itself rather than an imitation of nature.

THE REALISTS

In general the realists have been the more practical, businesslike, and financially successful. In England as early as the 1850s, Tom Robertson and the Bancrofts began using *box settings* (settings with a ceiling, back wall, and side walls) instead of the usual painted wings and drops. This led to the use of practical doors, practical windows, and such items as three-dimensional fireplaces. In America toward the end of the century, David Belasco established his reputation as the most painstaking realist of them all, sparing neither time nor money in his quest for the real and the lifelike.

In producing *The Easiest Way* Belasco went to a dilapidated rooming house, found the exact room he wanted, bought the entire interior, including doors, windows, and wallpaper, and transported it to the theatre, where it was reassembled with diligent care.[2] For other plays he even sent agents abroad to find exact and authentic props.

[2] David Belasco, *The Theatre Through Its Stage Door* (New York: Harper & Row, 1919), p. 77.

In theory, at least, Stanislavsky, Antoine, and other European directors carried scenery beyond the realism of Belasco into its most extreme form, known as naturalism. Actors and actresses began rehearsing in naturally furnished surroundings, not knowing which wall would eventually be removed to allow the audience to peer in on their private lives. Actors stood at the curtain line and gazed through windows in the imaginary fourth wall or warmed their hands at imaginary fireplaces. Chairs and even sofas might also be left standing with backs to the audience, as if the fourth wall had been slipped away without disturbing them.

But such extreme attempts only served to focus attention on the inherent limitations of realism and naturalism—limitations that many critics had realized from the beginning. For one thing, complete naturalism is impossible. Belasco could set up a real house but was defeated by such problems as lakes, mountains, and sky. Stanislavsky could set up a real room but eventually had to remove one wall. Much more important, complete naturalism is not only impossible but it is undesirable. How far would music have gone had it limited itself to a reproduction of sounds heard in nature? Imagine a great symphony orchestra rehearsing for weeks to produce the song of the blackbirds, the babbling of the brook, or even the rustling of the wind in the pines.

There are other charges against naturalism: It is expensive, cumbersome, and time-consuming; it can easily become distracting rather than helpful; and finally, stage naturalism could never hope to compete with motion picture naturalism even if it wanted to.

But while modern designers agree that extreme naturalism for its own sake is bad, there are many who still argue and demonstrate that modified realism can be very effective. Figure 11:7 suggests some of the modifications and simplifications possible within the realm of realism.

THE ANTIREALISTS

The antirealists were in revolt against not only painted scenery but also the realists.[3] In general, while antirealistic theories have been sound and stimulating, their realization has been muddled and impractical. Adolphe Appia, whose influence on the art of directing has already been

[3] John Dolman, Jr., *The Art of Play Production* (New York: Harper & Row, 1946), pp. 299ff.

(a)

FIGURE 11:7 Degrees of realism. (a) Total realism. A 1905 box set for David Belasco's *Girl of the Golden West.* (b) A 1930 design by Jo Mielziner for *The Affairs of Anatol.* Note that the sides and ceiling of the box have been omitted. (c) A 1947 production of *All The King's Men* at the University of Minnesota. Only the actors and a few properties stand out in the black void of a space stage.

(b)

(c)

considered, is a notable exception. This quiet, scholarly Swiss-German gave us a clear view of the functions and limitations of scenery. His settings were designed to harmonize with and assist the three-dimensional actors who played in them. He emphasized steps, levels, columns, and rhythm of line—the things stage art could do within the confines of the theatre. He also insisted that good lighting could fuse the actor and his environment into an organic whole. Both in theory and design he showed the way toward scenery that was both effective and practical.

FIGURE 11:8
Designs by
Adolph Appia.

FIGURE 11:9 Designs by Gordon Craig.

Gordon Craig, whom we considered earlier in our discussion of directing, held theories of design similar to those of Appia, though he verged more toward the impractical. In his passion for design he frequently forgot both the player and the limitations of the theatre. Still, it must be admitted that his scenes were stimulating and often beautiful. His influence on other designers and on twentieth-century theatre in general has been enormous.

Most students of scenic design devote some time to the study of such movements in modern art as symbolism, impressionism, expressionism, stylization, surrealism, constructivism, and abstraction. Such study can stimulate and open new horizons; on the other hand, artists also complain that it can be dangerous, especially if it becomes pedantic or rigid. There are no universally accepted definitions; moreover, such movements are rarely seen in anything approaching a pure form. Scenic artists of importance have emphasized the creative rather than the conventional. Howard Bay contends that the "isms" have melted together, or, as Robert Edmond Jones once phrased it, "What counts is expression, not expressionism."

But although rigid definitions are to be avoided, it is important to recognize that approaches to art can differ widely. Suppose, for example, that a naturalist, an impressionist, and an expressionist were to paint the same view of an old, abandoned mill. The naturalist's job would be clear and definite: a photographic reproduction of the old mill in full, accurate detail and color. The impressionist might say, "My impression of the mill is what counts, and my impression is one of vague, nostalgic gloom." In the impressionist's painting the mill might be softened in a mist. Hazy blues, gray-greens, and soft violets might replace the stronger hues of life; the hanging moss and vines might be heavily exaggerated. Still, the finished work would at least bear some resemblance to the old mill itself. But the expressionist might say, "I don't want to paint an old mill at all but rather my personal anger and indignation about man-made junk!" Accordingly, he or she might use harsh lines and colors, gross distortion, and splotches of raw pigment, with no more concern about whether the final result actually resembled the old mill than a composer would have about whether or not his music sounded like the harsh autumn wind as it moaned through the creaking timbers and grating hinges of the broken doorway. The painting might turn out to be an abstraction with no resemblance whatever to the old mill itself.

cheerleaders, and tumblers. A variation of the cyclorama setting is the space stage, which usually surrounds the playing area with black velours instead of the usual tan or gray, then sharply manipulates the lights so that only the players, the properties, and occasional fragments of scenery stand out in a black void. Finally, there is architectural formalism, which may consist of an expensive and elaborate arrangement of steps, levels, pillars, and screens, which, however, are never so elaborate or so specific that they could not be used for more than one play. The one common element of all types of formalism is that the background could become an accepted environment for many, if not all, plays.

THE FUNCTIONS OF SCENERY

Out of such theories and countertheories, can anyone hope to arrive at a rational understanding of the place and function of scenery? Perhaps not entirely, yet some of the confusion can surely be eliminated. We can begin where we just left off by considering the formalist's challenge and asking, "Is scenery necessary? What, if anything, does scenery really add to the sum total of the theatrical experience?" These questions are not purely academic. The success of *Our Town* and of a few other plays on essentially bare Broadway stages, as well as the current popularity of arena and modified arena productions, make the challenge a practical and serious one.

Obviously, if we limit scenery to its picture-proscenium style, if we think of it as painted flats, painted drops, columns, and levels, then scenery is not necessary, or at least not indispensable. But if we think of scenery in its larger sense, as the background against, upon, and in which a play is produced, there is no escape. In this larger sense all the so-called nonscenery plays actually do have scenery. Players cannot act in a vacuum. An environment of some sort is inevitable. In *Our Town* there was the back wall of the stage, with its dirty radiators; in the arena theatre there is the propertied acting area and the dim faces beyond; even in the space stage the black void itself is something—a very dramatic something. Consequently, in this larger sense the problem of whether or not there should be scenery vanishes. A background or environment of some kind is inevitable. The only question of importance becomes: Is the environment appropriate or inappropriate, effective or ineffective, an asset or a source of distraction? A designer who remembers this may avoid much senseless confusion.

But while in the final analysis scenery is a matter of effectiveness, this does not answer the question of what constitutes effectiveness. For obvious reasons, such a question has never been, and will never be, completely answered. Nevertheless, we can eliminate some of the vagueness by considering a few of the theatrical functions that a good setting can perform.

AID TO THE ACTOR

The relationship of scenery to the actor is no new idea. It was clearly recognized by Appia and others, yet many still think of scenery primarily as something to be looked at, not acted in or upon. As Robert Edmond Jones has implied, the question is not what the set will look like, but what it will make the actor or actress do. Harold Clurman calls the setting "an acting machine."

To those who ask "Why go to the trouble of making a real rope ladder for *Peter Pan?*" the answer lies not in the fact that real rope might look more convincing but in its contribution to the action. A real ladder can serve as a lookout post for Captain Hook. The Lost Boys can clutch at it to avoid falling overboard. It can save Peter by entangling Hook's claw just as he prepares to deliver the *coup de grâce*. Finally, it can provide one of the high moments of the great battle as terrified little Michael tries to escape up its rungs pursued by the biggest, most vicious of the cutthroats, until both disappear far above. The melee below can now be forgotten. Pirates and Lost Boys freeze in silence. Even Hook pauses in his mortal combat with Peter; all gaze aloft in horror. Then comes a blood-curdling death scream as the huge (dummy) body of the pirate hurtles through space and plunges into the sea. Try doing that on a painted backdrop!

The designer is under constant temptation to design a set that will look well, one that will bring a burst of applause from the audience as the curtain rises, for it is by the looks of the set that the average audience will judge the work. As will be explained later, it is important and legitimate for the set to be attractive, but never at the expense of the players'

FIGURE 11:11   Scenery that aids the action. *(above) Hang on to Your Head* at the Children's Theatre, Minneapolis; directed by John Clarke Donahue; designed by Jack Barkla. *(below) A Christmas Carol* at the Guthrie Theatre; directed by Stephen Kanee; designed by Jack Barkla.

ability to act in it. Scenery is essentially the environment in which the performers live and move.

CONCEALMENT OF DISTRACTIONS

As we have seen, there is always a background for the action of the play, but if this background is inappropriate, it becomes a source of distraction. Even in "no-scenery" productions some provision is usually made to get characters out of view when they are not supposed to be on stage. Moreover, in the conventional proscenium theatre the back wall of the average stage with its heating system, service doors, and piles of scenery provides neither an attractive nor appropriate background. *Our Town* got by largely because of the novelty of the idea and because of the fact that the play was presentational and frankly theatrical in nature. It is highly significant that very few other plays have followed its example. Of course, it is perfectly possible to design and build a theatre with a neutral and attractive background against which almost any play might be presented. The Greeks did it, the Elizabethans did it, Copeau did it, Guthrie did it at Stratford, Ontario, and now thrust stages are doing it everywhere. But unless some such formal setting is built into the architecture itself, curtains, cycloramas, or some kind of scenery must ordinarily be used to cover the ugly nakedness of the bare stage.

FIGURE 11:12 Thrust stages and modern lighting can render side wings and masking unnecessary, as indicated by John Gerth's design for *Doña Rosita, the Spinster.*

but as a rule the actor simply wore the best he had, regardless of the part. Some companies, in fact, managed to acquire cast-off clothing from the nobility, thus enabling them to appear in an elegance and splendor they could not otherwise have afforded.

Even during these periods, however, some attempt was made to fit the costume to the character. Thus the beggar usually appeared in contemporary rags, the servant in contemporary livery, and the prince in contemporary robes, but, at least in England, the practice of reflecting the historical period of the play in the costuming was practically unknown until 1773, when David Garrick's great rival, Charles Macklin, attempted to costume *Macbeth* in Scottish robes. (Lady Macbeth still insisted on using "modern" dress.) Odell reports that Garrick's pride was stung to the quick by the fact that Macklin and not he had introduced this innovation. Accordingly, Garrick dressed his King Lear in old English garments for his farewell performance of the role at Drury Lane.

By the beginning of the nineteenth century the idea of period costuming was generally accepted in England, as it had already been accepted several decades earlier in France. Even so, most stage costuming during the nineteenth century was restricted to a few period styles that tended to be unimaginative, standard, and conventional. Costumes for three or four periods, plus those of one or two national groups, made up the stock of most commercial costume houses. The usual practice, however, was for each actor and actress to provide his or her own wardrobe, and half a dozen favorite costumes were probably sufficient for most of the roles played during an actor's lifetime.

With the coming of men like the Duke of Saxe-Meiningen, Stanislavsky, and Belasco, standardized theatrical costumes were abandoned in a realistic search for greater and greater authenticity. While rigid adherence to historical accuracy, as sometimes practiced by such realists, is no longer regarded as important, we must nevertheless admire the painstaking care that Saxe-Meiningen and others lavished on costumes, as well as the conscientious effort they made to tie costuming into the organic pattern of the play as a whole. No longer did each player appear on opening night in the costume of his or her choice, regardless of scenery, other costumes, or lighting, for costuming, like acting, was made to function as one element in a larger pattern: the visual pattern of the play as a whole.

[5] George C. D. Odell, *Shakespeare from Betterton to Irving* (New York: Scribner, 1920), pp. 452–454.

(a)

(b)

(c)

FIGURE 11:15 Performing the classics in modern dress has again become popular. Plays thus produced tend to gain in meaning and relevance. *(a) Tartuffe* at the Asolo State Theatre; directed by Robert Strane; costumes by Flozanna John. *(b) A Servant of Two Masters* at the University of Minnesota; directed by Edward Payson Call; costumes by Irene Pieper; scenery by Donald Seay. *(c) Hamlet* at the Guthrie Theatre; directed by Tyrone Guthrie; designed by Tanya Moisewitsch.

That characterization and the organic life of the play are more important than historical accuracy per se is indicated by the fact that since the middle of the present century, directors have been more and more inclined to costume Shakespeare and other classics in modern (or semi-modern) dress. They argue that modern clothing can tell us much about the characters and the play, whereas authentic period costumes tell us very little.

COSTUME DESIGN

To one gifted with a knack for designing clothing, the theatre offers an exciting outlet, for stage costumes can be bold, colorful, and striking. They can display a theatrical flair, a dramatic imagination, and a streamlined simplification not possible in ordinary dress especially at the present time when realism is no longer sacred. In addition to a feeling for style in clothing, the costume designer must know period styles and be

(b)

FIGURE 11:16 Modern costuming, like playwriting and scene design, enjoys freedom from the dominance of realism. *(a) The Skin of Our Teeth* at Ohio State University; costumes by Michelle Guillot. *(b) The Comedy of Errors* at the Colorado Shakespeare Festival; costumes by David A. Busse.

(a)

2000 B.C.

400 B.C.

1400

1580

1775

1800

1860

1880

1900

FIGURE 11:17 A few lines, primarily those revealing silhouette, can capture the period of the costume.

able to reflect character. Obviously, everything he or she does must spring from the needs of the play. There can be no such thing as a good costume that does not fit the play and the character or does not harmonize with the setting, with other costumes, and with the lighting. Consequently, the costumer must work in constant cooperation with the director, the scene designer, and other members of the technical staff.

In establishing the period of a costume, sometimes color is important and sometimes texture; but ordinarily the essential element is the silhouette, as the sketches in Figure 11:17 indicate. Obviously, a keen sense of silhouette is one of the first skills the student of costuming should try to acquire. This is only a short cut, however, for in the long run there is no substitute for knowing as much as possible about major periods.

Adjusting designs to character is more important than adjusting them to period. *The Taming of the Shrew* can be played in modern dress without serious damage, but to costume Petruchio in delicate colors or effeminate lace, no matter what the period, would probably destroy the basic idea of the play as a whole.

In achieving costumes that reflect character, rules and formulas cannot replace taste and good judgment. A knowledge of color symbolism, for example, may be valuable, yet costumers can make fools of themselves by following too literally such oversimplified conventions as purple for royalty, pale blue for innocence, and red for vitality. The costumer, like the scene designer, must never forget that color is largely a relative matter; the color of the other costumes, the scenic background, the lights, and even the properties all have their influences.

One curious feature of style in clothing is its tendency to be in a constant state of change. In the modern world this is undoubtedly encouraged by clothing manufacturers and fashion designers, who obviously profit by stimulating the purchase of new wardrobes as often as possible. But a more fundamental explanation of shifting fashions lies in a strange psychological cycle. A new style is designed and modeled by the most shapely figures available. Movie and stage stars quickly adopt it, and soon, through association rather than merit, everyone scrambles to display the "new look." Inevitable disillusionment follows as the new sensation goes into mass production and is draped over the strange assortment of shapes that make up the average and less-than-average specimens of the species. A reaction sets in. Everyone now has the new style, most of them still look awful, and psychologically we are ready for the cycle to repeat itself. The last to discard the new style, by now the old style, are usually the underprivileged, the eccentric, and the poorest physical specimens of the race. Thus the impression of the style just past is generally negative, and a number of years may have to pass before we can view it impartially again.

Whether one accepts this explanation or not, the costume designer will do well to use care in dealing with styles that have aged less than a quarter of a century, unless he or she wishes to create a comic effect.

(a)

(b)

FIGURE 11:18 Costumes for Juliet.
Note that even after plays were
costumed in period, the styles
tended to reflect the period in
which they were worn as much as or
more than the period they were intended to portray. (a) Mrs. Jackson,
1775. (b) Julia Marlowe, 1888. (c)
Katharine Cornell, 1933.

(c)

During the 1920s women used to laugh at the horrible wasp waists that
had been worn during the Gibson Girl era. During the 1940s they
laughed at the shapeless sacks worn during the 1920s but were beginning to find the Gibson Girl styles rather pleasing. Beyond a certain period of time costume styles again become interesting and perhaps beautiful, but those of the immediate past are likely to seem simply dated and

old-fashioned. It is usually wise, therefore, to present most plays less than 25 years of age in modern dress unless they are period pieces to begin with or unless some other reason makes it necessary to adhere to the style of the period for which they were written.

The costume designer should not only be wary of the style that has just become dated but also conscious of the powerful appeal of the current vogue. Even in designing period costumes the modern style should wield its influence. Authentic period costumes are almost never effective. Good stage costumes for a Greek play produced in 1920 reflect the flapper silhouette as well as the classic lines of ancient Greece. The same Greek play, if well costumed in 1947, would have revealed the unmistakable influence of Dior's "new look." The good costume designer knows the past but instinctively modifies it by the present and finds it easy to adapt his or her designs according to the taste of the times. Rather than trying to rationalize the problem, for it is not necessarily logical, he or she simply accepts the fact that final judgment in style and beauty is largely a subjective matter that lies somewhere in the irrational subconscious of the audience.

CONSTRUCTION AND CARE OF COSTUMES

If the producing organization is small, does not employ a regular costumer, and for the most part produces modern plays, it is probably best to rent costumes when they are necessary. In such cases the problem is one of selecting the right costume company. Nationally known costume houses have large stocks from which to choose, and they know their jobs. On the other hand, they may be rather expensive and also inaccessible to most groups either for fittings or for individual consultation. Friendly relations with a local costumer, if there is one, can be advantageous. Personal contact, personal interest, and more moderate prices can often go a long way toward counterbalancing the inherent advantages of large, nationally known concerns. In any case, start early enough so that there is time to shop. A policy of asking for bids is wise, though quality, not price alone, must be considered.

But no matter where costumes come from, some efficiency in receiving them, caring for them, and returning them is essential. On the whole, costume houses have far greater cause for complaint than do most nonprofessional theatres. What can a costumer do if the order itself is garbled, inaccurate, and vague? He or she can hardly be blamed for not sending the best when he knows how thoughtless, careless, and destructive the untrained and confused amateur can be on opening night. He can hardly be blamed for exorbitant prices when only part of the costumes come back, and those late and in filthy condition. Most commercial costumers tend to be artists rather than entrepreneurs. They love costumes and often love theatre. If you are renting, take care of what you get, show intelligent interest and enthusiasm, start early, and you will probably be delighted with both the quality and prices that your costume house will provide.

For larger organizations like professional, community and university theatres, renting costumes is almost never as satisfactory as making them. Materials used in constructing costumes usually cost about the same as the rental for a week's run. If most of the work can be done by volunteer committees or by students, the saving over a period of years becomes impressive, for the wardrobe grows rapidly. In the school, moreover, the training and satisfaction that accompany original creation are of utmost importance.

A discussion of techniques of costume construction has no place here, though one or two basic ideas particularly applicable to the nonprofessional theatre are worth mentioning. Uniforms, for example, are beyond the skill of most amateur costumers, yet excellent results may be achieved by buying old uniforms (army, navy, band) and remodeling them to suit the play. They can be cut, fitted, dyed, and decorated with gold braid and medals. In fact, the gifted costumer is a genius at remodeling all sorts of wearing apparel. If the theatre has a real place in the community, and if it has adequate storage facilities, it is amazing how much of value can be acquired over a period of years if friends of the theatre know that gifts of old clothing are welcome. Some such gifts may be worth keeping just as they are. Others can be refashioned as needed. Good judgment will have to dictate what to keep and what to remake, but in either case gifts are valuable.

When working with stage costumes, the designer and the tailor must be constantly aware that the play's action may demand special techniques. The gentleman who must fight a duel may require a considerably different costume from one who does nothing but stand or sit in a formal drawing room. Elaborate costumes must sometimes be modified to permit quick changes. Such special requirements can be met if the director and costumer recognize and plan for the emergency in advance. Undetected until final dress rehearsal, quick changes can be disastrous.

In making new costumes, the selection of materials requires training, experience, good judgment, and a knack for shopping for bargains. Since the effect from a distance is always what counts, intricate patterns and delicate textures are lost. The good costumer is constantly alert regarding drape, weave, texture, and cost of materials. Skillful dyeing, top dyeing, spattering, and spraying can sometimes give inexpensive materials a luxurious and expensive stage appearance. Designs can be painted or appliquéd. There is no limit to the ingenuity of some costumers. Gorgeous pieces of costume jewelry can be fashioned from scraps of metallic cloth set with ordinary marbles. Some costumers turn out stunning effects at practically no cost, while others, working in elaborately equipped shops with expensive materials, achieve mediocre results.

As to general organization, there is no set pattern, although most large university and community theatres proceed about as follows. The costume designer first studies the play and then meets with the scene designer and director well in advance of the first rehearsal. By the time of the first general meeting the designs should be ready, the basic work schedule outlined, crews organized, and measurements taken of the players who must have costumes. A few days later materials should be on hand and construction under way. Further meetings with the director and the scene designer are almost always necessary. Actors and actresses must be fitted, unexpected problems solved, and changes in scenery or lighting noted.

Approximately a week before opening night comes the dress parade. Actors and actresses don costumes and appear on the set under the lights before the costumer, the director, and their assistants. Fittings, adjustments, and changes should be agreed upon and carefully noted. As dress rehearsals begin, costumes are usually checked out to the players, who then assume responsibility for their care until the run is completed. Unless a good tradition has been established, some pressure will have to be applied if the average actor or actress is to discharge his or her responsibility conscientiously. Even in the best of theatres, constant checking is necessary if costumes are to be hung up and cared for. Lost buttons, broken snaps, and other mishaps should be reported immediately.

Following the last performance costumes are checked in; those worth keeping are then sent to the cleaner's and stored for future use. The costumer in an active theatre has a full-time but fascinating job.

CHAPTER 12

STAGECRAFT: CONSTRUCTION, PAINTING, SHIFTING, AND PROPERTIES

Ideas and dreams without the skill and craftsmanship to express them can be as futile as skill and craftsmanship without ideas or dreams. Yet in spite of this obvious truth many students shy away from craft courses in theatre, many educators still oppose the inclusion of such courses in a college curriculum, and many American institutions of higher learning still refuse to allow the teaching of such skills. Some colleges permit the production of plays provided that only the literary values are emphasized, or, as a student at one large university recently expressed it, "We can do plays provided that we do not do them very well."

A sincere desire on the part of some students and educators to deemphasize skill, discouraging any tendency to transform a liberal education into a trade school education, is understandable; but surely the truly educated person should be able to do as well as to know what to do. Like the public speaker and the writer, the student in theatre should strive for a balance between having something to say and the skill used in saying it; both qualities are necessary. If a production of *Hamlet* is to excite discussion, stimulate ideas, and fulfill its function as either art or education, it must be staged with skill and craftsmanship. True, the crafts and techniques that go into such a production should be regarded as a means to an end, not as the end itself, but this does not mean that they should be ignored.

The foregoing discussion is not intended to give the impression that creation and craftsmanship, or, if you prefer, art and technique, are somehow antagonistic and that development of one is likely to inhibit the other. There is no evidence that skill in the use of even such practical objects as a saw and a hammer will cripple the mind or blight the creative soul. Yet one of the most persistent false assumptions made by so many with a taste for the literary is that good playwriting is somehow antagonistic to good production. Actually the reasoning of such purists goes through not one but two steps, for they begin by asking for an actor or actress who will "just say the lines," then ask that he or she be placed in the simplest possible setting, fearing that the acting will detract from the play and the scenery from the actor. Actually, the reverse is nearer the truth. Time after time, imaginative costumes, lights, sound, and scenery have stirred life into unimaginative actors, after which actors, costumes, lights, sound, and scenery together have stirred life into the play. To repeat: Something to say plus skill in saying it is the desirable combination, and this seems to require that the vision of the playwright, the director, and the designer be augmented by the skill and craftsmanship of the technicians.

Skill, however, is the critical word. Thus, although the average person may gain more from hearing a play skillfully read by good actors than by silently reading the script himself, an unskilled reading by poor actors can distort and destroy the play's values.

The same logic lies behind each technical element that is added: costumes, lighting, sound effects, scenery. Each may add or detract depending upon the skill and taste with which it is executed.

The tendency to feel that it is not a good production unless it has lots of everything must be avoided. If the budget is severely limited, it will be far better to do *The Importance of Being Earnest* in smart modern dress than to rent third-rate period costumes. The craftsperson's motto should be, "Do it well or not at all!" Bear in mind, then, that the crafts can range from being a tremendous asset to a cluttering distraction.

for example, to once more enjoy the art of old-fashioned painted back-drops and wings.

But in spite of the new, there is much that is still standard. To begin with, there are a few practical generalizations that almost always apply, especially in the noncommercial theatre: Scenery should be (1) light and portable, (2) tough, with all woodwork securely joined, (3) capable of rapid and inexpensive construction, and (4) capable of being reused or recycled.

The relationship between the designer and the technicians has also remained quite stable, especially in the case of realistic scenery. We have already seen that the scene designer is normally expected to provide either a model or a ground plan, elevation, and full-color rendering of the setting (Figure 12:1). From these the working drawings and detail drawings are prepared. Working drawings resemble elevation drawings except that they view the set from the rear and consequently indicate the basic plan of construction.

FIGURE 12:1   Based on the designer's sketch (*a*), ground plan (*b*), and elevation (*c*), the working drawings and detail drawings are drafted. These drawings are greatly simplified.

(a)

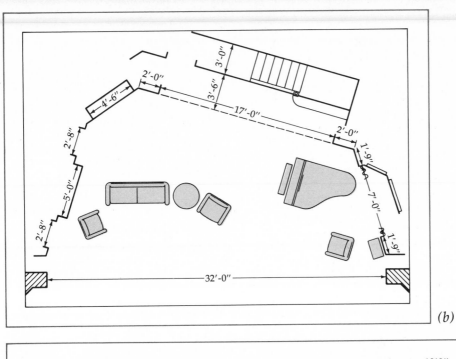

(b)

(c)

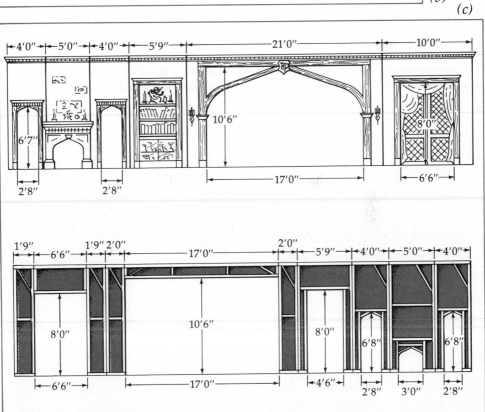

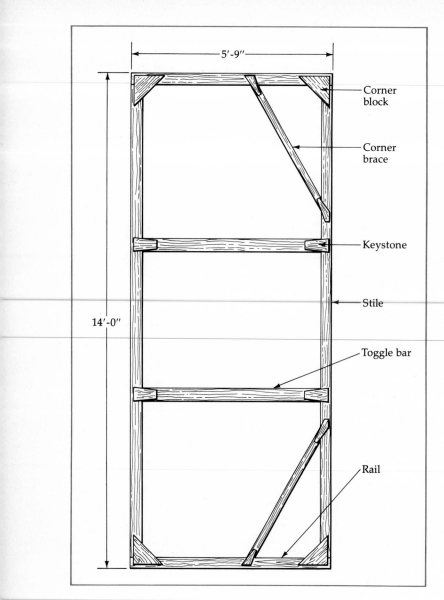

5'-9"

Corner block

Corner brace

Keystone

Stile

14'-0"

Toggle bar

Rail

FIGURE 12:2   The frame of the standard flat, traditionally made of 1-by-3-inch white pine. Keystones and corner blocks are made of quarter-inch plywood.

STANDING UNITS

In a proscenium theatre the setting usually consists of a number of standing units known as *flats* (narrow ones are called *jogs*). These have been, and can be, made in numerous ways and from numerous materials, but the traditional, and still standard, procedure is to construct a

light but tough wooden framework which is then covered with cloth —
usually canvas or muslin. Figure 12:2 indicates one way of constructing
such a flat. Figure 12:3 suggests some of the details involved in such construction.

FIGURE 12:3 Some construction details. (a) For strength the grain of corner blocks and key-stones should run at a 45- to 90-degree angle to the joint. (b) Hold corner blocks and key-stones in the width of a stile from the edges of flats. (c) Nails or screws inserted in straight lines make weak joints and split boards. (d) The use of screws when joining toggle bars to stiles enables the bar to be moved without damage. (e) To cover flats, tack or staple material along the inside edges of stiles and rails; turn back the free edges to apply dope or white glue.

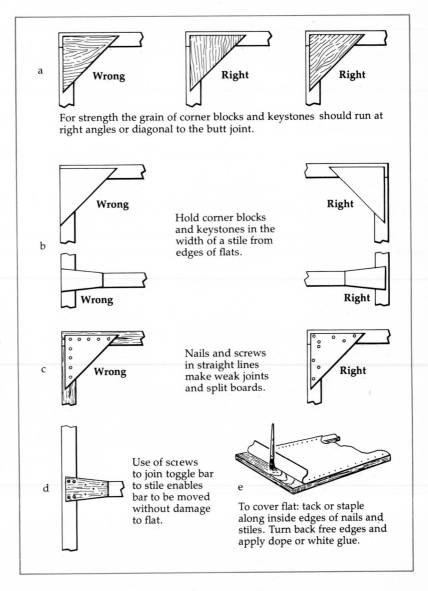

a **Wrong** **Right** **Right**

For strength the grain of corner blocks and keystones should run at right angles or diagonal to the butt joint.

b **Wrong** **Right**

Hold corner blocks and keystones in the width of a stile from edges of flats.

Wrong **Right**

c **Wrong** **Right**

Nails and screws in straight lines make weak joints and split boards.

d Use of screws to join toggle bar to stile enables bar to be moved without damage to flat.

e To cover flat: tack or staple along inside edges of nails and stiles. Turn back free edges and apply dope or white glue.

MODIFICATION OF FLATS

Once the technique of constructing a standard flat has been mastered, it is a simple matter to modify the construction to provide openings for doors, windows, archways, and so on (Figure 12:4 and Figure 12:5).

FIGURE 12:4 Flats modified to receive doors or windows.

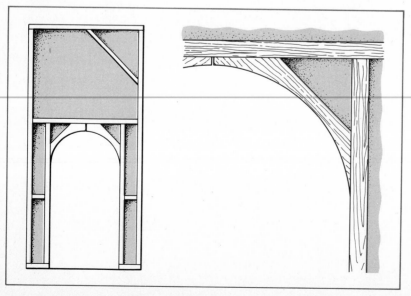

FIGURE 12:5 Flat modified as an archway.

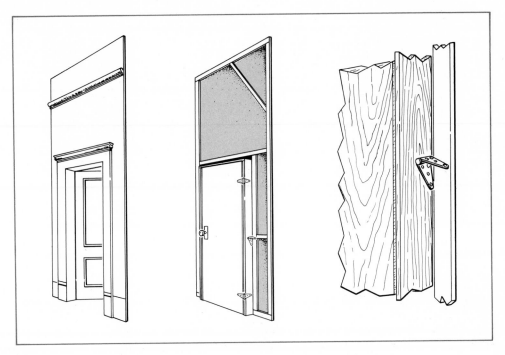

FIGURE 12:6   Door unit held into a flat by means of strap hinges.

Such flats of course provide only the openings. The window and door units themselves require techniques of carpentry that are much more involved. Such units are normally fastened into their flat openings by means of strap hinges (Figure 12:6).

METHODS OF JOINING FLATS

Flats seldom stand alone; they are combined with other flats to form larger units such as walls. Not many years ago the standard practice was to lash flats together as indicated in Figure 12:7.

Since lashing always leaves a visible crack between the flats, the practice has generally been discarded except at corners or in other cases where the crack can be disguised in some way. In a setting that can be assembled for the duration of a show, the flats are ordinarily battened

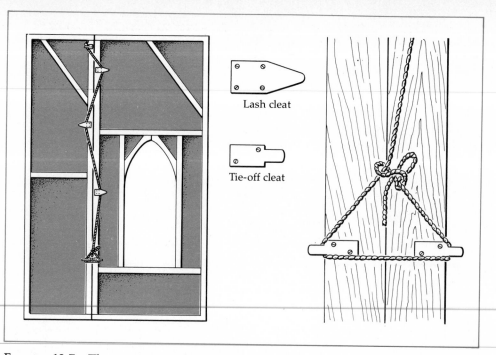

FIGURE 12:7 The traditional method of joining flats was to lash them together.

FIGURE 12:8 Two-fold and three-fold flats.

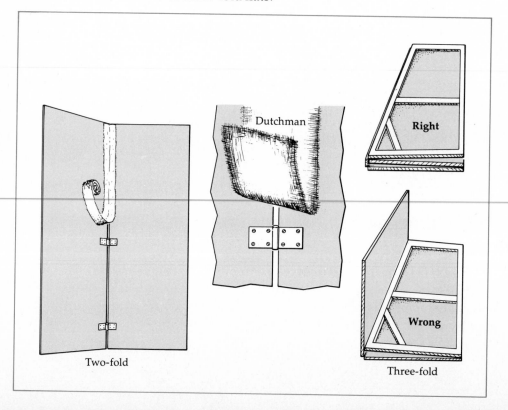

together and the cracks covered by pasting strips of tape or muslin (a dutchman) over them (Figure 12:8).

In cases in which flats must be folded in shifting and can no longer be battened together, two, and sometimes three, flats can be hinged together, forming two-folds and three-folds as indicated in Figure 12:8. Note that a three-fold requires the addition of an extra strip of lumber (a tumbler) between two of the flats to avoid having the third flat bind against the edge of the first.

<u>PROFILES</u>

Many pieces, such as two-dimensional trees, columns, foliage clumps, and ground rows representing mountains or city skylines, call for units with irregular edges.

If the unit is small—not over 4 by 8 feet—it is possible simply to outline it on a large piece of plywood or wallboard, saw out the silhouette, and paint it. If a larger unit is necessary, the scene technician will probably follow the type of construction shown in Figure 12:9. This consists of building a frame, using essentially the same technique as in flat construction except that the outside edge of the frame is lined with ply-

FIGURE 12:9   Profile construction.

wood. Units such as large ground rows are usually made in two or more pieces and hinged to provide greater ease in handling.

CUTOUTS

When the irregular outline lies within the frame, as in the case of an ornamental grill, a balustrade, or certain foliage units, the cutout technique may be the answer. Suppose it were necessary to construct the ornamental railing shown in Figure 12:10. The stage carpenter begins by building a flat. He or she then paints the posts, using plenty of paint and glue to provide stiffness. After the paint has hardened the carpenter cuts out and discards the unpainted material between the posts; finally he or she reinforces the posts by gluing scrim or netting across the back. If the unit is not framed but is flexible, as in the case of a backdrop or foliage border, rosin or some other adhesive that will not crack is used when gluing the cutout material to the scrim backing.

FIGURE 12:10   Cutout construction.

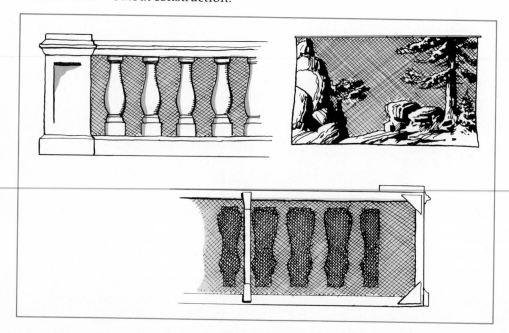

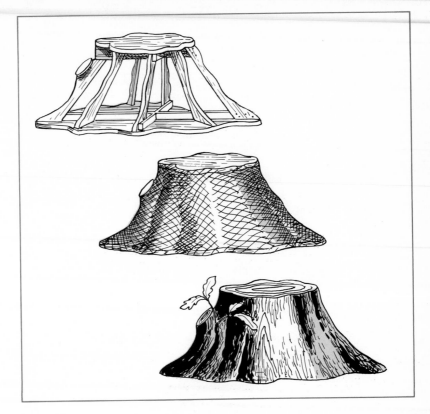

THREE-DIMENSIONAL OBJECTS

Traditionally when irregular three-dimensional objects, such as rocks, tree trunks, and capitals of pillars, were constructed, the mâché technique was employed (Figure 12:11). First the stage carpenter built a rough wooden framework of the object. He next nailed chicken wire over the framework and molded it into the desired shape. Finally he covered the wire with muslin or canvas that had been soaked in a solution of old pigment and glue.

Today a number of new products, including one known as Celastic, have largely replaced the mâché technique. Celastic hardens to a tough, leatherlike finish, and while many may find it too expensive for large objects such as tree trunks and rocks, they can still use it to excellent advantage in reproducing small objects, such as armor, statuary, and vases. The final product is light, tough, and comparatively unbreakable. Fiberglass may also be used and is especially sturdy. Where light weight but not strength is important, Styrofoam or polyurethane foam may be the answer.

PARALLELS

The construction of such items as doors, windows, stairways, and most platforms belongs in a more advanced course. There is, however, one unit that is so useful and unique to the theatre that it should be explained here. This is the parallel, which is a type of platform that can be

FIGURE 12:12   Parallels.

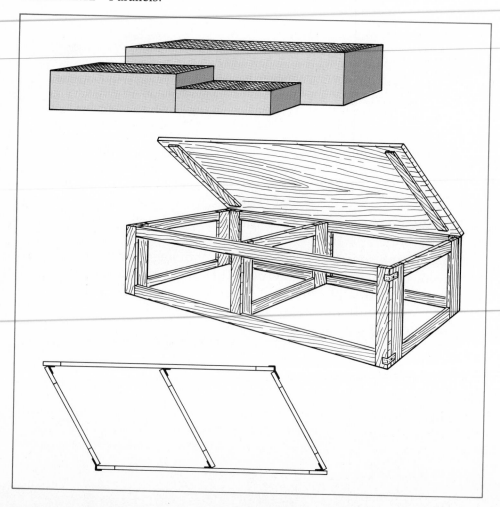

folded and stored when not in use. The top, usually cut from a solid piece of 3/4-inch plywood, is detachable. In most cases the sides and ends are cut from plywood or constructed in a manner resembling small flats (Figure 12:12). The essential element is the hinging arrangement. Two corners diagonal from one another are hinged on the inside, and the opposite corners hinge on the outside.

CYCLORAMAS AND CURTAINS

Curtains for stage use are ordinarily made in much the same way whether they are to be used as sky cyclorama, scrim, or drapes. Strips of material are sewn together, usually, but not always, with the seams running vertically. A heavy strip of burlap or canvas webbing is then sewn securely across the top of each section. Large grommets are then inserted in the webbing and finally tielines are inserted in the grommets (Figure 12:13). The hem at the bottom of the curtain is usually large enough to form a pocket that can be weighted with a chain or a pipe batten.

METAL AS SCENERY

The use of metal, both steel and aluminum, is becoming increasingly important in scene construction. As Howard Bay wrote in 1974, "the present drift is away from wood turning to sculpting and casting, to

FIGURE 12:13   Curtains.

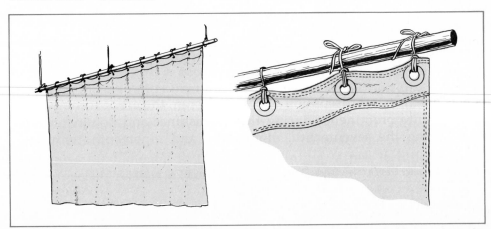

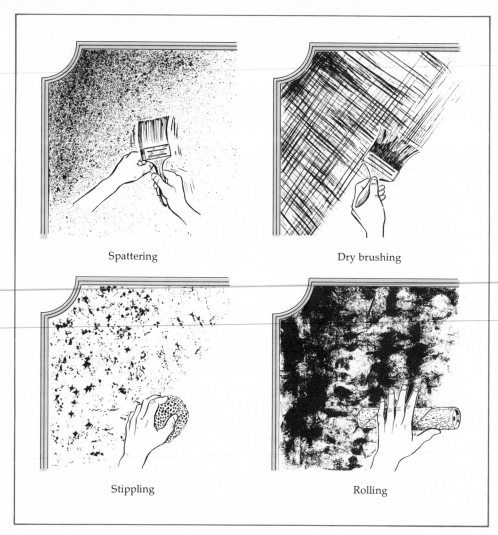

Spattering

Dry brushing

Stippling

Rolling

FIGURE 12:18 Some painting techniques.

Texturing in three dimensions is becoming increasingly important, especially in arena and thrust theatres, where objects tend to be seen and examined at close range. Improvisations in papier-mâché, paint mixed with sawdust, and new plastic foams are among the materials that are finding more and more use in giving texture to the surface of scenery. At times, of course, entire scenic units are carved from blocks of Styrofoam or molded from liquid plastics. Some examples of texturing are shown in Figure 12:19.

(a)

FIGURE 12:19   Some examples of texturing. *(a) The Three Cuckolds* at the Chanhassen Dinner Theatre; scenery by Tom Butsch; costumes by Sandra Nei Schulte. *(b) Medea* at the University of Wyoming; designed by Donald Seay. *(c) Amahl and the Night* Visitors at Idaho State University; designed by John Gerth.

(b)

(c)

FIGURE 12:20   The traditional method of enlarging a design when transferring it from the designer's rendering to a painted drop.

TRANSFERRING A DESIGN TO A DROP

One of two methods is commonly employed in transferring designs from an easel-sized painting to a large backdrop. The traditional method is to place a grid of small squares over the design and then transfer these squares on a much larger scale to the drop (Figure 12:20). A more modern method is to make a photographic slide of the design and then project this onto the drop. The main forms can then be quickly and accurately outlined.

Beyond the basic painting techniques already described lies the real art of scene painting—an art closely related to easel painting but on a much bigger and bolder scale.

THE SHIFTING OF SCENERY

Scene shifting is a far greater problem today than it once was. Audiences accustomed to an uninterrupted flow of action in movies are no longer content to pause from 5 to 25 minutes between scenes while stagehands laboriously shift the scenery. Some settings, moreover, are much heavier and more complex than the old painted wings and drops that once were standard. More numerous, too, are multiple-scene plays. Fast shifting has become a necessity.

Today many methods of shifting are employed, but none is perfect; all have advantages and disadvantages. No system can act as a substitute for careful planning, imaginative organization, and effective rehearsal. Shifts that would normally take four or five minutes can be cut to as little as 10 seconds by the split-second coordination of an excellent shifting crew. Nor is the shifting problem one that can be delayed until dress rehearsal. In a multiple-set show the requirements of shifting should be a major factor in determining the design of the scenery itself. Somewhere in the rehearsal schedule it may be necessary also to arrange for technical rehearsals that concentrate on the movement of scenery alone, and, finally, it will almost certainly be necessary to coordinate these with lights, sound, movement of properties, and movement of actors and actresses. Nowhere in theatre is coordination and high morale at a greater premium.

As to the basic methods employed in the handling of scene shifts, we have already considered the simultaneous setting, in which all the scenes were set up at once; the Elizabethan system, in which scenes alternated between the forestage and inner stage; and the Inigo Jones system, in which the scenes were shifted by sliding flats in grooves. Following Jones, the craze for spectacular scenery soon led to the development of the flying system.

FLYING SYSTEMS

Although first developed primarily to manage such spectacular effects as drifting clouds and airborne goddesses, the flying of scenery soon became a basic means of shifting, especially of shifting the painted back-

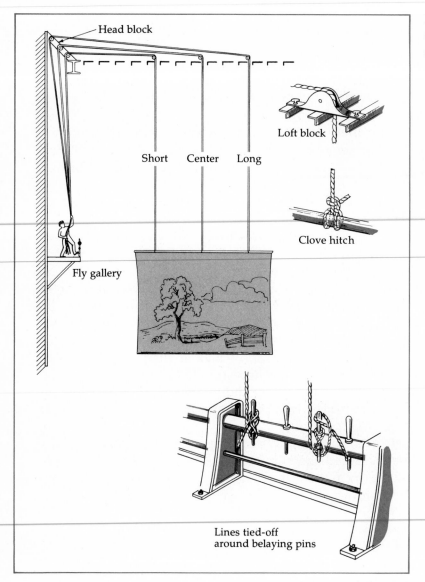

Head block

Loft block

Short   Center   Long

Clove hitch

Fly gallery

Lines tied-off
around belaying pins

FIGURE 12:21
Ordinary flying
system.

drops that were the essence of scenic spectacle until well into the twentieth century. With the coming of box-set realism, flying lost some of its importance, although it was still essential to the handling of ceilings, many exterior units, cycloramas, light borders, and certain act curtains.

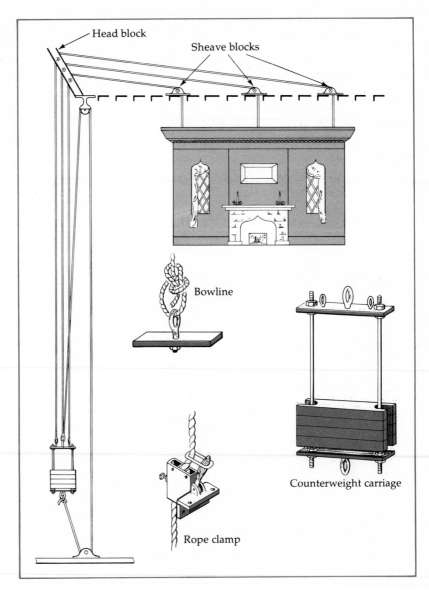

The ordinary conventional system consists of a number of sets of lines which are manually operated. Each set contains three lines: center, short, and long (Figure 12:21). Each goes from the top of the unit to be flown, over a loft block on the grid, over a head block above the fly gallery, and down to the pin rail, where the flyman, after raising the drop, ties off the lines on a belaying pin. For flying light weights, this system is foolproof and satisfactory, but if heavy weights are involved, trouble ensues. Sandbags can be temporarily clamped to the lines to help counterbalance the excess weight of the scenery, but the best solution, if available, especially for permanent equipment such as light battens and drop curtains, is to employ a counterweight system. As in the ordinary system, ropes or cables extend from the unit to be flown over their loft blocks and over their head block, but instead of tying off on the pin rail they are clamped to a counterweight, which will of course lower and raise the scenery. This is accomplished by an endless line, as shown in Figure 12:22. Pull one side and the scenery goes up; pull the other and the scenery comes down. In many of the newer theatres electric motors have replaced stagehands as the source of power in flying scenery; cables have replaced ropes; and guides of various types are usually used to help control the counterweights.

FIGURE 12:23   A jackknife stage.

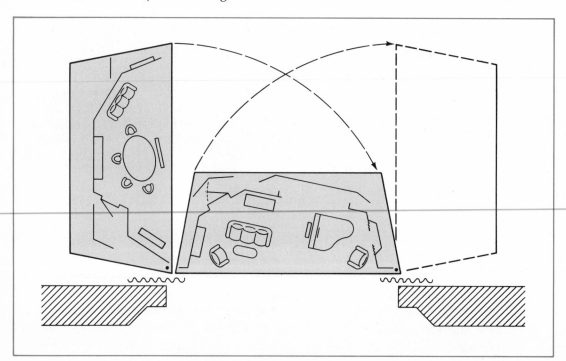

FIGURE 12:24 Hydraulic-lift casters, which enable heavy units to be lifted, shifted, then lowered to the stage floor for security; developed by technicians for the Guthrie Theatre and the Minnesota Opera Company. (Courtesy of Don Yunker and Terry Sateren)

HYDRAULIC CYLINDER

HYDRAULIC LIFT CASTER UNIT

WAGON STAGES

For multiple-set plays using heavy three-dimensional elements such as properties, step units, and levels, none of the systems of shifting described thus far is very satisfactory; either a revolving stage or a wagon stage is needed. The least expensive and the most common are the wagons. There is no standard size; they vary from small dollies to huge stages the size of the entire acting area on which complete sets, including properties and even the actors and actresses, can be rolled into place

FIGURE 12:25 Crew at the Festival Theatre, Stratford, Ontario, preparing to move the main stage balcony with the help of Red Baron (air-lift) casters.

in a single action. Construction of these is not difficult. A low, sturdy platform is built and equipped with rugged, rubber-tired casters. One of the most reliable forms is the jackknife stage (Figure 12:23), in which one corner pivots on a shaft securely anchored to the stage floor. Since this forces the wagon to travel always in the same arc, it makes possible the use of nonswivel casters that do not twist and bind against one another as do the swivel casters of the ordinary wagon. The result is that the jackknife can swing in and out both easily and accurately. Obviously its use requires moderate wing space. Jackknives can shift two large and complete sets. If additional scenes are necessary, these are handled in numerous ways. Flying is possible if there is a grid; a third wagon can be moved in from up center if the stage is deep; and sometimes changes are made on one jackknife while a scene is playing on the other.

For many plays the jackknife stage provides a reliable solution to shifting problems. It is, however, only one of many types of wagon stages which, as mentioned, come in all shapes and sizes. These wagons, together with their companions, lift jacks and tip jacks, provide the answers to many a stage problem. The twentieth-century theatre owes much to the rubber-tired, ball-bearing or roller-bearing casters that are the essential elements in all such devices (Figure 12:24). Even these are being replaced in critical instances by platforms that float on compressed air (Figure 12:25).

THE REVOLVING STAGE

The designer or technician who works for a theatre that has a large, permanent, motor-driven revolving stage is fortunate indeed, for there are times when no other method of shifting can equal its speed and effectiveness. With its use, it is frequently possible to design two, three, and even more sets that, when properly mounted, can be shifted in the space of a few seconds simply by pressing a button. On the other hand, the revolving stage has its limitations. The problem of designing sets so that the back of one becomes the front of another can become a headache. Also, there is a problem of filling in downstage corners missed by the arc of the revolver; and finally, there is some tendency for a revolving stage to force interior settings into angular sections that resemble pieces of pie. Fortunately, a revolving stage works well in conjunction with a

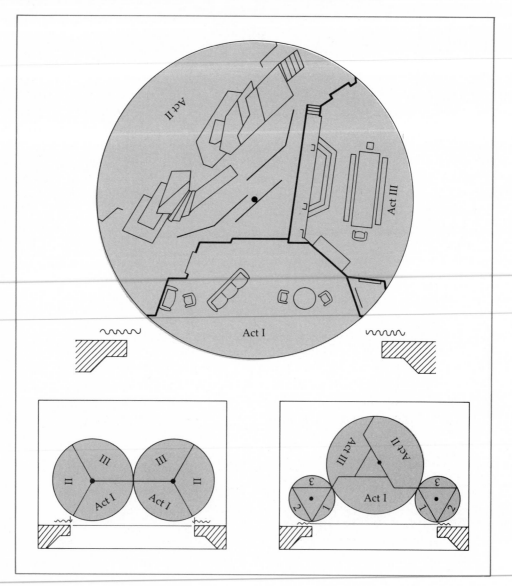

FIGURE 12:26   Revolving stages.

flying system, with wagons, and with most other systems. In spite of its inherent limitations, it does give the designer and the technician a powerful weapon with which to attack the problem of shifting.

Many directors do not realize that it is possible to build a temporary revolving stage (especially a small one or a combination of small ones) that rides on the regular stage floor (Figure 12:26). Such a stage is constructed something like a wagon except that it is round, is anchored to the stage floor by a shaft at its center, and is equipped with rigid, rather than swivel, casters. Such temporary stages, since they project 6 inches or more above the stage floor, can interfere with the use of wagons. Still, in certain instances they have rendered valuable service to the theatre.

PROJECTION OF SCENERY

Projected scenery perhaps belongs in the discussion of lighting rather than of shifting. Its use is, of course, limited, since it tends to work best in poetic, nonrealistic plays. There are times, however, when no other solution to the problem of changing scenery can approach the use of light. With this system there is no break whatever; one scene merges into another; such elements as mood, rhythm, and transition are sustained without distraction. Actors stay in character and the audience stays rapt in the spell of the play.

There are many shifting methods and devices that have not been mentioned. Elevator stages, which range from Steele MacKaye's famous invention for the old Madison Square Theatre to the various platform lifts such as those employed at the Philadelphia Convention Hall, can be very useful. Certain types of scenery—unit sets, selective realism, and drapery settings—owe much of their use to the ease with which they can be shifted. All in all, enough systems have been devised so that the well-informed technician with a reasonably adequate stage should be able to find some combination that will solve his or her problems. When shifting is slow, chaotic, and confused, the difficulty usually lies not so much in lack of equipment as in lack of imagination and organization. In shifting, the limitations of the human mind provide the chief stumbling block.

STAGE PROPERTIES

Plays can be, and frequently have been, staged without lighting, make-up, scenery, or costumes, but they have almost never been staged without properties. In fact, most plays cannot even be rehearsed without something to represent such items as chairs, tables, and benches, for these things are usually indispensable to the action of the players. Wherever one finds theatre, one will find props. Moreover, methods of securing them, their tendency to be realistic in style, and the techniques of handling them show only slight variation down through the ages. One striking exception to this generalization is the case of Oriental theatre, in which highly symbolic properties are common. A few other exceptions may be found in certain religious and ritualistic forms of drama, but for the most part property crews ever since Thespis seem to have gone their way borrowing, building, and improvising in much the same ageless pattern. Thus, according to its expense account, the passion play at Mons in 1501 used "apples old and new and also cherries to hang on the trees of the earthly paradise."[3] Also required were rabbits, lambs, fishes, birds, boats, real water, and other naturalistic items which tended to outdo even Belasco's craving for authenticity. Not all of the props could have been borrowed, however, for the list included dragons, serpents, devils, an artificial donkey, and other props or prop-costumes that must indeed have taxed the construction skill and ingenuity of the prop crew. Thus the story goes, even to the modern arena theatre which, managing nicely without conventional scenery, would be at a loss without properties. Even *Our Town*, while dispensing with most of the properties, could not ask the actors and actresses to sit on imaginary chairs.

In its most general sense the term *properties* is a catchall classification. During the eighteenth and most of the nineteenth centuries, it referred to just about everything on stage except scenery, players, and costumes. Later, with the advent of electricity, lights were removed to a category of their own. Today sound and musical effects have likewise broken away from the property classification and have either joined lighting or become a separate division; even so, the old attitude still prevails: "If it isn't anything else, it's a prop."

Four general classes may be distinguished.

1. Set props (chairs, tables, rugs, etc.) are furnishings that stand on the floor.
2. Hand props (letters, guns, food, etc.) are articles used by or carried on stage by actors and actresses.

---

[3]Quoted in Lee Simonson, *The Stage Is Set* (New York: Harcourt Brace Jovanovich, 1932), pp. 172–193.

3. Trim props (paintings, tapestries, draperies, etc.) are articles used to decorate the walls of the set.
4. Effects (snow, rain, wind, thunder, breaking glass, etc.) are anything not claimed by lighting or some other department.

These divisions are mentioned mainly to show the wide scope covered by the term *properties*. Such divisions are not absolute and should not be taken too seriously. Extended and ridiculous arguments can develop as to whether a given article is a hand prop or a set prop. Even more common is the argument as to whether the bookshelves in Act I are scenery or properties, or whether the hat and coat in Act II are properties or costumes. The standard rule in such cases has it that if the bookcase is built into the scenery, it is scenery, if not, it is a property; the hat and coat are costumes if worn, properties if not. However, such divisions are frequently more academic than useful. Actually, it matters not a whit whether the property or scenery crew provides the bookshelves, or whether the costume or property crew provides the hat and coat, as long as someone provides them. In a good noncommercial organization the stage carpenter may build both scenery and furniture, while the property crew may lend a hand in painting the scenery. Although such reshuffling of duties may be advantageous, it must be clearly understood in advance. Nothing is more amateurish than the last-minute confusion that occurs when Jones insists that the large rocks for Act III are scenery, while Smith maintains that he considers them props. At the first general meeting all such questions of responsibility should be pleasantly but firmly fixed, even if it means flipping a coin.

In the process of rehearsal, set props — or rather their substitutes — come first, for chairs, tables, tree stumps, and benches are necessary as soon as blocking rehearsals begin. Hand props come next, usually being introduced as soon as the players free themselves from their scripts. Trim props and effects ordinarily make their appearance at the time of the first dress rehearsal.

Needless to say, the selection, gathering, construction, care, and return of properties are of great importance to any theatre organization. Good prop crews usually pride themselves that there is nothing they cannot find or build, and if they stay in the theatre long, they are apt to find their boast challenged. Everything from a bloody head to a real steamboat has at one time or another found its way onto prop lists.

In most nonprofessional theatres a large proportion of the properties are usually borrowed. This means that a prop crew should know the town thoroughly, especially secondhand stores, florist shops, and antique shops. In this respect a large city has its advantages. Next, the prop crew should take such good care of borrowed items and return them so promptly that they will always be welcome to borrow again. Such courtesies as program notes and passes can also go a long way toward promoting good will. Some theatres can borrow practically anything in town, including expensive new furniture, while others can borrow practically nothing. It all depends upon the conscientiousness of the organization, especially the prop crew.

If storage facilities are available, permanent organizations like community and university theatres can simplify their problem by accumulating a permanent supply of properties. Some of the more expensive pieces of furniture may be made to serve double duty by adorning offices and lobbies when not in use on stage. Wise purchase and repair of secondhand items, plus the practice of encouraging patrons to donate antiques from their attics, can build up a gold mine for the theatre. Add to this the more permanent and useful of the gadgets that are constantly having to be constructed, and a large proportion of prop problems can be solved within the organization's own storage rooms.

In the construction of properties, the techniques employed are practically limitless. Skill as a cabinetmaker, as an upholsterer, and as an interior decorator are wonderful talents if one has them, but these barely scratch the surface. Knowledge of physics and chemistry, of zoology and botany, of almost every branch of human learning, will sooner or later prove an asset. One technique especially useful in constructing such things as statuary is the papier-mâché or, better still, the Celastic process already mentioned in the discussion of scenery. Mâché patterns may be made of almost anything by first taking a plaster cast of the object, then pressing mâché pulp into the greased cast, and allowing it to dry there before removing it. If you can afford Celastic, just follow the directions and the results will be even more satisfying.

There are other materials that are finding more and more use in prop shops. Fiberglass is superior for jobs requiring light but extremely tough construction. Sculpt-metal, commonly used in repairing automobile bodies, is invaluable in decorating shields, weapons, and so on. Styrofoam and plastic foams, already mentioned in connection with scenery, are even more useful in the prop shop.

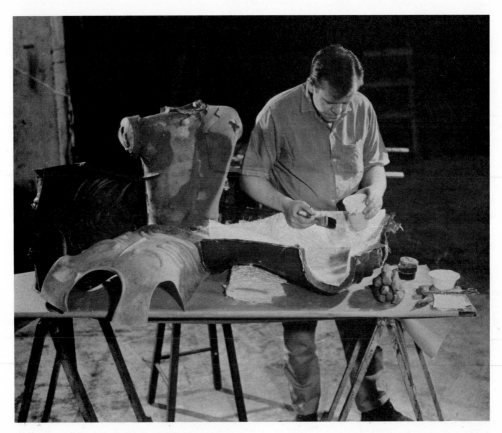

FIGURE 12:27 Armour construction at the Guthrie Theatre. Fiberglass, like many other modern materials, is becoming increasingly useful in scene shops, prop shops, and costume shops.

One final word in regard to organization: Since the job is usually too much for one person, a crew is ordinarily assigned to work under the property manager. The best division of labor for a given crew will depend on the play. If scene changes are complicated, one crew may be assigned to gather the props while another crew shifts and cares for them during rehearsals and performances. A cupboard or table containing hand props is usually placed backstage, and actors and actresses are required to assume responsibility for selecting and returning whatever they use. Further rules would need to be modified by individual circumstances if they are not already obvious.

CHAPTER 13

LIGHTING AND SOUND

The greatest technical advantage that the twentieth-century theatre enjoys lies in its mastery of the art of stage lighting. Of all the technical crafts a director can employ to reinforce the work of the actors and actresses, good lighting can be the most unobtrusive, the most flexible, and in many ways the most expressive. Not only can the director illuminate the stage and the actors but he or she can select what to illuminate. In other words, lighting can focus audience attention on the significant and the attractive, while quietly ignoring the insignificant and the distracting. Thus on the well-lighted stage, the players, generally the most important element of the visual design, tend to work in a pool of light, while the scenic background retires into the softer shadow. Nor should the scenery itself be evenly and equally illuminated. Even when lighting an ordinary realistic interior the more significant elements—perhaps furnishings, fireplace, large window, and stairway—will be highlighted, while the ceiling and upper portions of each wall will blend into shadow. Furthermore, good lighting is not static. It changes its focus to suit

404

FIGURE 13:1 In modern stage lighting, the characters usually stand out in highlight while the scenery recedes into the background. *(a) Of Mice and Men* at Ohio State University; directed by Roy Bowen. *(b) The Glass Menagerie* at the Alley Theatre; directed by Nina Vance. *(c) Revelation* at the University of Minnesota; directed by Edward Payson Call, designed by Donald Seay.

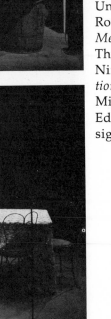

(b)

(c)

FIGURE 13:2 *She Stoops to Conquer,* University of Minnesota, 1944. In realistic productions, ceilings and corners usually blend into the background.

the varying action pattern of the play. In a poetic, nonrealistic drama, such as *The Dream Play,* this change of focus may be noticeably swift, provided that it is in harmony with the rhythm and mood of the action. Even in a realistic play a subtle ebb and flow of intensity among the acting areas can be effective, though it should never be obvious enough to call attention to itself. Thus if Grandma and Grandpa play a scene by the fireplace down right, anyone taking the trouble to check would discover that they are playing in the brightest area on the stage. As the old folks leave and the young lovers settle themselves on the sofa down left, a further check would reveal that the focus of the lighting had quietly shifted until the brightest area on the stage had become the one surrounding the sofa.

But focus of attention, or selective illumination, is not the only function that lighting can perform. It can enhance beauty. The golden hair of the leading lady may get the credit, though no small portion of its luster may come from just the right touch of back lighting. A romantic setting in a small high school recently brought a shower of compliments to its designer, when the element responsible was the lighting, which turned a dirty gray wall behind a huge Indian archway into an evening sky that was a transparent blend from turquoise to midnight blue. The effect in this case was completed by cross beams from two spotlights which transformed a flat cardboard urn filled with plain dried weeds into a gorgeous display of lacy gold and green foliage. Many a setting that seems entirely satisfying and attractive under stage lights looks cheap and shabby under work lights. A group limited in funds, yet still wishing to build a reputation for attractive and high-quality staging, will do well to look to its lighting. In capable hands it can work wonders.

The third and most vital contribution of lighting lies in its power to create atmosphere. In *Macbeth* our fears and anxieties for Banquo and Fleance grow deeper as the lights fade into dimness, leaving the murderers barely visible in heavy shadows. The Never Land in *Peter Pan* lies ominous and gloomy when we first look at it, for the nervous Lost Boys are without their leader and pirates are on the prowl. Then as Tootles shoots the great white bird, the Wendy, there is a moment of rejoicing, and the

FIGURE 13:3 The primitive power of *King Lear* is increased by the lighting; a design by Norman Bel Geddes.

sunshine obligingly sparkles forth only to fade a few seconds later as the realization grows on them that the Wendy may have been a lady. The gloom of a cloudy evening lies across the island as Peter arrives to confirm their worst fears: Wendy is dead. But the sun obligingly bursts forth again as they discover that by a miracle "She lives, the Wendy lady lives!"

The brilliance of Wilde's wit in *The Importance of Being Earnest* can be reinforced by brilliance of illumination. The daughter's cry of anguish in *The Dream Play* can be accentuated by a stab of light from the darkness. Then, as her anguish dies into a tired sob, the light shaft disintegrates, leaving only a cold, diffused glow. Lighting is the mood music of vision and if skillfully done can achieve maximum results with a minimum of distraction.

Thus light has the power to focus attention, enhance beauty, and reinforce atmosphere. Authors of texts on the subject also point out its value in revealing form, suggesting time and place, and reproducing such naturalistic effects as clouds and sky. In the case of projected scenery, such as that used for *The Dream Play*, light provides practically the entire visual background. It is unfortunate that in spite of such tremendous potential, good lighting is seldom realized. In skilled hands it becomes a sort of twentieth-century genie—dependable, responsive, willing—a servant content to enhance the work of players, costumer, designer, and property crew without demanding a spotlight for itself.

THE HISTORY OF LIGHTING

The functions and services just described did not even begin to become available until the late nineteenth century. Prior to this, stage lighting was almost entirely concerned with one problem: the search for sufficient illumination. Greeks, Romans, and Elizabethans generally conceded defeat as far as artificial illumination was concerned and staged their productions under the open sky. Though some purists have accordingly argued that daylight is therefore superior to artificial light for theatrical work, there is no basis for such an assumption. On the contrary, even primitive peoples generally recognized the emotional effectiveness of ritual by firelight. Shadowy objects that terrify the child at night surren-

FIGURE 13:4 Sources of illumination before and during the time of Shakespeare: torch, floating oil wick, tallow candle.

der their power under the full light of day. It was undoubtedly necessity rather than choice that kept the classic and the Elizabethan public theatres outdoors.

Shakespeare's plays contain numerous references to the use of light. Such directions as "Enter with torches" have led some to the assumption that artificial illumination was highly developed in his day. Research, however, finally pointed out that torches, tapers, and lanterns were used not for illumination but as a convention to designate time of day.[1] Thus the entrance of servants with lighted torches was a cue that night had fallen rather than an attempt to illuminate the stage. This symbolic use of light does not necessarily hold true for indoor theatres like the Blackfriars, where artificial illumination was probably a necessity.

During the Elizabethan period the principal sources of illumination were wicks floating in oil and tallow candles (Figure 13:4), and these, with the addition of wax candles, continued to be standard until almost the close of the eighteenth century. The units were grouped into chandeliers, and later into footlights and border lights, in an effort to satisfy the constant need for brighter and brighter illumination. About the time of the American Revolution, oil lamps with wicks and chimneys began to

[1] Lee Mitchell, "Shakespeare's Lighting Effects," *Speech Monographs* 15 (1948).

FIGURE 13:5   Common nineteenth-century illuminants: camphine burner, kerosene lamp, gas (open flame), gas with incandescent mantle.

replace candles. A few years later, in 1803, the Lyceum Theatre in London installed gaslights (Figure 13:5).

With the development of gaslight the problem of illumination finally approached a solution. During the last half of the nineteenth century long rows of gas jets in borders and foots flooded stages with light—but they also flooded both stage and auditorium with heat and fumes. Above all there was a constant fire hazard, for gas lighting was the cause of some of the worst disasters in theatre history.

Nor was gas lighting the only development of the period. The calcium light, or limelight, made possible the first spotlights. A piece of lime, heated to brilliant incandescence by an oxyhydrogen flame, emitted a clear white light of excellent quality and brilliance (Figure 13:6). However, it was expensive and needed constant attention.

FIGURE 13:6   Some important sources of stage illumination: limelight, carbon arc, early incandescent lamp.

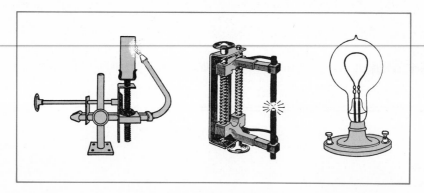

FIGURE 13:7 The new electric lighting system installed at the Paris Opera around the turn of the century consisted of long strips of borderlights and footlights, which covered the entire stage with bright, but unselective, general illumination.

As early as 1808 Sir Humphry Davy had demonstrated the electric arc, but it was almost half a century before this powerful source of light began to find use in theatres. Even then it flickered, was noisy, could not be dimmed, and required much attention; but in spite of all its defects the electric arc, especially in spotlights, made an enormous contribution. Then in 1879 (the year Ibsen wrote *A Doll's House*) Thomas Edison invented the incandescent lamp. Theatres were among the first to recognize this new source of illumination. The Paris Opera led the way by installing the new system in 1880. Within a few years incandescent lights found their way into theatres all over the world. By the turn of the century they were in general use, except in spotlights, where lamps with a sufficiently powerful concentrated filament were not available until shortly before World War I.

Today new light sources—fluorescent, neon, sodium vapor, and others—are competing with incandescent lamps in homes, on streets, and in factories, but on the stage incandescents still tend to dominate. Though somewhat inefficient, they are safe, inexpensive, foolproof, and can be dimmed. In the past few years some striking improvements have been made. Quartz has replaced glass, and halogen gases have been used to surround filaments. The result has been incandescent lamps that are much smaller in size, yet much longer lasting and much whiter and brighter in their light output.

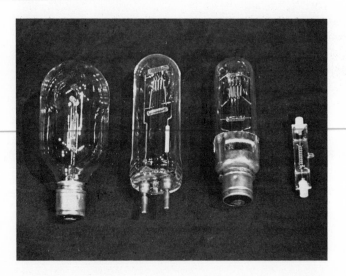

FIGURE 13:8 Spotlight lamps: 500-watt T20 used in small Fresnels, 500-watt T14 bipost commonly used in ellipsoidals, 500-watt T12 medium prefocus also used in ellipsoidals, tungsten-halogen lamp which is replacing older lamps in striplights and floodlights as well as spotlights.

THEORY AND PRACTICE

Although until the twentieth century the primary quest in stage lighting was simply for brighter and brighter illumination, there were scattered attempts to achieve other values. Both Serlio and Sabbatini experimented with lighting effects. Inigo Jones is said to have brought continental lighting to England and may have invented reflectors. In Germany Joseph Furtenbach invented footlights; David Garrick introduced them into England almost a century later. But for the most part inadequate illuminants held lighting in check until the end of the nineteenth century, when gas and electricity opened the way for stage lighting to become an art.

Among the first to sense the new possibilities were Sir Henry Irving, whose well-lighted plays awakened much interest; Steele MacKaye, whose lighting plans and inventions were far ahead of his time; and David Belasco, MacKaye's one-time partner, whose practical business sense and executive ability enabled him to demonstrate in actual production many of the naturalistic lighting effects that MacKaye had left on paper or in the dream stage.

Belasco also developed the baby spotlight, a spotlight employing an incandescent lamp rather than the carbon arc or limelight used by his predecessors. This light was called a "baby" because only small-wattage incandescent lamps were available at that time. Belasco brought stage lighting into the consciousness of the theatrical world with scenes like his naturalistic sunset over the Sierra Nevadas in *The Girl of the Golden West* and especially with his reproduction of a Japanese night, sunset to sunrise, in *Madame Butterfly*, where actors stood motionless while music and light held the stage. "Lights are to drama what music is to the lyrics of a song," he wrote. "No other factor that enters into a play is so effective in conveying its moods and feeling."[2]

In spite of Belasco's great contributions, he is overshadowed in the history of lighting by Adolphe Appia, who by the close of the nineteenth century was writing about the potential contributions of light with an insight and vision half a century ahead of his time. He was the

[2] David Belasco, *The Theatre Through Its Stage Door* (New York: Harper & Row, 1919), p. 56.

first to protest in clear terms against the flat, even illumination that came from the overuse of footlights and border lights. Appia named this diffused, uninteresting light "general illumination" but pointed out that artistic stage lighting could be achieved only through "specific illumination"—the type of light produced by spotlights and hence subject to control, light that could be localized, emotional, and form revealing. Lee Simonson, writing about Appia, vividly describes the difference between these two kinds of light.

> Diffused light produces blank visibility, in which we recognize objects without emotion. But the light that is blocked by an object and casts shadows has a sculpturesque quality that by the vehemence of its definition, by the balance of light and shade, can carve an object before our eyes. It is capable of arousing us emotionally because it can so emphasize and accent forms as to give them new force and meaning. In Appia's theories, as well as in his drawings, the light that in paintings had already been called dramatic was for the first time brought into the theatre, where its dramatic values could be utilized.[3]

Appia's awareness of the psychological potentials of lighting was reinforced by others, especially Gordon Craig. The importance of the art has grown until today the lighting designer is usually awarded program credit along with the director, scene designer, and costume designer as one of the creative forces in the production.

THE MCCANDLESS PLAN FOR STAGE LIGHTING

Any attempt to set up a standard plan for lighting the stage is hazardous, for the art is still young. No two plays are alike, and even the playhouses, as we have seen, present a wide variety of shapes and sizes. As a result, flexibility and adaptability have become major characteristics of any good modern lighting system. This is a marked contrast to the old standard system which, with but few exceptions, held sway on the professional stage from before the time of Ibsen until the 1920s. The old system was an unimaginative carry-over from the day when, in order to

[3] Lee Simonson, *The Stage Is Set* (New York: Harcourt Brace Jovanovich, 1932), p. 358.

illuminate the acting area to a satisfactory degree of brilliance, it was necessary to employ long strips of footlights and border lights, even though these covered everything with an unselective and undramatic flood of general illumination. To make matters worse, these footlights and border lights were ordinarily wired to a standard switchboard which, though expensive, was as inflexible and inadequate as the instruments it was meant to control. Practically every authority on lighting since Appia condemned this old layout as obsolete, and yet unscrupulous manufacturers and salesmen still managed to install such systems in new school and civic auditoriums until the close of the Second World War. It was not unusual, therefore, to see amateur craftspeople in poverty-stricken summer theatres turn out a quality of lighting that put to shame the new local high school with its thousands of dollars worth of obsolete equipment.

In modern proscenium theatres the most essential lights are the beam spotlights that shine through slots in the auditorium ceiling, their beams of light striking the downstage areas of the stage at about a 45-degree angle from the horizontal.

Consider the problem of illuminating an actor or public speaker who stands downstage center. Light him from the foots and the result will be distracting distortion, for the light shoots up from below and spills on the set. Light him from the borders and only the top of the head and shoulders will be illuminated. Light him from the tormenters and only his sides will be illuminated. Light him from the balcony front and sharp shadows will appear on the set. There is only one solution: Light him primarily from above and in front, in other words, from the auditorium ceiling or *the beams.* Two or three spots rather than one should be used. This causes less glare, provides two-tone possibilities, and insures protection should a lamp burn out during performance.

As soon as one understands this basic plan for lighting a single area, it is easy to understand the system for lighting the acting areas of a proscenium stage that was developed by Stanley McCandless of Yale shortly after World War I (Figure 13:9). The three downstage areas (right, center, and left) are each covered by two spots from the beams. The system is repeated for the three upstage areas, except that the light for these areas comes from six spots placed immediately behind the front curtain and mounted on either a teaser batten or a light bridge. If the lights are well focused and controlled, the actor or actress now plays in a flexible pool of

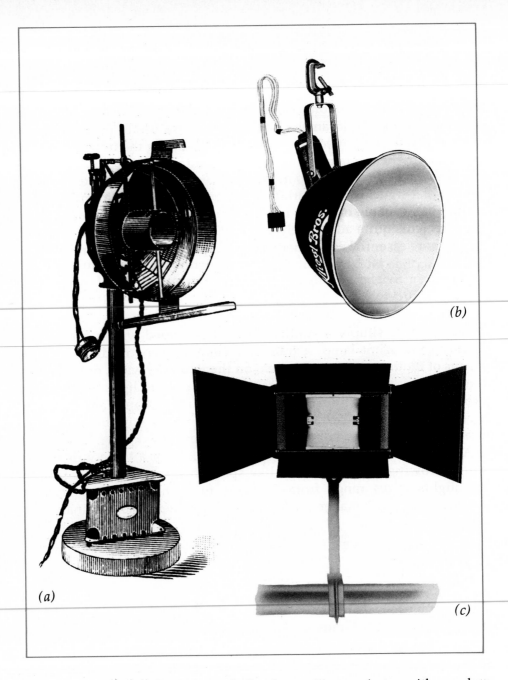

FIGURE 13:11   Floodlights. *(a)* Parabolic glass mirror projector with a carbon arc source of illumination, in use during the late nineteenth century. *(b)* Ellipsoidal reflector floodlight, or scoop, a basic instrument from 1930 to 1970. *(c)* A modern tungsten-halogen floodlight with barn doors for masking.

FIGURE 13:12   Lamps with built-in reflectors: an R 40 reflector lamp, a PAR 56 (seal-beam) projector lamp, a PAR 38 projector lamp.

beam. Such spots are inefficient, transmitting to the acting area but a small percentage of the total light emitted by the filament.

New-type spotlights, which have come into general use since 1930, have made the old plano-convex spot obsolete for most purposes. The Fresnel spot (Figure 13:14) approximately doubles the efficiency of the ordinary spot by using a stepped lens which, although optically crude, gives a soft edge to the beam, a quality that is usually desirable.

The ellipsoidal reflector spotlight (Figure 13:15) increases efficiency above that of either the Fresnel or the plano-convex spot by reflecting rays that the others waste. The reflector simply gathers the rays coming from the filament and directs them through a second focal point and toward the lens. In contrast to the soft edge projected by the Fresnel, its beam can be sharply framed.

Other developments in spotlight design include (1) follow spots that are both efficient and flexible, (2) mirror spots, which rely entirely on re-flected light for their high efficiency, and (3) spots using tungsten-halo-gen lamps for greater compactness and efficiency.

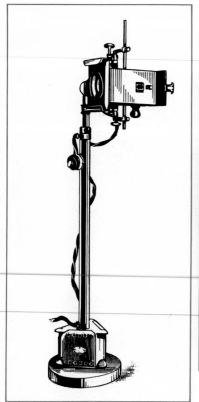

(a)

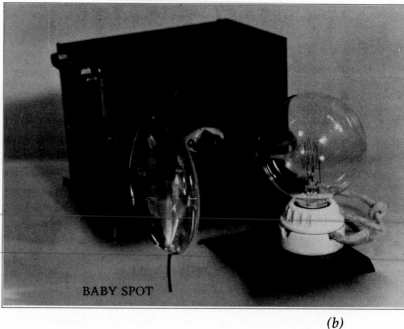

BABY SPOT

(b)

FIGURE 13:13 Plano-convex spotlights. (a) Lens-box with carbon arc, about 1890. (b) Baby spot of the type that came into common use following the First World War. Exploded view with lamp and lens (the essential elements) removed from hood. (c) Diagram of the simple plano-convex spotlight makes it clear that most of the light rays from the filament are wasted.

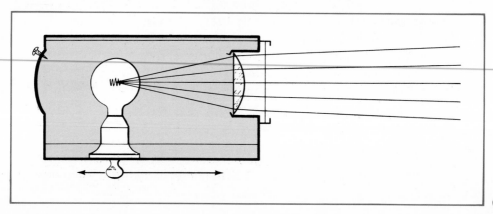

(c)

500w FRESNEL

FIGURE 13:14 The Fresnel spotlight. This type collects and emits a greater percentage of the rays from the filament than does the plano-convex (exploded view).

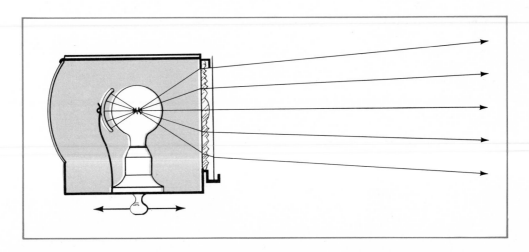

FIGURE 13:15 The ellipsoidal spotlight. Rays wasted by other spotlights are reflected through a second focal point into the lens.

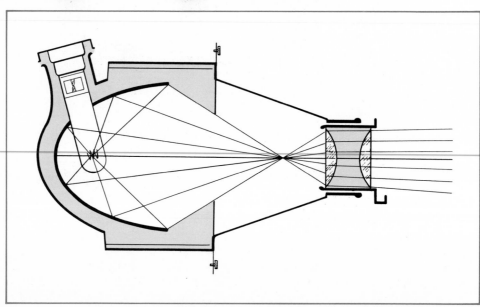

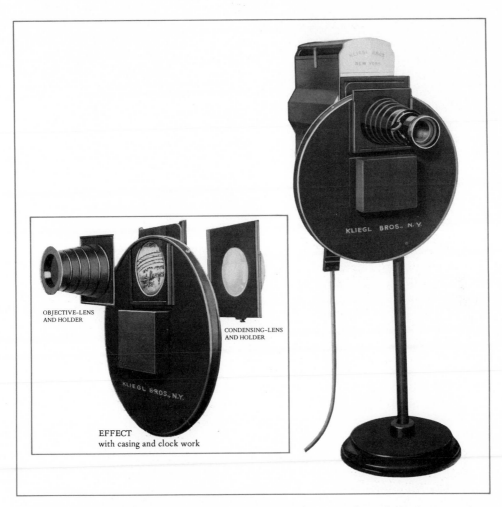

OBJECTIVE-LENS
AND HOLDER

CONDENSING-LENS
AND HOLDER

EFFECT
with casing and clock work

KLIEGL BROS., N.Y.

FIGURE 13:16 Sciopticon, a scene projector that employs lenses to project moving clouds, flames, and other effects.

EFFECT MACHINES AND SLIDE PROJECTORS

Modern productions often require the projection of clouds, skylines, and other scenic forms. Two types of projectors are used: (1) a Linnebach lantern, which is merely a shadow box that projects a crude but large image from a short throw, and (2) the lens projector (Figure 13:16), which is superior where detail and sharpness are required. With ordinary lenses a long throw is necessary in order to secure a large image. However, if some distortion does not matter, an objective lens of extremely short focal length can increase the size of the image.

Not only stationary images but also moving effects, such as drifting clouds, driving rain, rolling waves, and raging fires, can be provided by lens projectors.

COLOR MEDIA

Since early in the century the standard color medium for stage lighting has been gelatine. It comes in thin sheets, the color range is excellent, and it is inexpensive; but it is also fragile. Plastics such as Cinemoid and Roscolene are now preferred by many electricians, since they are much more durable, though more expensive.

DIMMERS AND CONTROL BOARDS

While both lighting practice and lighting instruments have been influenced by modern technology, it is lighting control that is truly a child of the twentieth century. I can best illustrate the pace of this development by citing my own experience. During my early years of touring, the switchboards of most theatres consisted of six to ten open-knife switches. I had heard of dimmers by the time I was in high school, but the first one I ever saw was one I made: a saltwater contraption I "invented" in 1925 for the death of Minnehaha in Longfellow's *Hiawatha*. It was the first time that our audience had ever seen lights dim except when the local power plant failed. My first look at a resistance dimmer came a year later when I entered a university that had three: one permanently wired to the red foots and borders, one to the white, and one to the blue!

In New York in 1930 I first became acquainted with the huge banks of resistance dimmers that covered a 10- to 30-foot section of wall and required three or four muscular men to operate the innumerable handles (Figure 13:17). In 1932, in the depths of the Depression, I actually built a 24-circuit control board with open-knife switches, fuses, and a by-pass

FIGURE 13:17 Lighting control board at the Metropolitan Opera in New York, 1903.

system, where one dimmer could jump from one circuit (or group of circuits) to another. The total cost, minus the dimmer, was $38.60! At the University of Iowa in 1935, Hunton Sellman introduced me to three new wonders: (1) the newly invented autotransformer (Figure 13:18), (2) the reactance dimmer, which could be remotely controlled, and (3) switchboards located at the back of auditoriums where the lighting artist could finally see what he was doing.

Then, following the Second World War, George Izenour at Yale developed the first all-electronic board, which used thyratron tubes and remote control. This permitted the massive control board to be reduced to the size of an organ console and also permitted an easy method of presetting complicated cues. A number of Izenour boards were manufactured, but they were expensive, difficult to maintain, noisy, and in television studios sometimes interfered with the transmission of the pic-

500w VARIAC   2000w VARIAC

(a)

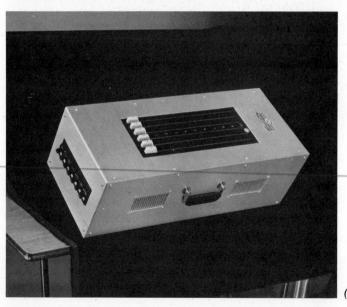

(b)

FIGURE 13:18
Autotransformers.
(a) Variacs. *(b)*
Davis dimmer.

FIGURE 13:19   Dimming unit of an SCR system.

ture. Then, before such bugs could be removed, the silicon-controlled rectifier (SCR) dimmer hit the market in 1958 (Figure 13:19). Anything thyratron could do SCR could do better. The dimming unit itself was a tiny element no bigger than the end of your finger, yet its performance soon rendered other dimmers obsolete except for small installations where autotransformers are sometimes still preferred. Even from the standpoint of economy, nothing else could equal the 600-watt simplified version of the SCR, designed to fit into the standard wall switch of any home and available in 1976 at Sears Roebuck for $3.89 each.[4]

With the development of the SCR, the problem of lighting control has become a problem of philosophy rather than electronics. Presetting

[4]These tiny dimmers are not recommended for stage use. Stage-type SCR dimmers are quite large and rather expensive.

FIGURE 13:22   Rock Hall, a sound technician, in action at the University of Utah.

and literally hundreds of other effects are frequently called for by play-wrights.

Since radio came of age, recorded sound effects have gradually im-proved in quality and range until they have almost pushed the old man-ually operated devices from both the studio and the stage. Skill in opera-tion and split-second timing, so necessary if the sound is to reinforce mood and not detract from it, are more difficult to achieve on records and even on tape than they were when produced by hand. Yet an opera-tor with a sense of rhythm, steady nerves, and an alert awareness of the show can soon master complicated cues. Rehearsal, skill, and timing are essential, for good sound must reinforce, and not compete with, the show. Both sound and music are probably best when the average mem-ber of the audience is not even consciously aware of them.

PART
FOUR

PROFESSIONAL WORK IN THE THEATRE

CHAPTER 14

PROFESSIONAL WORK IN THE THEATRE

Many intelligent students who would like to major in theatre resist the temptation to do so because they see in it no future. Others plunge into the program, finding it stimulating and worthwhile during the years in college only to face the eventual disillusionment of graduating into a world that has no place for them. Unemployment, a chronic ill of the American theatre, still exists on a scale that may well cause intelligent students to consider carefully before burning their bridges and dedicating their lives to the stage. Definite figures and rigid answers are hazardous in this area; sources of information do not agree. The only real certainty about theatre employment appears to be uncertainty, and yet in spite of this, some general advice seems necessary. We shall therefore look at the problems and possibilities on six levels: (1) the commercial theatre, (2) the nonprofit professional theatre, (3) the semiprofessional theatre, (4) the community theatre, (5) the educational theatre, and (6) the children's theatre.

FIGURE 14:1   Stagestruck. A 1903 sketch by Charles Dana Gibson.

THE COMMERCIAL THEATRE

Although the commercial professional theatre may no longer be America's most important theatre, it does include Broadway, where fame and big money still provide irresistable lures to so many talented students. As far as Broadway is concerned, the employment situation appears to have changed very little since Elmer Rice wrote the following in 1959:[1]

> There are about sixty Broadway productions each season, including musical comedies, with casts ranging up to fifty. If we assume that these productions employ, in the aggregate, fifteen hundred actors and another fifteen hundred for touring companies, stock companies, summer theatres and off-Broadway productions, we arrive at an approximate total of three thousand job opportunities. However, this is by no means the actual employment at any one time. The summer theatres operate only for about two months, tours are seldom longer than four or five months, and most of the

[1] According to a 1976 report by Actors' Equity, the lowest percentage of membership employment in recent years was 17.7 in 1951–1952; the highest, 25 in 1969–1970. The average for 1975–1976 was 19.8.

plays that open in New York run less than twelve weeks, many only for a week or two. I should say that the actor who works in the theatre for more than fifteen weeks a year is exceptional. Certainly the overwhelming majority of Equity's ten thousand members are unable to make a living in the theatre or even to find employment. It has been estimated that the average theatrical income of Equity members is under two thousand dollars a year.

How do they manage to live? In all sorts of ways. A good many find occasional work in movies or in radio and television, including dramatized advertisements. Others have private means or are supported by a husband or wife. Many are engaged in occupations that have nothing to do with acting. I have known unemployed actors who worked as secretaries, receptionists, truck-drivers, ushers, department-store employees, laboratory technicians, models, night-club hostesses, photographers and teachers. Most of their free time is spent in theatrical job-hunting: hanging about the offices of casting agents; writing appealing or petulant letters that are never answered; trying to get to see a producer or a director, and mostly meeting with a quick dismissal if they succeed. It cannot be said that these conditions are beneficial to the morale of the actor or conducive to his development as an artist.[2]

As far as the would-be young professional is concerned, there has been one important addition to the commercial theatre's employment picture since Rice wrote the above: the establishment of professional dinner theatres in many cities throughout the nation. These for the most part feature small companies performing light entertainment, although a few produce full-scale musicals. Since they are mostly based outside of New York, they have had a tendency to absorb local talent into their groups, and many young performers, designers, and craftspeople are now gaining their first foothold into the professional world of theatre through these dinner theatres.

Small professional stock theatres, mostly East Coast summer theatres, still give many newcomers a chance, but in general the commercial theatre still offers no logical or organized approach—no national system of auditions—to help newcomers break into its ranks. Theatrical agents can help, but the road to success is usually a very frustrating and difficult one.[3]

[2]Elmer Rice, *The Living Theatre* (New York: Harper & Row, 1959), pp. 189–190.
[3]Anyone contemplating a professional career in the theatre is urged to read Dick Moore's excellent paperback, *Opportunities in Acting Careers* (Louisville, Ky.: Vocational Guidance Manuals, 1975).

THE NONPROFIT PROFESSIONAL THEATRE

As we have already seen, the most encouraging development in the American theatre during the third quarter of the twentieth century has been the establishment of nonprofit professional companies. The real breakthrough in this much-needed movement came during the early 1960s. The most powerful figure in its development was Sir Tyrone Guthrie, the inspiration behind both the Festival Theatre at Stratford, Ontario (1953), and the Tyrone Guthrie Theatre in Minneapolis (1963). A lesser figure might have been accused of having gone to the provinces because he could not make it in New York or London, but Guthrie loomed so high in the profession that he was unassailable. His books on the subject helped to make matters clear, and almost immediately other professionals were able to follow in his footsteps without having their motives questioned, while those already in the field picked up strength and prestige from his association. Foundations and national agencies were impressed by the new trend in American theatre, and resident professional companies quickly became the hope of the future.

Theatre Profiles /2, published in 1975, contains information and photographs covering 100 of these nonprofit professional theatres located in 50 American cities. They include an amazing variety: black theatres and a Chicano theatre, theatres specializing in new plays, theatres dedicated to the classics, musical theatres, and a theatre of the deaf. According to Peter Zeisler, "the diversity of the work and the size of the audience demonstrate that theatre in this country is not an arcane art form serving a small select audience but a burgeoning movement."[4]

The fact that these companies are organized on a nonprofit basis means that financially they resemble symphony orchestras and art galleries rather than show business. This gives the theatre a long-needed halo of cultural prestige in the eyes of civic leaders, educators, legislators, and foundations, which in turn leads to financial support—directly through gifts, subsidies, and the sale of tickets and indirectly through tax exemption and other concessions, including the fact that labor unions are usually much more reasonable. Actors and actresses and

[4] Peter Zeisler, introduction to *Theatre Profiles /2* (New York: Theatre Communication Group, 1975).

other employees are willing to work for much less than in Hollywood or on Broadway, since they are employed for an entire season rather than for a single show which might run three years but will probably run three days. Perhaps the greatest appeal of all is that the resident company, especially if it is a repertory company, offers the theatre artist a chance to grow in his or her profession. During the course of a season each actor or actress plays a number of roles instead of walking the streets unemployed because his or her play ran only a week, or else suffering the boredom of playing the same role in the same play month after month because it is a hit.

Finally, and of special importance to those seeking entry into the profession, there is a central organization, the Theatre Communications Group, which, among other things, conducts national auditions. Although these TCG auditions are frequently criticized and are obviously imperfect, they do represent a gigantic improvement—a rational and organized attempt on the part of the professionals to discover and encourage the best young talent not only in acting but also in lighting, designing, costuming, and craftsmanship.

These professional nonprofit theatres have also displayed an excellent tendency to encourage new playwrights. This tendency was undoubtedly stimulated by support from the Office of Advanced Drama Research (OADR), a project directed by Arthur H. Ballet and initially funded by the Rockefeller Foundation. Through this project many talented young playwrights have received the invaluable experience of seeing their plays skillfully produced.

THE SEMIPROFESSIONAL THEATRE

Closely related to the resident professional nonprofit theatres are a number of semiprofessional groups, located mostly on college campuses or in some other way affiliated with college or university programs. Although those who work in such theatres are paid, most of them do not belong to professional unions. The University Resident Theatre Association (URTA) is made up of 30 or 40 such groups. There is wide variety: Some, like the Minnesota Showboat, operate only during the summer; others, like the Hillberry Theatre at Wayne State University, perform

(a)

(b)

(c)

FIGURE 14:2   New plays sponsored by the Office of Advanced Drama Research (OADR). *(a)* Hyde Clayton, Judith Olauson, and Michael Ruud in Tim Kelly's *Beaux Johnny;* directed by Robert Hyde Wilson; setting by Vern Adix; costumes by B. W. Peterson. *(b)* Jo Ann Schmidman and Joe Guinan in *Walking Into the Dawn: A Celebration* by Rochelle Holt at The Omaha Magic Theatre; directed by Jo Ann Schmidman. *(c)* Cynthia Harris and Laurence Luckinbill in *The Shadow Box* by Michael Christofer at The Mark Taper Forum.

(a)

(b)

(c)

FIGURE 14:3 Shakespeare festivals. (a) Festival dancers performing before the show at the Utah Shakespearean Festival in Cedar City. (b) A performance in progress at the Oregon Shakespearean Festival in Ashland. (c) Laurie O'Brien, David Miller, and Ed Sampson in *The Tempest* at the Colorado Shakespeare Festival at Boulder, directed by Lee Potts.

during the nine months of the regular school year. Some use only student actors; others rely heavily on professional artists-in-residence and guest stars. Some are Shakespearean festivals and some, musical festivals. Members of the companies are often paid via scholarships instead of regular salaries, and in most cases their work partially fulfills requirements toward a graduate degree, normally the M.F.A. Auditions for these companies are held annually in four regional locations.

These programs, together with the closely related work of the great outdoor dramas, such as *The Lost Colony* and *Unto These Hills,* provide much-needed stepping-stones for those who wish to move from student to professional status. A very successful variation of the above has been the program of the Drama Division at the Juilliard School, where highly selected students, after a period of thorough training, have been formed into a professional group known as the Acting Company.

But above all, what is needed at the professional level is not the stage-struck actor or actress who wants to act and act and act if only someone else will provide the theatre, the audience, the director, the technical necessities, and the salary; what is needed is the young director-producer: the imaginative, pioneering artist-executive who can organize and build an exciting theatre from the materials at hand — someone with a touch of Thespis, Molière, or Guthrie. Such a rare spirit need not be of the male sex. It was a woman, Hallie Flanagan Davis, who headed the enormous Federal Theatre Project during the Depression; it was a woman, Margo Jones, who founded and directed the famous Theatre-in-the-Round in Dallas, which until her death in 1955 was probably the finest professional theatre in America outside of New York. In Washington, D.C., it is again a woman, Zelda Fischandler, who has been the inspiration behind the Arena Stage. In Houston the guiding spirit of another arena, the Alley Theatre, has been Nina Vance; while in Kansas City the creative force behind the Missouri Repertory Theatre has been Patricia McIllrath. Such leaders could probably move into any one of hundreds of American cities and soon have the town alive with theatre excitement. Opportunities still exist for those with the imagination and energy to create them.

THE COMMUNITY THEATRE

According to *Theatre in America* there are some 18,000 community groups concerned primarily with the production of plays.[5] About 3000 of these meet "acceptable" standards of production, while about 200 maintain standards that are "more or less professional." Community theatres,

[5] *National Directory for the Performing Arts and Civic Centers* (Dallas, Tex.: Handel and Co., 1973).

which began as the Little Theatre Movement, originated early in the century as a crusade against the commercial theatre. Then, as the commercial theatre outside of New York disappeared, community theatres together with university theatres expanded to fill the vacuum. In doing so they lost much of their original drive and purpose, but even so, they have served, and have often served very well, in providing good theatre for their audiences plus creative satisfaction for their participants.

As far as employment is concerned, most community theatres begin by paying only a director, and even then on a show-to-show basis. Eventually the more successful groups add paid staff members in about the following order: full-time director, technical director, business manager, costumer, and perhaps a children's theatre director. Rarely does either the philosophy of the group or the money permit them to go further. Most of the work is done by volunteers. Good community theatres usually draw their support from a wide segment of the population, ranging from professional people like doctors and lawyers to dedicated teenagers.

It should be obvious, therefore, that those employed in community theatres need qualities of leadership in addition to theatrical knowledge and talent. Consideration and tact, ingenuity and enthusiasm, common sense and compromise, are basic ingredients in promoting the health and vitality of a community theatre. Such theatres have obvious limitations, yet in spite of these limitations, many have achieved reputations for the high quality of their productions. Moreover, many theatre majors who did not choose to pursue professional careers on the stage have had their lives enormously enriched through wholehearted participation in these community theatres.

THE EDUCATIONAL THEATRE

For those talented in theatre and at the same time genuinely interested in teaching, the prospect of finding a financially modest but rewarding profession is more encouraging than for those pursuing a career on the professional stage. Years ago Norris Houghton warned against the danger of "teaching teachers to teach teachers to teach," but if the things taught by these teachers are sound enough, if the teachers who go into

the teaching of theatre. Speech clinicians and school nurses, since they hold positions in which ignorance can do great harm, have long been carefully certified; teachers of mathematics, English, and other well-established disciplines must pass a required course of study. But the general attitude toward theatre, especially among high school executives, is that anyone can teach dramatics. Consequently, anyone does, and with such wretched results that all values are lost.

The problem is difficult, for actually the ideal high school director would need everything a professional director has plus the patience and genius to lure fine performances out of beginners. For the most part anyone so gifted simply tries to become a professional. But fortunately we do not need to have the ideal. There are undoubtedly hundreds, if not thousands, of men and women now wasting their time trying unsuccessfully to break into the professional theatre who, had they wanted to do so, could have been excellent high school directors. Why didn't they elect to do so? Probably because the high school plays they had seen were abysmally poor. Bad plays make it difficult to attract gifted leaders, and this in turn leads to more bad plays. One hopes this unfortunate cycle is about to reverse itself; if it does, the sleeping giant will rise.

There is no standard aptitude test or self-inventory that can determine whether or not one should be a teacher on any level—elementary, high school, or university. The following questions are simply intended to provoke thought and initiate the process of evaluation:

(a)

(b)

(c)

FIGURE 14:4 High school productions. *(a) My Fair Lady* at St. Louis Park, Minnesota; directed by Roger DeClercq. *(b)* Two scenes from *The Capture of Sara Quincy* at Eisenhower High School in Hopkins, Minnesota; directed by Tony Steblay, music by Gary Parker. *(c) Giraffe Story*, an original musical by Robert Stoddard at a Brigham Young University workshop for high school students; directed by Charles W. Whitman.

1. Do I have enough theatrical talent to make theatre training under my direction worthwhile? Just being an excellent scholar or teacher in general is not enough. Educational theatre can be justified only if it maintains high artistic standards.

2. On the other hand, am I willing to accept the fact that the school exists for the student? While artistic standards must be high, these alone do not guarantee a good education. Art and education sometimes come into conflict, and in such cases the decision must be made in favor of education. People to whom the art of the theatre means everything, even to the extent of riding roughshod over the rights and lives of students and/or other faculty members, do not belong in educational theatre.

3. Can I endure long hours of extra work without martyrdom? Hours are unimportant to one genuinely involved in creative work. Twelve-hour days are no hardship if one enjoys every minute of them, but they can be sheer misery to those who begin to compare hours and salaries with those of former grade school pals who now drive trucks or fix leaky faucets.

4. Can I enjoy a life of service rather than one providing wide recognition or personal fame? This may sound idealistic, but it is really very practical. Teachers, even the finest, tend to remain unknown except to their students and a few personal friends. People whose egos need constant nourishment should avoid teaching.

5. Do I enjoy young people, or do they annoy me? This is a personal rather than a rational matter. People who are annoyed by youthful immaturity, lack of professional dedication, and natural irreverence—especially toward teachers—should avoid trying to work in a school.

THE CHILDREN'S THEATRE

The above list of self-inventory questions for potential teachers becomes especially important to those who choose to work in the children's theatre. Of course, not all of the workers in children's theatre are teachers by profession. Many of the best are connected with Junior Leagues, church groups, social agencies, or cultural centers. Moreover, there are

(a)

(b)

FIGURE 14:5 Childrens' theatre productions. (a) A Peppermint Tent (University of Minnesota) production of Carl Sandburg's *Rootabaga Stories;* directed by Debbie Anderson, designed by Mimi Gramatki. (b) A Children's Theatre Company (Minneapolis) production of Hans Christian Andersen's *The Snow Queen;* directed by John Clark Donahue, designed by Dahl Delu.

many kinds of children's theatre: those in which children perform for children, those in which adults perform for children, and a few in which professionals perform for children. There is also creative dramatics, in which children act out stories or improvise but not for audiences.

Professional children's theatres obviously offer the same opportunities to actors, designers, playwrights, and technicians that would be found in any other nonprofit theatre. Other than this, work in the children's theatre is limited mostly to teachers and leaders, who, like its founder, Winnifred Ward, usually consider theatrical work with children to be a labor of love.

SUMMARY

In closing this discussion of theatre as a profession, we should remind ourselves that the theatre's real function in higher education is not one of training a few students to earn a living. Its true function, as pointed out in our first chapter, rests on the less tangible but more lasting values of a liberal education. Let us summarize, then, the possibilities that a theatre education has to offer.

If you are primarily interested in a liberal education, interested in acquiring understanding, including a touch of that rare quality known as wisdom, then you might well consider majoring in theatre. This does not guarantee results, but the opportunities for learning and experience should be second to no other course of study in the curriculum.

If in addition to the cultural values mentioned above you must eventually face the prospect of earning a living, the by-products of theatre training should prove valuable in almost any profession you may later choose to follow.

But if you feel that you must earn a living in the theatre itself, the problem becomes more serious. Those who are genuinely interested in teaching and at the same time possess qualities that would make them good teachers face prospects that are moderately favorable. Teaching, however, must not be something disagreeable that one intends to fall back on in case one fails to succeed in the professional theatre. One's interest should spring from a love of theatre and a desire to share it with young people. It should include affection and respect for the whole educational environment.

FIGURE 14:6   Curtain call at the Asolo State Theatre, Sarasota, Florida.

If you are determined to be a professional — actor, director, designer, playwright, or technician — well, good luck. If in spite of the hazards you become the Sarah Bernhardt, Tyrone Guthrie, or Robert Edmund Jones of tomorrow, all will cheer and clamor to claim some share of your glory. Second-guessers and fair-weather friends will cry, "I knew you could." But the courage to try rests with you alone.

Finally, if you are the director-executive type, if you have ability, work well with others, have the patience to acquire sound experience and training, have a love for the theatre and not just a secret love of personal fame — then the theatre needs you, whether you need it or not. There are communities and schools the length and breadth of the country that offer opportunities to those with the initiative and imagination to go out and create opportunities.

While many students who want to go into theatre should be discouraged, others, like Richard Brinsley Sheridan, make the unfortunate mistake of forcing themselves to become politicians, lawyers, and doctors, whereas if they had only devoted themselves wholeheartedly to the theatre, they might have found an infinitely more rewarding life for themselves and offered immense pleasure to others.

BIBLIOGRAPHY

PERIODICALS

To keep abreast with the theatre, periodicals are a necessity. Among the most useful are the theatre section of *The New York Times*, *Variety*, *Educational Theatre Journal*, *Drama Survey*, *Players*, *Theatre Crafts*, *The Drama Review*, and *Plays and Players*.

ANTHOLOGIES

BENTLEY, ERIC (ed.). *From the Modern Repertoire*. Series 1–3. Bloomington: Indiana University Press, 1949–1956.

BENTLEY ERIC (ed.). *The Modern Theatre* (6 vols.). Garden City, N.Y.: Doubleday, 1955–1960.

BENTLEY, ERIC (ed.). *The Classic Theatre* (4 vols.). Garden City, N.Y.: Doubleday, 1958–1961.

BROCKETT, OSCAR G., AND LENYTH BROCKETT (eds.). *Plays for the Theatre: An Anthology of World Drama*. New York: Holt, Rinehart and Winston, 1967.

CLARK, BARRETT H. (ed.). *World Drama* (2 vols.). Englewood Cliffs, N.J.: Prentice-Hall, 1933.

CORRIGAN, ROBERT W. (ed.). *The Modern Theatre.* New York: Macmillan, 1964.

DICKINSON, THOMAS H. (ed.). *Chief Contemporary Dramatists* (3 vols.). Boston: Houghton Mifflin, 1915, 1921, 1930.

DICKINSON, THOMAS H. (ed.). *Continental Plays* (2 vols.). Boston: Houghton Mifflin, 1935.

DUCKWORTH, GEORGE E. (ed.). *The Complete Roman Drama* (2 vols.). New York: Random House, 1942.

GASSNER, JOHN (ed.). *A Treasury of the Theatre.* New York: Simon & Schuster, 1935, 1940, 1951, 1963, 1967.

GASSNER, JOHN (ed.). *Twenty Best Plays of the Modern American Theatre.* First Series, 1929–1939. Second Series, 1939–1945. Third Series, 1945–1950. New York: Crown, 1939, 1945, 1952.

MACMILLAN, DOUGALD, AND HOWARD MUMFORD JONES (eds.). *Plays of the Restoration and Eighteenth Century.* New York: Holt, Rinehart and Winston, 1931.

MANTLE, BURNS, AND JOHN GASSNER (eds.). *A Treasury of the Theatre.* New York: Simon & Schuster, 1935.

MOODY, RICHARD. *Dramas from the American Theatre, 1762–1909.* Cleveland: World, 1966.

MILLET, FRED B., AND GERALD E. BENTLEY. *The Play's the Thing.* Englewood Cliffs, N.J.: Prentice-Hall, 1936.

OATES, WHITNEY J., AND EUGENE O'NEILL, JR. *The Complete Greek Drama* (2 vols.). New York: Random House, 1938.

QUINN, ARTHUR HOBSON (ed.). *Representative American Plays.* Englewood Cliffs, N.J.: Prentice-Hall, 1953.

WHITE, MELVIN R., AND FRANK M WHITING. *Playreaders Repertory, An Anthology for Introduction to the Theatre.* Glenview, Ill.: Scott Foresman, 1970.

HISTORIES

BROCKETT, OSCAR G. *History of the Theatre.* Boston: Allyn & Bacon, 1968.

CHENEY, SHELDON. *The Theatre: Three Thousand Years of Drama, Acting, and Stagecraft.* New York: McKay, 1929.

CLARK, BARRETT H., AND GEORGE FREEDLEY (eds.). *A History of Modern Drama.* Englewood Cliffs, N.J.: Prentice-Hall, 1947.

FREEDLEY, GEORGE, AND JOHN A. REEVES. *A History of the Theatre.* New York: Crown, 1941.

GASSNER, JOHN. *Masters of the Drama.* New York: Random House, 1953.

HEWITT, BARNARD. *Theatre U.S.A.: 1668 to 1957.* New York: McGraw-Hill, 1959.

MACGOWAN, KENNETH, AND WILLIAM W. MELNITZ. *The Living Stage: A History of World Theatre.* Englewood Cliffs, N.J.: Prentice-Hall, 1955.

McGraw-Hill Encyclopedia of World Drama. New York: McGraw-Hill, 1972.

NAGLER, A. M. *Sources of Theatrical History.* New York: Theatre Annual, 1952.

NICOLL, ALLARDYCE. *World Drama.* New York: Harcourt Brace Jovanovich, 1950.

ODELL, G. C. D. *Annals of the New York Stage* (15 vols.). New York: Columbia University Press, 1927–1949.

PARROTT, THOMAS MARC. *William Shakespeare, A Handbook.* New York: Scribner, 1934.

QUINN, ARTHUR HOBSON. *A History of the American Drama, from the Beginnings to the Civil War* (1 vol.); *A History of the American Drama, From the Civil War to the Present Day* (2 vols.). New York: Harper & Row, 1923, 1927. Rev. ed., Englewood Cliffs, N. J.: Prentice-Hall, 1936, 1943 (2 vols.).

ROBERTS, VERA MOWRY. *On Stage.* 2nd ed. New York: Harper & Row, 1974.

THEORY AND CRITICISM

ARTAUD, ANTONIN. *The Theatre and Its Double.* New York: Grove Press, 1958.

BENTLEY, ERIC. *The Playwright As Thinker.* New York: New American Library (Meridian Books), 1946.

BRUSTEIN, ROBERT S. *The Theatre of Revolt.* Boston: Little, Brown, 1964.

BUTCHER, SAMUEL H. *Aristotle's Theory of Poetry and Fine Art with a Critical Text and Translation of The Poetics.* 4th ed. London: Macmillan, 1927.

CLARK, BARRETT H. (ed.). *European Theories of the Drama.* Rev. ed. New York: Crown, 1947.

HEFFNER, HUBERT. *The Nature of Drama.* Boston: Houghton Mifflin, 1959.

SELDEN, SAMUEL. *Theatre Double Game.* Chapel Hill: The University of North Carolina Press, 1969.

THOMPSON, ALAN R. *The Anatomy of Drama.* 2nd ed. Berkeley: University of California Press, 1946.

DIRECTING AND PLAY PRODUCTION

CANFIELD, CURTIS. *The Craft of Play Directing.* New York: Holt, Rinehart and Winston, 1963.

CLURMAN, HAROLD. *On Directing*. New York, London: Macmillan, 1972.

COLE, TOBY, AND HELEN KRICH CHINOY (eds.). *Directors on Directing*. Indianapolis: Bobbs-Merrill, 1953.

DEAN, ALEXANDER. *Fundamentals of Play Directing*. Rev. ed. by Lawrence Carra. New York: Holt, Rinehart and Winston, 1965.

GALLOWAY, MARIAN. *The Director in the Theatre*. New York: Macmillan, 1963.

HEFFNER, HUBERT C., SAMUEL SELDEN, AND HUNTON D. SELLMAN. *Modern Theatre Practice*. 4th ed. Englewood Cliffs, N. J.: Prentice-Hall, 1959.

HEWITT, BARNARD, J. F. FOSTER, AND MURIEL S. WOLLE. *Play Production, Theory and Practice*. Philadelphia: Lippincott, 1952.

HODGE, FRANCES. *Play Directing: Analysis, Communication, and Style*. Englewood Cliffs, N. J.: Prentice-Hall, 1971.

MCMULLAN, FRANK. *The Directorial Image*. Hamden, Conn.: Shoe String Press, 1962.

SELDEN, SAMUEL. *The Stage in Action*. Englewood Cliffs, N.J.: Prentice-Hall, 1939.

SIEVERS, W. DAVID. *Directing for the Theatre*. Dubuque, Iowa: William C. Brown, 1961.

WELKER, DAVID. *Theatrical Direction*. Boston: Allyn & Bacon, 1971.

ACTING

ALBRIGHT, H. D. *Working Up a Part*. Boston: Houghton Mifflin, 1947, 1959.

ALBRIGHT, HARDIE. *Acting, the Creative Process*. Belmont, Calif.: Dickinson, 1967.

BOLESLAVSKY, RICHARD. *Acting: The First Six Lessons*. New York: Theatre Arts, 1933.

COLE, TOBY, AND HELEN KRICH CHINOY (eds.). *Actors on Acting*. New York: Crown, 1949.

CORSON, RICHARD. *Stage Make-up*. 5th ed. Englewood Cliffs, N.J.: Prentice-Hall, 1975.

DOLMAN, JOHN, JR. *The Art of Acting*. New York: Harper & Row, 1949.

KLEIN, MAXINE. *Time, Space, and Designs for Actors*. Boston: Houghton Mifflin, 1975.

LEES, C. LOWELL. *A Primer of Acting*. Englewood Cliffs, N.J.: Prentice-Hall, 1940.

LEWIS, ROBERT. *Method—or Madness?* New York: Samuel French, 1958.

LINKLATER, KRISTIN. *Freeing the Natural Voice*. New York: Drama Book Specialists, 1976.

MCGAW, CHARLES. *Acting Is Believing*. New York: Holt, Rinehart and Winston, 1955. Rev. ed., 1966.

SPOLIN, VIOLA. *Improvisation for the Theatre.* Evanston, Ill.: Northwestern University Press, 1963.

STANISLAVSKY, CONSTANTIN. *An Actor Prepares.* New York: Theatre Arts, 1936.

STANISLAVSKY, CONSTANTIN. *Building a Character.* New York: Theatre Arts, 1949.

STANISLAVSKY, CONSTANTIN. *Creating a Role.* New York: Theatre Arts, 1961.

THEATRE ARCHITECTURE, DESIGN, AND CRAFTS

ADIX, VERN. *Theatre Scenecraft.* Anchorage, Ky.: Children's Theatre Press, 1956.

BARTON, LUCY. *Historic Costumes for the Stage.* Boston: Baker, 1935.

BAY, HOWARD. *Stage Design.* New York: Drama Book Specialists, 1974.

BELLMAN, WILLARD F. *Lighting the Stage.* New York: Intext, 1967.

BURRIS-MEYER, HAROLD, AND EDWARD C. COLE. *Scenery for the Theatre.* Boston: Little, Brown, 1938.

BURRIS-MEYER, HAROLD, AND EDWARD C. COLE. *Theatres and Auditoriums.* New York: Reinhold, 1949.

COREY, IRENE. *The Mask of Reality, An Approach to Design for Theatre.* Anchorage: Anchorage Press, 1968.

FRIEDERICH, WILLARD J., AND JOHN H. FRASER. *Scenery Design for the Amateur Stage.* New York: Macmillan, 1950.

GILLETTE, A. S. *An Introduction to Scenic Design.* New York: Harper & Row, 1959.

JONES, ROBERT E. *The Dramatic Imagination.* New York: Duell, Sloan & Pearce, 1941.

KERNODLE, GEORGE. *From Art to Theatre: Form and Convention in the Renaissance.* Chicago: University of Chicago Press, 1943.

MCCANDLESS, STANLEY. *A Method of Lighting the Stage.* New York: Theatre Arts, 1932.

MIELZINER, JO. *Designing for the Theatre.* New York: Potter, 1970.

NICOLL, ALLARDYCE. *The Development of the Theatre.* New York: Harcourt Brace Jovanovich, 1927. 3rd ed. 1937.

PARKER, W. OREN, AND HARVEY K. SMITH. *Scene Design and Stage Lighting.* 3rd ed. New York: Holt, Rinehart and Winston, 1974.

PECTAL, LYNN. *Designing and Painting for the Theatre.* New York: Holt, Rinehart and Winston, 1975.

ROBINSON, HORACE W. *Architecture for Educational Theatre.* Eugene, Ore.: University of Oregon Press, 1970.

RUBIN, JOEL E., AND LELAND WATSON. *Theatrical Lighting Practice.* Theatre Arts, 1954.

SELDEN, SAMUEL, AND HUNTON D. SELLMAN. *Stage Scenery and Lighting*. Englewood Cliffs, N. J.: Prentice-Hall, 1941.

SIMONSON, LEE. *The Stage Is Set*. New York: Harcourt Brace Jovanovich, 1932.

WALKUP, FAIRFAX PROUDFIT. *Dressing the Part*. Englewood Cliffs, N.J.: Prentice-Hall, 1950.

THE THEATRE AS A PROFESSION

BENNER, RALPH. *The Young Actor's Guide to Hollywood*. New York: Coward, McCann & Geoghegan, 1964.

DAVIS, JED H., AND MARY J. WATKINS. *Children's Theatre: Play Production for the Child Audience*. New York: Harper & Row, 1960.

MOORE, DICK. *Opportunities in Acting Careers*. Louisville, Ky.: Vocational Guidance Manuals, 1963, 1975.

OMMANNEY, KATHERINE ANNE, AND HARRY H. SCHANKER. *The Stage and the School*. 4th ed. New York: McGraw-Hill, 1972.

The Performing Arts, Problems and Prospects. Rockefeller Brothers Report. New York: McGraw-Hill, 1965.

PLUMMER, GAIL. *The Business of Show Business*. New York: Harper & Row, 1961.

YOUNG, JOHN WRAY. *The Community Theatre and How It Works*. New York: Harper & Row, 1957.

INDEX

81 82 83 84 85 86   10 9 8 7 6 5 4